HMS COLOSSUS

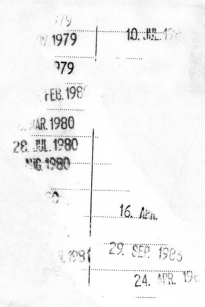

Roland Morris

HMS COLOSSUS:

The Story of the Salvage of the Hamilton Treasures

Foreword by
BRIAN F. COOK FSA
Keeper of Greek and Roman Antiquities
The British Museum

HUTCHINSON
OF LONDON

By the same author

ISLAND TREASURE

Hutchinson & Co. (Publishers) Ltd
3 Fitzroy Square, London W 1 P 6JD

London Melbourne Sydney Auckland
Wellington Johannesburg and agencies
throughout the world

First published 1979
© Roland Morris 1979
Illustrations © Roland Morris 1979

Set in Monotype Bembo

Printed in Great Britain by The Anchor Press Ltd
and bound by Wm Brendon & Son Ltd
both of Tiptree, Essex

British Library CIP data

Morris, Roland
HMS Colossus
1. Vases, Greek 2. Underwater
archaeology 3. Archaeology –
Scilly Islands 4. Colossus *(Ship)*
1. Title
914.23′79   NK4645

ISBN 0 09 134660 6

ENDPAPER

*The return of Hephaistos (Tischbein
drawing with fragments of the Colossus
Vase superimposed)*

I dedicate this book to all those who have worked with me during my sunken men-o'-war adventures. Those who have shared with me the arduous and the easy times, the jolly and anxious times, the hilarious and the solemn times, the exciting and the placid times.

Especially I mention the two who have stood by me in the recording of those adventures: Elisabeth, my companion for nearly twenty short years, and Edith Horsley, my ever patient editor.

My most grateful thanks to each and every one.

Contents

Illustrations

Halftones

Line drawings

Acknowledgments

I acknowledge with many thanks the courteous assistance extended to me by the keepers of the nation's records, in particular the Trustees and staff of the British Museum, National Maritime Museum, Science Museum, Victoria and Albert Museum, Portsmouth Victory Museum, Plymouth City Museum, and Plymouth Naval History Library. Their help made my lengthy research work all the more pleasurable. I am also indebted to Mrs Pam Vincent, formerly of the Marine Division of the Department of Trade, for her invaluable advice over the years on the complexities of salvage law. I should also like to express my appreciation of the research carried out in Plymouth records by my brother, Arthur H. Morris, and in London by my nephew William A. Morris. I also acknowledge with fond remembrance the assistance given to me by the late Mr H. Lee Duncan, Fellow of the Royal College of Surgeons, Edinburgh, who identified for me many biological specimens associated with nautifacts from the seabed. For the scientific analysis of material salvaged by us, I should like to acknowledge the help of the laboratories of British Ropes Ltd. and of the British Non Ferrous Metals Technology Centre.

I am particularly grateful, too, to Mollie Hardwick for the loan of two Rehberg prints from her own personal collection, and to which I was led by the reproductions in her own authoritative biography of Emma Hamilton. The underwater photographs reproduced in the book and on the jacket are the work of Paul Armiger, who was always ready at the flip of a face mask to come to our aid when needed, and our versatile diving team member, Slim Macdonnell.

I also owe hearty thanks to the 'Benbow Laboratory Staff' – Elisabeth, Denise and Ian Morris – for their invaluable hours of painstaking work, often undertaken into the small hours, in the preliminary sorting of the various 'droits' of the Hamilton pot-sherds.

Foreword

by Brian F. Cook FSA
Keeper of Greek and Roman Antiquities
The British Museum

The story of the recovery of the remains of Sir William Hamilton's second collection of Greek vases from the wreck of HMS *Colossus* is an intriguing one. No one is better qualified to tell it than Roland Morris, who not only discovered the elusive site of the wreck but undertook the difficult and sometimes hazardous job of recovering the broken vases from the sea-bed. Although the work was carried out under the general archaeological direction of an Assistant Keeper in the Department of Greek and Roman Antiquities of the British Museum, Dr Ann Birchall, the unavoidable brevity and infrequency of her visits and her previous inexperience of work under water left the day-to-day running of the enterprise in the hands of Mr Morris.

I first met him myself in February 1975, when I was taking an off-season holiday in Penzance. I had already heard that he had found a wreck that he thought was *Colossus*, and I had seen photographs of some of the material that had been brought up as evidence. I was naturally interested in Mr Morris's discoveries, not only because my own researches had been largely in the field of Greek pottery, but also because the British Museum already possessed two groups of vases that had once belonged to Sir William Hamilton; the whole of his First Collection (which had included bronzes, jewellery and other materials as well as pottery) and a few of the vases from his Second Collection that had been sent to England on board other ships and eventually sold. My holiday provided the opportunity to call on Mr Morris at the Admiral Benbow in Penzance to see the finds myself. He was a little disappointed when I had to say that none of the fragments yet found looked like ancient Greek work to me, but he remained confident that he would eventually be able to prove that he had actually found HMS *Colossus*. Indeed he convinced me that he was on the right track when he showed me the enormous copper bars from the wreck: their size, he argued, proved that a large ship was involved, and in that particular area there was no record of any large wreck except *Colossus*.

At that time neither Mr Morris nor his colleagues had yet had the opportunity to handle fragments of ancient Greek pottery. That opportunity was soon to come in abundance, but in the meantime I presented him with a scrap of Athenian black-glazed pottery from my own sherd collection to give him a better idea of the kind of material he was looking for. To my surprise and delight he insisted on giving me in exchange one of the silver 'pieces of eight' that he had recovered from the wreck of HMS *Association*. This exchange and the gift of an autographed copy of his earlier book, *Island Treasure*, marked the beginning of our friendship.

I am therefore happy to have this opportunity to pay tribute to the achievement of Roland Morris and his crew in recovering so many thousands of fragments of pottery from Sir William Hamilton's collection. The sea has unfortunately taken its toll, and we can all share the sorrow that Hamilton would have felt at the fragmentary state of his prized vases. At the same time we can also share the approval that he would surely have given to the men who, so late in the day, spared no effort to recover what was left of the cargo of HMS *Colossus*.

Brian Cook
September 1978

PART ONE

The Legend of Colossus

I

The Bay of Ships

Whenever I think of HMS *Colossus* – ship of the line in the fleet of George III – a picture of Naples, as I once saw it from the sea, comes to my mind. The splendid marble waterfront lies pink-tinged in the early-morning sunlight, Vesuvius is away to the east in deep blue silhouette, and a brilliant sky arches above the city, reflecting all the hues and tints of the dawn in carmine and amber, topaz and gold.

When *Colossus* left her moorings on that last voyage of hers, all was light and an enchantment of colour. And then I bring to mind the raw sea-bed off the Scilly Isles; the chill, rugged sea-bed on which the great ship broke apart, spilling out her precious cargo of ancient vases from Greece and southern Italy. This is a lacklustre underwater world of scattered boulders, hazy sandy gullies, dim shapes of great rocks, and weed – giant, glossy brown weed. Its clutching roots cling to the bedrock like countless gnarled monkey fists, and the massed fronds dance in slow, graceful rhythmic unison, choreographed by the tireless currents of the sea.

In the late autumn of 1798 the beautiful Bay of Naples was cluttered with shipping. It held a forest of masts; billowing, drying sails were like low-lying clouds; and warships lay yard-arm to yard-arm. Many of the vessels – certainly the armed brigs and larger warships – had recently limped into the anchorage from Aboukir Bay, scene of Nelson's great victory in the Battle of the Nile. In all that tired and battered assemblage, none was in greater need of a refit than HMS *Colossus*. She was at that time a battleship-cum-storeship attached to Nelson's marauding wartime Mediterranean squadron; a squadron, be it told, made up of the best and fastest 74-gun ships in the British navy.

An armed storeship, and there were but four in the Navy Lists of 1798, was a most important unit. It provided a base in a foreign sea, such as the Mediterranean, where no land base then existed, and supplied ammunition, gear and accoutrements, and even food, to the ships of the fleet. Her crew were skilled craftsmen and could undertake almost any kind of repair. The life of such a ship was short, more especially in the hot sun of the Mediterranean. Always overworked, perpetually overburthened and consequently overstrained, *Colossus* had developed faults and breaks which, like the shoes of cobblers' children, were never attended to.

It had been some two years earlier that *Colossus* had been despatched to join Admiral Sir John Jervis, in his fight against the combined might of France and Spain. Her newly appointed commander was Captain George Murray, a friend of Nelson, and she took up her position on the so-called Mediterranean Station. This area of sea embraced the estuary of the great river Tagus in friendly Portuguese territory, as well as the stretch of enemy coastline to the east, where the Spanish stronghold of Cadiz lay in its sheltered haven, some seventy miles west of Gibraltar.

During their turns of duty, watch-on and watch-off, in the blockade of this Spanish base, the Advanced and Inner Squadrons were commanded by Murray and Nelson respectively. Murray was so greatly admired by the enemy, both for his tactics and his personal conduct, that the Spanish admiral sent him an invitation to a gala bullfight under a flag of truce, offering to leave his own nephew aboard *Colossus* as a guarantee of Murray's safe return. The captain was tempted, but on reflection declined the honour.

His reputation had been hard won, almost to the loss of his ship. In the previous year, on 14 February 1797, *Colossus* had been a casualty in the Battle of Cape St Vincent, which had led to Sir John Jervis being ennobled under the title of Earl St Vincent. The Spanish fleet, commanded by Don José de Cordova, had been on its way from Cadiz to rendezvous with the French off

Brest. The combined fleets were intended to make a landing in Ireland, for the Irish politician and rebel, Wolfe Tone, had visited Paris in the autumn of 1796 to plot this diversionary invasion with the members of the Directory. For good measure, Tone had also infiltrated agitators in the British ships to stir up mutiny.

The plan came to an abrupt end on 14 February 1797 when Sir John Jervis, with his fifteen sail of the line, sighted the Spanish fleet, numbering twenty-seven sail of the line – thirteen three-deckers and fourteen frigates. He engaged at once. *Colossus*, in company with such great ships as *Victory*, under Sir John himself, *Blenheim*, under Captain Frederick, *Culloden*, under Captain Troubridge, and *Captain*, under Commodore Nelson, was in line-ahead formation with the rest of the squadron hard astern. Because the Spanish ships were superior in numbers as well as guns, the British planned to tack and pass through the enemy line, thus cutting off a third of the Spanish ships from the main fleet.

The manoeuvre was highly successful, but as *Colossus* received the signal 'tack in succession', at the very moment her helm was put down, as she luffed into the wind and ranged up on her new course, her foremast was blasted by enemy fire. The damage was severe, the slings of the fore tops'il yard were carried away, and her fore-topmast went just above the cap. Since the 'slings' carry the main weight of the yard and sail, the loss of them meant that the ship fell away to leeward, completely out of control.

As she lay helpless she came under a withering enemy barrage, and was only saved from further severe damage by the prompt action of Captain James Saumarez in *Orion*. He most gallantly backed his main topsail and lay by to provide cover for his friend until the danger had passed. In this memorable battle of Cape St Vincent, *Colossus* could play no further part, though later, with her battle damage repaired, she was detached to convoy merchant ships and transports to Naples. Here she was to come under the immediate orders of Nelson, although still under the overall command of Earl St Vincent.

During Nelson's subsequent chase after the French fleet, *Colossus* underwent great strain, beating to and fro from one end of the Mediterranean to the other in all weathers for month upon month, and all the time laden with tons of anchors, spars, round-shot and the like. She was eleven years old and already cranky, so that it is a wonder she survived to be present when Nelson cornered the French at last on 1 August 1798. The Battle of Aboukir Bay, sometimes called the Battle of the Nile, was fought out at night in shallow water, and was bloody and destructive.

Of thirteen French sail of the line, only two of these escaped; nine were captured and two were later destroyed by fire. Of the four French frigates, one sank under the British guns, one beached and burned itself rather than surrender, and two managed a getaway.

For the victors the burial of the dead was a prodigious task, and even more so the care of the wounded. Many of these, both French and British, were lodged within the orlop-deck space of *Colossus*, where they remained right until the time she was wrecked. More agreeable was the task of stripping the prizes of everything of value. Wines, pictures, furniture, carvings, stores, navigational instruments and the like, were all temporarily onloaded into a transport ship – the booty of war.

Though the British victory was complete, the damage inflicted by the French had been enormous. Not one of Nelson's twelve 74-gun ships of the line was capable of making sail. It was small consolation that the French were in even worse condition, three of the prizes being in such a parlous state that, after everything of worth had been taken from them, they were destroyed. Not a ship, whether French or British, that didn't need repair and refitting, and all had to be undertaken at speed as Nelson's squadron could not afford to be long out of commission.

It was now that Captain Murray experienced the inglorious side of being commander of a storeship. In such conditions every captain, every master, scrambled for shipwrights and spares to put his vessel to rights, and the more illustrious the commander, the more imperious his demands. For, the sooner his ship was seaworthy, the sooner he would be anchored off Naples or back home in England, basking in the reception which always awaits the victor.

Spars and anchors, ropes and sails – no storeship could have carried the quantity required at that time. Murray would have found himself between the devil and the deep. He had not, so it seems, the stonewall resistance needed to withstand the entreaties of his fellow commanders, and, to keep the peace, seems to have allowed them to cannibalize his rigging of some of its more important gear. Later he was to rue his ill-timed generosity.

Having exhausted both their own resources and those of the storeship, the battle-damaged squadron had to remain in Aboukir Bay for jury-repairs to fill the remaining gaps before their ships could be considered seaworthy. An ingenious shipwright could fashion a temporary 'jury-rudder' from a spare topmast, and a 'jury-mast' could be improvised from the lengthy lateen-spars carried on the mizzenmasts of those days, and so on. These makeshift repairs complete, the British ships at last limped from the scene of the great battle.

The squadron now divided, the prizes being escorted down the Mediterranean to Gibraltar by part of the fleet, and the rest – including *Colossus* – heading for Naples, the nearest port for those needing major permanent repairs. Among the latter was a 74-gun ship of the line, built on the same scale as *Colossus*, impressively menacing even though she lacked a mast. 'The poor wretched *Vanguard*', as Nelson described his flagship at the time, couldn't even make the voyage under her own canvas, but had to be towed into the bay by the frigate *Thalia*, where she was to have her repairs completed at Castlemare, the Royal Neapolitan dockyard a little to the south of Naples itself.

It was a special privilege, graciously granted by the King of the Two Sicilies, and one which would never have been granted a few weeks' earlier when His Majesty had been intent on preserving the appearance of strict neutrality. Now that Nelson had won so decisive a victory over the Napoleonic fleet, his neutrality could be rather more 'friendly'. The King no longer feared to wake up one morning and find French sails bearing down on his little kingdom.

As a storeship *Colossus* would receive minimum attention, but cherished *Vanguard* had the broad bands of chequered black and yellow running fore and aft along her length freshly painted, and the massive lids of her gun ports, drawn open to let in the balmy

Italian air, revealed newly red-painted interiors. Shipwrights, caulkers and riggers swarmed over her, working with their best skill and at top speed, for her commander, knighted after Cape St Vincent, was due for further honours, and was to be created Baron Nelson of the Nile for trouncing the French in Aboukir Bay.

Squatting deeply in the water, this floating fortress was also the focus of attention for a constant stream of small craft. Nelson's brother officers and the nobility of the Italian Court made courtesy calls, and with Napoleon's armies overrunning the north of Italy, there was much business of state to attend to. Nelson was planning his future campaigns.

For him this visit to Naples was almost a return home. He had first made landfall there as captain of HMS *Agamemnon* – 64 guns – in 1793. He had carried despatches for Sir William Hamilton, the British Minister to the Court of Naples, who quickly saw in the young captain 'signs of rare capacity and the promise of signal greatness'. Indeed, he made such a favourable impression at the Court that Queen Marie Caroline and King Ferdinand overwhelmed him with attention, and neither of them wasted time on nonentities. They had not been influenced by his looks. Sir William, wishing to introduce Nelson to his beautiful wife, Emma, warned her that 'he is a little man and far from handsome'. She had still found him of more than ordinary interest, and now, with the gunsmoke of the victory of the Nile fresh in everyone's nostrils, the whole of southern Italy was eager to welcome him.

Pendants, flags and coloured bunting had flown from mast-head and yard-arm of every ship in the great anchorage when *Vanguard* appeared. Hundreds of little boats laden with sightseers were held in check within the harbour confines to allow Sir William and Lady Hamilton to lead the welcoming procession of gala barges to meet her. These beflagged and beribboned craft were gunnels down, not only with all the 'well-affected' élite of Naples, but with their accompanying musicians, whose rendering of British patriotic airs filled the firmament.

The hero himself was not looking his best. His face was pale and drawn with exhaustion, and he bore a recent deep, ugly wound in his forehead. During the five years since he had last seen Emma and her husband, he had also lost the sight of an eye at Calvi in 1797, and in the same year his right arm had been amputated following an abortive landing at Tenerife. Writing home to his wife, Nelson described the reunion as the Hamiltons' barge closed with his vessel: 'Alongside came my honoured friends. The scene in the boat was terribly affecting. Up flew her ladyship and exclaiming "O God! is it possible?" she fell into my arm more dead than alive.'

Scarcely had the three friends dried their tears than the King arrived in the Royal Barge, having come three leagues out into the bay to escort *Vanguard* to her anchorage. With a great show of bonhomie and gratitude, His Majesty named Nelson as his deliverer and preserver – '*Nostra Liberatore*'.

By this time the boats penned up in the harbour had been allowed to set out, and the bay became alive with small craft, bright with colour and fluttering with flags from stem to stern. As the Royal Barge turned back to lead the way, the thunder of a twenty-one-gun royal salute welcomed them in, and the sailors cheered with more than usual goodwill. Lady Hamilton was already the self-styled 'Patroness of the British Navy', and every man jack of them (well versed in their admiral's amorous activities), warmly approved this new 'poll' of his.

2
Journey in Haste

Day after day *Colossus* swung at her moorings, and day after day Captain George Murray kicked his heels in exasperation while he awaited his long-overdue sailing orders. These would be issued by Admiral Lord St Vincent, as overall commander in the Mediterranean, either from Lisbon or Gibraltar – depending on where his flagship happened to be stationed.

In the meantime Murray ceaselessly wrote to friends and superiors alike, telling of his ship's rotten and cranky condition. Faced with a voyage to England, which threatened with every day's delay to become more and more hazardous, he was a worried man. Undertaken in winter it was a voyage that would be a devilish gamble, not only with the weather, but with fate itself.

Nelson was already tiring of Court life. His opinion of the depravity and weakness of the people about him, including King Ferdinand and his wife, was expressed in a disillusioned note to Admiral Lord St Vincent himself: 'It is a country of fiddlers and poets, whores and scoundrels.' As repairs to *Vanguard* neared completion, and his own body grew stronger and his mind more relaxed, his thoughts strayed from Lady Hamilton to sterner things more often. He yearned to be at sea again, and welcomed the day when he could issue the interim order: 'The ships of the squadron at this place are to use all possible despatch in victualling and fitting for sea and report to me the moment they are ready.'

No one was more delighted to receive the signal than George Murray, but one or two things remained still undone. The flagship had requested an anchor. *Colossus* had none in stock, but if the admiral required an anchor, then an anchor the admiral must now have, even if it were the only spare anchor she had for her own use in emergency. By surrendering it, Murray would be courting strong protests from his bo's'un John Shaw, for they would both know that he would be risking the safety of his own ship.

On 15 October Nelson sailed with four ships of the line 'to observe the blockade of Malta' – and took the vital spare anchor with him. The island had been taken from the Knights of St John in June 1798 by the very French fleet that Nelson had out-manoeuvred at the Battle of the Nile, and the admiral now assisted in the rapid turning of the tables. In the final peace treaty of 1814, with the wholehearted backing of the Maltese, Malta became British.

Murray's own orders, as he had expected, were for the return voyage to England:

> By Earl St Vincent, Knight of
> the Bath, Admiral of the Blue,
> and Commander In Chief of
> His Majesty's Ships Vessels
> employed & to be employed
> in the Mediterranean etc. etc.
> etc.

You are hereby required and Directed, to take under your Convoy, such trade of His Majesty's Subjects and of His Allies, as may be ready to proceed with you to the Tagus, and on your arrival there, you are to use the utmost dispatch, in filling the water of His Majesty's Ship under your command, and to Complete her Provisions to ten weeks of all Species, and you are to receive on board such remittances, in specie, bullion, cochineal, and indigo, as the Merchants of Lisbon may have occasion to make: The two latter Articles, paying freight in bullion, with the Corpse of the late Admiral, Lord Viscount Shuldham, and taking under your protection any ships or Vessels bound to England, as may be ready at the time the Colossus is – you are to make the best of your

way consistently with their safety to the Downs, acquaint the
Secretary of the Admiralty, of your arrival, and wait further
Orders.

To George Murray Esqr.
   Captain of His Majesty's
   Ship The *Colossus*.

Given on board *Le Souverain*
Gibraltar 12th November 1798

St Vincent
By Command of the Admiral

Murray would long since have onloaded the war loot taken by
his fellow commanders from the French ships at the Nile battle.
They would have entrusted it to him, rather than keep it aboard
their own vessels, because such lightweight goods were a hazard
on board a fighting ship, and to have them there was a serious
offence. Before an engagement every stick of furniture would
normally be cleared from the ship. In practice this meant from
the admiral's great cabin, his sleeping apartment and the officers'
quarters, for furniture was not for seamen; they lived and slept
amongst the guns. It would all be stacked in the ship's longboat,
covered with sailcloth and then towed astern, out of harm's way.
More fatalities, more ghastly injuries were received in battle from
wood splinters than from any other cause. A round-shot glancing
off even the ship's own heavy timbers could produce a lethal
shower of them, so that any unnecessary wood inboard was
regarded as asking for trouble.

A warship such as *Colossus* had one large hold divided into two
by a central bulkhead. The forehold would normally contain
barrels of water, beer and provisions, as well as all kinds of spare
equipment. In the afterhold there would be tons of ammunition,
and barrels of gunpowder buried for safety in coarse sand. At
this end of season time, however, the holds would probably have
been vast empty spaces, apart from the forest of timber pillars
supporting the deck above.

The afterhold was the more secure of the two, for a way led
down to it from the officers' quarters immediately above, and
constant surveillance was possible. The records have it that it was

indeed the afterhold where Murray had the prize goods stowed, but there was still enough room there for another very special consignment. It was being carried as a result of a personal request from Admiral Nelson himself, on behalf of his very good friends Sir William and his wife Emma.

Sir William has come down to history in popular legend merely in the role of cuckolded husband, but in fact was a considerable person in his own right. His Scottish ancestry, as a grandson of the third Duke of Hamilton, was blue as could be desired, but as a younger son and rather unenthusiastic soldier his bank account went so far into the red that the first little art collection he amassed as a very young man had to be sold to assuage his creditors. He reluctantly retrieved his fortunes by marriage with a plain heiress, but found the remedy increasingly pleasant. His wife was exceedingly amiable and was as adept with keyboard instruments as he was himself with the violin – a picture of her playing the clavichord, with Sir William in attendance, survives – and the only drawback to their happiness was her delicate health.

Sir William's mother had been Mistress of the Robes to the Princess of Wales and (so rumour had it) also mistress of the bedchamber of Frederick, Prince of Wales. Consequently, Sir William had grown up in such close friendship with the royal couple's eldest son, the future George III, that the two boys were always spoken of as foster brothers. By the time of George III's accession in 1760, Sir William, having given up the army on his marriage, had put his wife's estates to rights, and was eager to avail himself of his foster brother's patronage. He entered Parliament as a King's man, and in 1764 was appointed Envoy Extraordinary to the brightest, most civilized – and most corrupt – capital in Europe, the Court of Naples.

It was an ideal post from the point of view of his wife's health, and from that of his own interests in music and art, and also in the more scientific field of vulcanology. He was so assiduous in climbing Vesuvius during his term of office to make personal investigations that he must almost have established his own trackway to the top. When he arrived in Naples, which was to remain Italy's largest city until the twentieth century and, at the time, was only second to Paris in the whole of Europe, the young king was only thirteen: they had thirty-seven years of friendly association before them.

The Kingdom of the Two Sicilies, as the young Ferdinand IV's domains were known, included the island of Sicily itself and 'mainland Sicily', practically all the Italian peninsula south of Rome. All was then peace, and the preoccupation of the moment was the excavation, or rather, the plundering, of Pompeii. Sir William was very much in advance of his time in objecting strongly to holes being dug into the site, and paintings being stripped from walls, and bronzes and other works of art carted off, all without any record of the location in which they were discovered, not to speak of the vandalism being completed by shovelling the rubbish back into the holes. He favoured the modern approach of careful excavation of the site so that visitors could walk round it with the works of art *in situ*, or, if material had to be removed, of making meticulous drawings before it was disturbed, and keeping the finds together for exhibition.

Hamilton was never raised to the rank of ambassador, though he did manage to rise from envoy to Minister Plenipotentiary, and there was no 'embassy', so that his headquarters were in a private house, the Palazzo Sessa. It looked over the great Bay of Naples and had a series of rooms for the display of the treasures which he began to collect as soon as he was installed. As a connoisseur, anything was grist to his mill – bronzes, glass, statues, coins, gems and jewels – but more particularly the Greek 'vases' which were not, in fact, vases in the modern sense of purely decorative objects, but intended for use as tableware in the ancient world. He was among the first to perceive their outstanding beauty of design and workmanship, for although scholars studied the *content* of the vase decoration with interest, such points as the ancient Greek disregard for certain aspects of perspective prevented others from a full appreciation of them.

Hamilton was also the pioneer in recognizing something which we now take for granted, and which the Greek inscriptions on some vases would seem always to have made obvious but curiously did not – that the vases were of Greek origin. Leading scholars were adamant that the vases were Etruscan, the work of that strange people of northern Italy whose written language still remains largely a mystery. It was a belief that led Wedgwood to call his great pottery Etruria, and which was upheld fiercely by the Tuscans of the day, proud in the new nationalism of the period. It was to take Hamilton to point out that the close resemblance between the vases found in Greece and those found in the Two Sicilies suggested either a single source or, more probably, that Greek immigrants had brought the manufacture to southern Italy from an original 'home', which the subject-matter of the decoration suggested must be Athens.

In pursuit of his quarry Sir William showed all the verve of collector's fever, thinking nothing of dirtying his court dress by staggering home with treasures discovered by a peasant in some local tomb, rather than miss the chance of a purchase. In 1766–7 he published four folio volumes illustrating his finest vases with plates that were engraved and hand-painted, dedicating the work to George III. A series of engravers – including Giuseppe Bracci, Antoine Cardon, Carlo Nolli, and Carmine Pignatoro – was employed, and the text was supplied by the art historian Pierre François Hugues, who wrote under the aristocratic pseudonym of 'the Chevalier P. V. d'Hancarville'. Even the type was specially imported from Venice, where the Renaissance tradition of the Aldine Press was not yet quite dead, and in the initial volume the text was duplicated in English and French. The production cost Hamilton in the region of £6000. Not surprisingly, the books won the approbation of Sir Joshua Reynolds, confirmed Hamilton's reputation as a pioneer connoisseur, and incidentally helped to price him eventually out of the market that he himself had created, since they set other, wealthier, collectors, on the trail.

These handsome volumes, however, were intended as something much more than a record of what had been achieved in antiquity. They were designed to assist in the inspiration and development of the modern arts in general, and in particular of contemporary ceramic style. In this they succeeded beyond what even Sir William could have hoped. Among the artists whose work bears their mark are John Flaxman, Henry Fuseli, and Angelica Kauffmann, but the most greatly influenced was Josiah Wedgwood. In addition to providing him with general inspiration, they prompted the creation of vases with designs directly based on the plates, and the medallion profile he produced of Sir William himself has been described by Stephen Bayley as 'among the most telling British portraits of the later eighteenth century'. The drawback to the work – and the rare quality of Sir William is shown in his perceiving it as such at that period – was that it was too expensive for young artists and craftsmen to afford to buy. When it came to commissioning a record of his next collection, it contained outline drawings only – still of the finest quality, but more economical to reproduce and so more easily available to beginners in the arts, to whom he was always eager to give personal encouragement when they approached him.

After seven years in Naples the ambassadorial couple returned to England on leave, and the occasion was taken to dispose of the Hamilton First Collection of antiquities, of which the four sumptuous folio volumes formed a kind of advance catalogue. With the aid of a Parliamentary grant, the Trustees of the British Museum acquired it for £8400, despite some protests at public funds being used for such a purpose. In his correspondence Hamilton refers to the sum as having been £7000, the discrepancy possibly being due to the collection having included bronzes, gems and other items, as well as pottery. Another of his acquisitions at this period had been a seven-ton marble vase found at Hadrian's Villa, which he wanted to give to the British Museum. Unable to afford the costly gift, then valued at £350, he sold it to the Earl of Warwick, who housed it in a specially built orangery. Removed from this shrine by the seventh earl, before his sale of Warwick Castle to Madame Tussaud's in 1978, the 'Warwick Vase' (now valued at £250000) became the controversial subject of an application for an export licence to the United States.

For some time Hamilton had been vainly hoping for transfer – and promotion – to Vienna, and although he had been disillusioned on this point before his homecoming, he must have felt cheered by being able to take back with him to Naples the red riband and star of a knighthood in the Order of the Bath. His ambassadorial susceptibilities needed some such soothing token at the court of a monarch with the tastes of Ferdinand, who gloried in boar 'hunts' in which the animals were gathered for him in droves for slaughter, and a dozen dead dogs were a minimum daily expenditure.

Sir William at once began his 'Second – and even finer – Collection', since although prices were rising, he had the advantage of being on the spot and of having useful connections. Indeed, he gradually lost all ambition except as a collector, and his achievement in the field was remarkable. For the modern student of antique art the loss of the Second Collection has been an ever-lamented tragedy, and the recovery of the sherds which we were to effect is an unexpected miracle. As far as they could go, the Tischbein drawings were a useful enough record, but to look at these is rather as if the Mona Lisa had been destroyed soon after Leonardo da Vinci painted it, and all that was left was an outline sketch by a necessarily inferior later artist. The drawings are not always even accurate in quite significant detail, partly because some of the work was delegated by Tischbein to his students, but partly also because the originals were judiciously improved according to the standards of the day. This process can be seen in operation in the case of our famous 'satyr-sherd', in which the face has been rendered in more formal perspective and has lost much of its eager life in consequence.

Hamilton, despite being so much in advance of his age in appreciation of the vases, was naturally far behind ours in the amount of knowledge which has since been accumulated by the devoted research of scholars. The names of many of the vase painters are now known, and the location of their workshops, but the outlines of the Tischbein copies interpose a maddening barrier to any such recognition in the case of the vases in the Second Collection, whereas even fragments of the original may enable today's expert to supply 'a habitation and a name', and fill out a previously bare catalogue entry with a wealth of fascinating information.

Even more exciting has been the discovery that many of the sherds come from about a hundred previously quite unknown vases of the finest quality. Obviously, Hamilton did not stop collecting in the interval between the publication of the Tischbein volumes, completed in 1795, and the date of the despatch of the vases to England in 1798, and some of his most delightful finds would appear to have belonged to this period. 'Delightful' is the right word for many of these graceful, beautifully decorated pieces, and some of the loveliest are naturally the products of Greek artists settled in Italy. Among scholars there is a certain snobbery that only vases of Attica, on the Greek mainland, are of the true classical perfection, but to the modern eye, and perhaps increasingly among younger scholars themselves, there is a preference for the freer, livelier touch of artists working in the Neapolitan area, especially those of Paestum. A number of the vases of the Second Collection of which we recovered fragments naturally came from this particular happy hunting ground exploited by Sir William, and their re-emergence to the light of day will certainly reinforce the claims of the Greek expatriate artists to recognition as being second to none.

The next landmark in Hamilton's more personal life was the loss of his wife in 1782. He is said not to have been a faithful husband, and in the aristocratic circles of his day would have himself been something of a collector's item had he never taken a sideways step. However, the loss of the quiet, companionable woman who had loved him so deeply probably affected him more than he would have anticipated, and he never destroyed her affectionate letters to him. A year after her death, and perhaps as a distraction from this loss, he was back in England. His purpose was the disposal of the Roman cameo-glass vase which, after a sojourn in the Portland family, was to become known as the 'Portland Vase', and finally became one of the most famous items in the British Museum collection. In this connection the paths of Sir William and Josiah Wedgwood crossed again, for the latter devoted years to perfecting a method of copying this superb piece in the ceramic medium. Legend also has it that, when in later years a madman smashed the Museum original to smithereens, it was a Wedgwood copy which was used as a guide to its restoration. However, Wedgwood had been more concerned with matters of technique than fidelity to the design, and it was a plaster cast of the original that helped in the restoration. Indeed, one version of the Wedgwood copy is notoriously inaccurate, Cupid's legs being crossed in the reverse direction for the sake of 'modesty'. Another amusing sidelight on Hamilton's link with this famous vase – as Wolf Mankowitz relates in *The Portland Vase and the Wedgwood Copies* – is that he told Josiah Wedgwood of his conviction that it had originally been brought out of Asia by Alexander the Great, and had served as the hero's funeral urn. Since it is definitely Roman, and most likely of the Augustan era, although its exact provenance is unknown, this claim is revealing of the impulsive connoisseur and eighteenth-century gentleman, rather than the cool assessment and scholarship of modern experts.

Another distraction during his leave was the company of his nephew, Charles Greville, who looked after his business affairs for him in England and also shared his intellectual interests. Greville, too, was a connoisseur, though with a more calculating eye to cash values than aesthetics. It was at his nephew's house that Hamilton met the loveliest girl in the England of her day.

Amy Lyon was the daughter of a Cheshire blacksmith, who had died when she was only six weeks old. She grew up with her widowed mother, who returned to her own parents' home on the Welsh border, at Hawarden in Flintshire. At thirteen little Amy became a nursemaid, and it may be that the complexion which was one of her great features owed its preservation to her first employer being a doctor skilled in smallpox vaccination. Later, she and her mother moved to London, and in her late teens she moved from a nursery milieu to the Temple of Health run by a quack doctor who sold potions claimed to restore the virility of his debilitated, but well-born, clients. The so-called 'temple' was more like a pretentious sort of brothel where Amy, and the other young ladies in attendance, displayed their scantily clad charms by posing as the goddesses of Wisdom, Beauty and Health. The price – five shillings a peep – was the equivalent of several pounds today, and it was obviously at this establishment that Amy began to perfect the subtle art of creating 'attitudes' for which she was later to become famous.

One of the temple customers was Sir Harry Fetherstonhaugh, a young blood of sizeable means, who quickly carried off 'Emma Hart' – as she had now rechristened herself to meet the fashionable taste of the day – to his home at Up Park on the South Downs.

Here she entered into the carousing high-jinks and dissipation enjoyed by the young squire and his sporting friends, and is rumoured to have entertained them by dancing naked down the lengthy dining-table.

Among Sir Harry's guests was Hamilton's nephew, Charles Greville, and when Emma found herself pregnant after something under a year at Up Park, it was to him she turned for help. Fetherstonehaugh had been furious at discovering her condition, jumping for some reason to the conclusion that the child was not his and turning her out of the house. Much later he did acknowledge paternity, and he and the forgiving Emma became friends again. In the meantime, Greville gave her immediate help, and installed both Emma and her mother in his house in the then rural district of Paddington. The baby, also christened Emma, was despatched first to her grandmother, and then permanently to boarding school.

The two women made the Paddington house a haven of comfort for the bachelor Greville, and he amused himself by instructing his young mistress in the arts of conversation, singing and playing, and by having his apt and beautiful pupil painted by George Romney. The artist fell head over heels in love with her, and was to produce portrait after portrait. Equally charmed, though after a more sober fashion, was Sir William Hamilton.

Noting how greatly taken his uncle had been with Emma, Greville soon conceived the scheme of transferring her to Hamilton's protection. As Sir William's intended heir, it would be advantageous for Greville to give his uncle a young woman who was so low in rank that it would be unthinkable to marry her, and who would yet be so engaging that he would not marry anyone else. Greville was not anxious to part with Emma from a personal point of view, but he had in his sights 'a lady of at least £30000', and if he married he could neither keep Emma in his house nor afford to pension her off in the style to which she had become accustomed. Hence, soon after his return to duty in Naples, an expostulating Sir William found Greville urging the transfer. In 1786 Emma was despatched to the Palazzo Sessa, ostensibly on a visit, during which Greville would join her and

Rowlandson's version of the Attitudes, inspired by the unfounded rumour that Emma had once modelled at the Royal Academy.

only later discovering the intended permanency of the arrangement.

She raged and pleaded on finding out the truth, but Greville never replied to her letters, even the threat: 'if you affront me, I will make him marry me'. He thought it impossible, but it wasn't. Sir William was eventually to make her his wife in 1791, and all Greville could do was transfer the 'standing order' for 'little Emma's' upkeep from his own bank account to that of his uncle. Greville never married. The £30000 turned out to be £20,000 and perhaps he never later quite found the combination of a fortune and a face and disposition like Emma's.

In Italy Emma gradually transferred her affection, though not the girlish love she had felt for Greville, to his uncle, and he in turn enjoyed ensuring the further perfection of this beautiful item in his varied collection of beautiful objects by having her taught Italian and French. Her singing lessons also continued, and she reached a pitch of expertise which led to serious offers of opera house engagements. Her more unusual accomplishment of assuming poses had not been forgotten while she lived with Greville, and with Hamilton's encouragement she now developed them into 'attitudes' of classical beauty and dramatic conviction which won the warm approbation even of the Neapolitan élite, some of whom were far from enamoured of the lowly born beauty.

For these tableaux-vivants, or living pictures, Hamilton designed a special Greek costume, which was to become all the rage in Naples and Sicily. The large vases were used not only as an inspiration for the poses, but as 'stage-props' in the actual performance. The curves of their exquisite shape drew attention to her own, always shown to advantage through the diaphanous folds of her long draperies. With a vase resting on her hip, or shoulder, or poised gracefully on her head, she would melt seductively from one pose to the next.

At the time of his starting to amass his Second Collection, Sir William was called upon at the Palazzo Sessa by Goethe, then visiting Italy as part of the Grand Tour. Accompanying him was the artist Wilhelm Tischbein, who was so delighted with Naples that he decided to stay, accepted an academic post and became a member of Hamilton's intimate circle. The pair arrived in the spring of 1787, when Emma had been Hamilton's mistress for about three months, and they were among the earliest to see her perform her perfected series of classical poses. Goethe recorded his impressions in his *Travels in Italy*:

Sir William Hamilton who still lives here as ambassador from England, has at length, after his long love of art, and long study, discovered the height of these delights of nature and art in a young woman. She lives with him; an English girl of about twenty years of age. She is very handsome with a beautiful figure. The old knight has made a Greek costume for her which becomes her extremely. Dressed in this, letting her hair fall loose, and making use of a couple of shawls, she exhibits every possible variety of pose, expression, and aspect, so that in the end the spectator almost imagines himself in a dream. Here one sees in perfection, in ravishing variety, in movement, all that the greatest artists have loved to express. Standing, kneeling, sitting, reclining, grave or sad, playful, triumphant, repentant, alluring, menacing, anxious, all states of mind flow rapidly one after another. She suits the folding of her veil to each expression with wonderful taste, even adapting it into every type of head-dress. The old knight holds the light for her and enters into the exhibition with his whole soul. He thinks he can see in her a likeness to all the most famous antiques, to the beautiful profiles on Sicilian coins – yes, to the Apollo Belvedere himself! This much at any rate is certain, as an entertainment it is quite unique. We saw it on two evenings with complete enjoyment.

It should be noted that the 'old knight', as Goethe called him, was then in his fifty-seventh year: old age arrived early in the eighteenth century.

After Goethe returned to Rome, Tischbein wrote to him of a variation on the concept of the attitudes, this time involving the male form, of which Hamilton was equally an admirer. As an escape from the heat of Naples and the Palazzo Sessa, Hamilton had two 'holiday villas', one at the bottom of the cone of Vesuvius and the other to the north of the city on the coast at Posillipo. This, which was later to be called the Villa Emma, had a balcony overlooking the sea. 'After dinner', wrote Tischbein, 'we saw a dozen boys swimming in the sea, and a beautiful sight it was with their many varied groupings and postures in the water. He pays them for swimming so that he can enjoy this pleasure every afternoon.' Emma herself also included masculine roles in her repertoire of attitudes, her strong build giving them versimilitude.

Altogether, it was a very strange transformation for the young English girl, taken from her poverty-stricken background to become the admiration of the highest intellectual and social circles of Europe. She liked the gifts with which she was showered, and revelled in the admiration she excited, but such pleasures became familiar. It was inevitable that, as she matured into womanhood, she should become conscious of a certain emptiness, and feel a need to be loved as a woman and not as a possession.

When Nelson came along, with all the prestige and excitement linked to his name, her imagination was kindled and – as we have seen – she was genuinely touched when she saw him return to Naples, worn and ill, and mutilated by the loss of the sight of an eye and an arm. She undoubtedly enjoyed sharing in the fame, and was histrionic in the expression of her emotions on this and other occasions, but Nelson shared these faults himself. They were two of a kind.

As for Nelson, the scholars argue about his feelings for his wife, which were certainly appropriately expressed in his letters up to the time he met Emma that second time. All the same, there were other ladies in his life before Emma, but there was none after. The degree to which Hamilton had befriended and helped Nelson in his career makes the admiral's eventual betrayal of the older man seem dastardly, and Emma has been accused of ingratitude. Yet, Emma at least has a case. Passed from nephew to aged uncle like a chattel, she must have had it borne in upon her by the calculated coolness of the exchange that, if some ravaging disease had ruined her treasured beauty, she would have been discarded by either with conventional regret and not a moment's hesitation. By both of them she was considered below the level of a possible wife, and it was to be five years before she could exact marital status from Hamilton, rather than being offered it as her due.

Sir William's role was eventually to be one which he had dreaded overtaking him when his nephew first proposed to un-load Emma upon him, and, when it came, he accepted it with a certain philosophy. In too feeble health to play the part of a husband to a young woman in her twenties – even Nelson fell

to dozing when she played cards to all hours of the night –
Hamilton was also too greatly taken up with the preservation of
his art collections and his reputation as a scholarly connoisseur to
dwell too much upon the loss of the kind of ardent love from
Emma which he must have known he had never really possessed.

Emma still remained attentive and affectionate towards him
as ever, and for Nelson the old diplomat was to retain an admiration that was unstinted. In the beginning of their triple relationship Hamilton adopted the motto of the Order to which both
men belonged, that of the Knights of the Bath (*Tria juncta in uno*
– Three joined in one) to describe it. In 1798, as Sir William
rejoiced over what seemed the providential coincidence of
Colossus being about to leave for England just as Napoleon's
gains in northern Italy made it imperative that his precious vases
be shipped home out of harm's way, Emma was still his loyal
wife. Hers was no sudden surrender, and it was to be a long
time before it was Sir William and not Nelson who was the
'odd man out'.

In the meantime, Sir William lost no time in obtaining Nelson's
permission to place the cream of his Second Collection on board
ship. How and when the vases were onloaded is not precisely
known; what is certain is that Murray would have had his ship
loaded and ready for instant sailing for some time. According
to the muster table, he also took on board a few passengers,
including George Purvis, an Admiralty Secretary, and a Captain
Peyton, both bound for England; and two men – Goodwin and
Jennings – being taken home by order of Lord St Vincent himself,
as well as an Isaac Dalton who was only going as far as Gibraltar.
Still crammed in her orlop, or lower deck, were the British and
French casualties of the Battle of the Nile, and immediately
beneath them in the hold was the battle loot from the French
prizes – and the vases.

The ship made excellent progress through the length of the
Mediterranean and along the Atlantic coast of southern Spain;
arriving in the mouth of the Tagus she took aboard a Vincent
Deauvau as Pilot Extra to bring her up the river to Lisbon. Well
over half her homeward journey had been completed, and Murray
must have congratulated himself. He was also not surprised to

learn, for the Navy Board correspondence was full of complaints as to the inefficiency of the storekeeper – a Mr Hodson – at Gibraltar, that the warships which had sailed there directly after the Battle of the Nile for repair had not had their requirements met. Stocks of spares had been quite inadequate, and they had had to come on to Lisbon to get the attention they needed.

Although he had made such excellent sailing time from Naples, Captain Murray was still in a fever of anxiety to reach home waters. To his vexation, he now discovered that several merchantmen were not yet ready to join his convoy. Their captains implored him to postpone his sailing date, but he was adamant that he must press on. Little did he realize that he was sealing his own fate by doing so. Had he waited till 8 December, the extra two weeks would have meant his missing the contrary winds which are such a menace in the Western Approaches in November and December. Instead, he sailed straight into a seven-day spell of easterly and sou'easterly gales.

To ease his conscience over this decision he wrote a letter of explanation to his flag officer:

Colossus in the Tagus 22nd Nov. 1798

My Lord

I have the honour to inform Your Lordship, His Majesty's Ship under my Command arrived in the Tagus with all her Convoy (except two which parted between Cape St Vincent & Cape Espichel) on Tuesday last the 20th Inst. On My Arrival I requested Mr Crishir would inform The Merchants I would take any vessels under my Convoy for England that might be ready to sail on Sunday next the 25th Inst: – I have today received an application to put off the sailing of the *Colossus* 'till the 28th Inst & the Merchants were in hope that the *Colossus* would wait 'till the 8th of Decr: when a large Convoy would be ready – I wrote for answer that from Your Lordship's Orders I did not feel myself authorized to put the sailing of the *Colossus* off a single day after she was ready to proceed. I trust my sailing on the day I first fixed, will meet with your Lordships approbation – more particularly so as the state of the *Colossus* is such as to require her getting to England, if possible, before the EasterlyWinds set in, in the Channel and every days delay may be of consequence. Etc. Etc.

I have the honour to be etc. etc.

To add to his problems, Murray also found himself charged with taking home the lead coffin which encased the remains of Admiral Lord Shuldham. His Lordship had created something of a record by being appointed Admiral of the White in 1793, when he was in his mid-seventies, and had died when he was touching eighty. Crews were incurably superstitious at the best of times about this kind of cargo, but now there were still, even in *Colossus*, smouldering repercussions of the previous summer's great naval mutiny at the Nore. Murray dowsed the potential spark of trouble by hiding the coffin in a large wooden crate, which was then placed on top of those already in the hold.

Murray was an inveterate letter writer, and among the many he wrote at Lisbon was one to Evan Nepean, Secretary to the Admiralty, which was sent via the British Agent there:

Colossus in the Tagus November 24th 1798

Sir

Be pleased to inform Their Lordships His Majestys Ship under my Command arrived at this Port on 20th Inst. from Gibraltar with a Convoy & persuant to the orders of the Commander in Chief to compleat my Water and provisions to Ten Weeks with the utmost dispatch, to receive the Corps of the late Admiral Lord Shuldam, and take under my protection any ships or vessels bound to England as may be ready at the time the *Colossus* is, & make the best of my way consistant with their safety, to the Downs – I shall sail tomorrow with such ships that are ready & shall endeavour to keep (on approaching the Channel) nearly in the Stream of the Scilly Islands – & in case of falling in with any of His Majesty's Cruisers I will hoist a *White flag* at the *Fore Topmast head* – which I would wish to be answered by a *White Flag* at the *Main Topmast Head* – & in case of falling in with them in the night – I will hoist *two lights* one under other at the *Fore Topmast Head* – to be answered by *three lights* at the *Main Topmast Head* – I will then burn a *false fire* to be *answered by two false fires* one after the other – it is to be understood that the *Colossus* will answer these signals if made to her instead of her making it first – I forward by the Packet some dispatches from the Commander in Chief which

His Lordship directed me to send in a Packet sailed before the
Colossus –
> I have the Honour to be
> Sir your obed. & humble Servant
> Geo. Murray –

The false fires referred to, and which sound so alarming in the context of a wooden ship, were commonly blue flame signals made by burning certain combustibles in a wooden tube. All these elaborate precautions, routine at this period, were to prevent *Colossus* being mistaken by the Royal Navy for an enemy ship. Sinking into his bunk that night, Murray must have considered that he had done all in human power to secure the safety of his ship.

3

Disaster

The following day, 25 November, *Colossus* sailed from Lisbon, having made a number of last-minute additions to her company: Simon Harcourt, Sam Geararm, Ralph Mitton, Thomas Parker and William Caven, and another shipless commander, Captain Draper. Down the Tagus she went, through the tidal lake, and, bearing first westerly, then rounding into the open Atlantic, she headed her blunt bows to the north. She was now on the final leg of her last voyage, but with a crossing of the Bay of Biscay and over eight hundred miles of hard sailing still before her.

What passed on that voyage from Lisbon to the 'soundings' in the Channel will never be known, for the ship's log for the whole of 1798 is missing. Neither the Public Records Office nor any museum has it in their care. It is a pity, since it could have told us many things of interest, especially regarding the condition of the ship. Murray's overriding anxiety to get to home waters as quickly as possible, even to the extent of refusing to wait for an important merchant convoy, tells us that *Colossus* was pretty nearly *hors de combat*.

The question is, was she so far gone as to make Murray guilty of hazarding the lives of his people by bringing his ship home? Was she in such a state of disrepair that she was likely to founder, so that Murray was in fact taking a calculated risk?

The only surviving proof that she was giving rise to serious anxiety during the voyage comes from the list of defects made out by the ship's carpenter on her arrival in Scilly. 'Ship complains much,' he wrote, 'and when on the Larboard Tack blowing a fresh gale makes from two to three feet of water a hour.' In landsman's language that meant the great ship could take in a ton or more of water every minute, as she hogged her seams agape under the strain of those particular conditions.

The document, which he headed 'The Defects of His Majesty's Ship *Colossus*', goes on to specify:

Sheer Strake, Strings, Channel Wales, Gun Deck & Upper Deck Spirkettings, Gun Deck Clamp and Several Timbers on the Starboard Side brok, the work starts as low down as the Orlop Deck. Timber for the Security of the Anchor on the Larboard Side brok.
Figuer and Main Top Decayd –
Knee of the Head Channel, Ladders, Grateings, hatches, half Port Deadlights. Carve work, Shot lockers, Bulkheads, Boats and Copper on the Bottom want Repairs.
Lower Mast Complains much.
Masts, Yards, Pumps, Capstan & Blocks want Inspection.
Decks and Boiler much worn –
Ship wants Caulking
Glass wanting

Coppered Jan-y 1793
Painted May 1796

J. Loney   Carpenter

The 'strakes', 'strings', 'wales' and 'deck clamps' of a ship were all important longitudinal members of great strength, running fore and aft along the length of the vessel. Their function was essential to the structural soundness and rigidity of the ship. Imagine a ship sailing in a head, or a following sea; she might at times, if only momentarily, be supported on a single wave-crest under her middle, what time her bow and stern were comparatively unsupported. It would be then that the 'strakes' and 'wales' would take the enormous strain and prevent the ship breaking in half. With her main fore and aft members 'brok', *Colossus* would have been as crazy and gimcrack as a floating palliasse.

As Captain George Murray brought his ship into the Western Approaches on 6 December, he found what he had long feared he might, a strong wind blowing from the east along the English Channel. As this was a contrary, or 'head' wind, to that he needed

to take him up-Channel, he veered his convoy to the west and
headed for the Isles of Scilly. Two of the ships under his protection now left him, for they were making for northerly ports and
the wind was in their favour.

At dawn on 7 December, with the wind growing stronger,
Colossus and the rest of her brood approached St Mary's Island
from the south. St Mary's Sound lay open and clear ahead of
them, with the rocks of Spanish Ledges showing off on their
larboard bow, and Pininnis Head, the most southerly point of
St Mary's, away on their starboard beam. Here Captain Murray
took aboard his Pilot Extra, Henry Nance (whose descendants
are still in Scilly), who would guide the eight merchantmen
and the weary man-o'-war into the safety and shelter of the
island's main anchorage.

The pilot would need to stand at the breast rail of the poop-
deck, the better to see his navigational 'marks', as he conned
Colossus through the storm-thrashed St Mary's Sound, and
shouted his directions to the helmsman standing at the wheel
under the break of the poop. Captain Murray, never before
having been to Scilly in a large vessel, would undoubtedly have
stood alongside the pilot, and probably the two shipless captains,
Draper and Peyton, as well, for to sail into the islands is always
an event.

To the west lies the small islet of Gugh, and on the eastern side
of the sea-way the island of St Mary's rises in gentle slopes to the
rounded mound of Garrison Hill topped by Star Castle, a squat,
rugged granite fort with the ground-plan of a seven-pointed star.
It was built in 1593, and the portcullis has the initials ER – for
Queen Elizabeth – carved above it. As *Colossus* and her convoy
made their way in line-ahead formation, any crew members not
busy preparing the anchors and cables would have plainly seen
the 24-pounder guns in the embrasures of the outer defences,
which consist of a weather-scoured, fortified wall of massive
proportions encircling the castle grounds on the lower slopes of
the gorse-clad mound.

Soon the man-o'-war's sails would slacken, as she sailed further
into the lee of the island's high land, in towards the main anchorage. The haven of St Mary's Pool, a little under a sea-mile in

circumference, and surrounded by islands, reefs and rocks, forms an anchorage of good, bad, and indifferent holding ground.

As Pilot Nance brought *Colossus* to the spot he had chosen for her berth, he would have had her helm put hard down, and the ship would slowly have turned into the now muted wind, with her fore- and mainsails rippling and flapping. At that moment the best bower anchor would have been let go with its great rope cable running out freely.

Anchors were hung from a wrought-iron release gear bolted to the end of the catheads – so-called because it was customary to carve a cat's face on the square end of the great greenheart beams which were out-thrust from each side of the bow of a ship like giant gibbets. A pull on a lanyard sprang a trigger, which in turn released the anchor and allowed it to drop. *Colossus*, with her courses (the fore- and mainsails) now taken aback by the wind coming from dead ahead, would gradually gain stern-way. The anchor cable would deliberately be allowed to veer out almost to its entire length in order to reduce the degree of strain, for a hawser-laid rope cable has a certain amount of 'spring' or elasticity in its length. The longer the cable, the 'softer' the link between ship and anchor.

The two large sails which had brought the ship through the Sound would now have been brought in, furled and securely lashed. A sounding was made and the leadsman reported that she had eleven fathoms of water round her. Everything on board that called for it would be lashed and secured, for once an easterly wind sets in at Scilly it may be expected to go on blowing for days on end.

The rumble and slither of the anchor cable through the hawse-hole would evoke a sigh of relief from the sick and wounded below deck, where only 'purser's glims' – candle lanterns – broke the dank and dismal gloom. The voyage across the Bay of Biscay they had just endured was a heart-sinking experience, with gales from all quarters; the continuous clank of the chain pumps night and day; water seeping in through the deck above, and no means of keeping warm.

Now, because the wind was offshore, *Colossus* was becalmed. For the first time in weeks she rode on an even keel, enabling her people at long last to move about normally. For two days – 8 and 9 December – all was peace and quiet aboard. True, the wind was increasing still, as it veered from sou'east to east-sou'east, but aboard the ship it would be heard rather than felt, for it swept across St Mary's and went whistling from the high ground well over her people's heads and barely disturbing the ship.

On 10 December there was an ominous change. The wind had grown to a full gale. With the sea making-up, and becoming confused, Murray sent his Master to sound round the ship, to make quite sure that the sea-bed beneath was free and not foul with isolated boulders or abandoned anchors and the like. As a ship of some seventeen hundred tons burthen, she was carrying a good deal of weight for her size – 172 feet of length and a 48-foot beam – with her armament of 74 guns and two carronades. She would need plenty of water under her if the sea became really rough. Her captain feared that the sea might build up into a pattern of high crests and deep troughs, for in the troughs such a heavy ship might conceivably touch bottom. This would be serious enough if she came down hard on the sea-bed, but to squat on an anchor or a rock would be disaster. However, the Master reported no obstruction of this kind, and, provided the anchor held all would be well. The question now in everybody's mind would be, 'Will she hold?' The two remaining, smaller anchors were made ready to let go if needed, but Captain Murray must assuredly have suffered a pang at the thought of that very good anchor which he had allowed Admiral Nelson to take from him at Naples.

As the ship began to buck and tug at her mooring in the strengthening gale, Captain Murray ordered the top-gallant masts and yards to be struck (taken down), in order to reduce wind pressure on the rigging. It was not an order to be lightly given, for in such conditions, with the mast-heads raking violently to and fro across the sky, the task of lowering the upper masts and yards from the fore-, main- and mizzenmasts was never welcome to any crew.

The usual complement of sails was carried on each of her three masts. On the foremast was the foresail, the lowest and largest; above that the fore topsail; and above that again, in the uppermost position, the fore topgallant sail. Each of these t'gallant sails was spread from its own t'gallant yard which, in turn, was hung by slings from the (removable) t'gallant mast. The latter formed the upper section of each three-sectioned mast. The lowering of all this gear, inevitably to the accompaniment of barked knuckles and grazed elbows, and much blasphemy, would have entailed the transfer of scores of ropes and running-rigging gear. But it was all in vain. At eight bells that afternoon – four o'clock – the time of high-water springs, the cable parted.

Every soul on board must have felt a breath-stopping spasm of apprehension, for they would have known to a man what had happened. 'The cable's parted!' must have been a simultaneous shout from every part of the ship. It is possible for an anchor to drag surreptitiously, more often than not it does just that, craftily, stealthily, without anyone at first noticing. But, when an anchor cable parts, the whole demeanour of the ship is transformed. One minute she is a tethered, wild, living thing, tugging and

straining against captivity, with the fortissimo string-music of the gale in her taut rigging. The next, she is free. The sea and the wind flow with her, she is no longer struggling, and with her freedom comes a silence – sudden and dramatic. The difference is unmistakeable.

In the case of *Colossus* her liberty was short-lived. 'The small Bower Anchor was instantly let go. . . .' Instantly would mean exactly that, for the reaction of the men on anchor-watch would be simultaneous with their realization of what had happened: '. . . and after veering to a Whole Cable the Ship brought up.' In his autograph 'Narrative of the loss of *Colossus*', which was read by the Judge Advocate at the eventual court martial, Captain Murray was precise.

The last moments of HMS
Colossus

Having, then, only the Sheet Anchor left, and every appearance of its blowing hard, I determined to put to Sea but the Pilot, whom I had kept constantly on board, judging it impossible to clear the Rocks, before it would be too dark to justify the Attempt, it became necessary to prepare the Ship for riding out the Gale: the Sheet anchor was accordingly let go; and having Struck the Yards & Top Masts, I flattered myself the cables and anchors would then hold: but about half past five, we had the Mortification to find the small Bower come home & I was obliged to Veer and let her ride between both.

Everything was combining to prevent Murray saving his ship. She was then in the middle of the anchorage, in the full blast of the gale, with no shelter whatever. The tide was ebbing and taking him in a nor'west by westerly direction, towards the nearest rocks; it would continue to ebb until ten o'clock that night, which was bad, as he wanted as much water under him as possible. His main cable, one which he thought was 'new', and which he had therefore trusted, had proved to be rotten. There was no other sizeable spare anchor, and his smaller anchors were proving incapable of holding the ship.

Murray's vessel was doomed and he must have realized the fact. She was moving relentlessly nor'west, towards a rocky reef over which the sea could be seen foaming and thundering. What, in those days of shipwreck, did the commander of a doomed ship do in such circumstances? In my research into ships which have been wrecked on a 'lee-shore' – a dread description meaning a shoreline towards which the wind and the ship is blowing, and which leaves a sailing vessel no means of escape – I found there was a routine pattern of conduct on the part of those in command.

Once the conclusion had been arrived at that the ship was indeed doomed to a total loss, every endeavour was made to prolong the break-up of the vessel in order to gain time to save the lives of the people. For instance, if there were a sandy beach or cove in the rocky lee-shore, then by a variety of means, by drogues (floating canvas 'anchors') or by wisps of sail on the right yards, the ship was inveigled to beach herself rather than smash herself against the rocks.

The secret of driving ashore in a ship 'not under control' was to make every effort to strike broadside on; then, immediately, to persuade the vessel to heel towards the land, thus presenting her strong rounding bilge to the smashing seas. In such cases, and there have been many, the hull acts as a breakwater while the people scramble ashore. If by some mischance the ship were to heel towards the sea, she would present her flat deck to the full force of the breakers; a ship's deck is her weakest part, in a matter of hours the sea breaches it and traps everything, and everyone, inside the hull.

Ships may be made to heel, to one side or the other, by various means. In the case of an armed vessel, such as *Colossus*, guns would have been brought inboard on one side and run-out on the opposite side; once the inclination had been started the gale-force winds, acting on the masts and rigging, would complete the heel. Masts inclined over the sea have never saved anybody, but masts leaning landwards have provided escape routes for hundreds of seamen in the past. In some instances as a last resort, the masts have been cut and allowed to drop on the land, thus forming a 'bridge' between ship and shore.

Murray had no sandy beach for which to aim, in fact he had very little time to prepare his ship for taking the shore. He gave some thought to the idea of casting his heavy guns overside, in order to lighten his ship and give her more buoyancy. As there would have been a danger of the vessel actually foundering on her own guns he gave up the notion.

About 6-o'clock the Ship Struck the Ground, but not so hard as to appear to me of much consequence, and which the throwing the Guns overboard and cutting the masts away might in some degree have relieved: but as these were objects of considerable Moment, I thought it prudent to hold a Consultation with Captains Peyton and Draper (of His Majesty's Navy, then onboard) the First Lieutenant and Master of the *Colossus*, who, with me were, unanimously, of Opinion, that, as there was not room to veer clear of them, the throwing of the Guns overboard might be attended with very grave consequences; And as there were still hopes of getting to Sea at Daybreak, with the Flood Tide, it was thought most advisable not to cut away the Masts; also, as another reason for postponing this measure, it was considered that in case the Ship should strike so hard as to Bulge, the Tide would

flow over her, and, by keeping the Masts standing, it might be the
means of saving the lives of the People. Everything else to lighten
the Ship was done.

Murray would already automatically have lightened the ship
a little by jettisoning the hundreds of round-shot contained in the
shot-garlands – racks of cannon-balls, each resting in a shallow
depression – which lined the gun-decks and formed ready-to-
hand supplies of ammunition. However, it is very doubtful, with
his holds cluttered with merchandise and flooding fast, whether
he would have been able to reach what remained of his main
store of round-shot. But we can be sure that all else of weight
that was moveable would have gone overside.

With the tide still ebbing – it had two hours to dead low-water
springs – it is uncertain whether all this effort was worth while,
apart from the psychological benefit of keeping everyone aboard
occupied during a very anxious period.

By eight o'clock that evening, when the wind veered round
to the south, it would have funnelled straight through St Mary's
Sound, whipping up the sea in the anchorage to even greater
fury. To see such a gale in Scilly is a fearful and awe-inspiring
sight. Hugh Town on St Mary's is the island's only town, and
sprawls across a low sandy isthmus, clinging to the slopes of a
rocky peninsula, so that it has two seafronts. With a southerly
gale shrieking and roaring over the island the sea smashes across
the low neck of land in great inroads of solid, writhing, spume-
ridden water, slashing at everything in its path. On land it can
be alarming enough; at sea it is terrifying.

Returning to Murray's spare account:

About 8 o'Clock the Wind unfortunately veering round to the
Southward, the Ship tailed more in Shore, but notwithstanding this
Circumstance, and it blowing tremendously hard, we were able to
keep her free; and having tried with the Boat, and found that there
was more water ahead of the Ship, I had hopes, by heaving on one
Cable & bousing in the Slack of the other, I should be able to keep her
afloat – accordingly we hove in to half a Cable On each Anchor: But
as the tide ebb'd, the Ship, again Struck with great Violence, and
shortly after, the Water having gained on our Chain Pumps, we
man'd them all, and baled with half Tubs and Buckets.

It is one thing to ride to two small anchors, in a raging gale, as did *Colossus*; but it is entirely another thing to heave the ship in on them, against sea, tide and wind, and to expect them to hold. To illustrate how divers of today may become involved in historical events of over 175 years ago, I can say that we – the diving team – now know why Captain Murray had trouble with those two small anchors. When we located them we found that they were broken; they had broken where anchors usually broke in those days, where the shank was forged to the crown. The shank being the upright bar with the ring at the top, and the crown being the curved part with a fluke at each side – each anchor had half the crown with one fluke missing.

To heave in an anchor cable in those days was not so simple as it sounds. It involved more than tramping round a upright drum pushing on the capstan bars, which stood out like the outspread, horizontal spokes of a rimless wheel. The great hawser-laid cables themselves were too large, too stiff and too unmanageable to take a turn round the capstan barrel. So, short lengths of flexible rope, called 'messengers', were attached to the main cable, and it was these messengers which were taken around the capstan and in turn hauled in the main one.

In the dim confines of the tween decks, scores of men would be sweating and swearing, arms akimbo, with their chests pressing against the capstan bars, straining for every inch of movement to heave in on those anchor cables. Only the strength of their own muscles lay between them and the raging seas on the nearby rocks. To keep the men there, in those overcrowded, dark, bucking swashy gun-decks, urging them on to ever greater efforts as they jostled fiercely against one another, filled with one instinctive, overpowering desire – to get out from below – would not have been a matter of words only.

Captain Murray gives no slightest hint in his account of any revolt against his orders, but in our work on *Colossus* we were to discover, in an unexpected way, a speaking clue to the tense horror of the situation at that moment. We found the remains of a pistol belonging to one of the officers, showing unmistakeably (as I shall later explain) that at the time of the shipwreck it had been loaded and half-cocked – ready for immediate use on anyone who disputed their commands.

Murray's official narrative, however, continues precise and unemotional:

About Midnight the Rudder was beaten off: and the Wind continuing to blow very hard, and the Night extremely dark – , the Signals of distress, which we had made from the first of the Ship's driving, were constantly repeated, tho' situated as we were, there was but little hope of Relief until day light.

During this time notwithstanding the great exertions of the Crew, and the Activity of every Officer in the Ship, the water gained on us fast: and having more Reason to apprehend that the next flood would be over the Ship, it was a matter of the greatest Satisfaction to think, that I had foreborn to Cut away the Masts as, before daylight, I was obliged to Order the People on the Quarter Deck and Poop, the Water being up to the Cills of the Ports of the Upper Deck.

By midnight the tide would have been flowing some two hours, and it would have been at about half past four in the morning that the water reached the cills of the upper deck gun-ports – in other words, *Colossus* had sunk and was resting on the sea-bed. The quarter-deck and poop deck would have remained above the reach of the tide, but with the enormous seas running that night they would have been as swamped by waves as half-tide rocks, and the whole ship's company would seek safety in the rigging. Many would have scrambled up clear to the fighting-tops, others less fortunate would stand on the ratlines, the rope-rungs attached across the shrouds, which form mast-stays and resemble rope-ladders.

Those in the worst plight would be the wounded. The ammunition of the period inflicted terrible mutilation, and included round-shot, chain-shot, bar-shot, grape-shot, and – perhaps worst of all – the favourite of the French, langrage. This consisted of scrap iron, such as cut-up horse-shoes with the nails left in, and Nelson himself suffered his severe head-wound from just such a fragment. The men who had survived such injuries and were still unable to walk would be carried up from their lower-deck sick-bay and lifted into the rigging wrapped in scraps of sailcloth. Lashed into position above the sea, they would still be continuously drenched with showers of spray.

This operation would also have provided the occasion for mutiny, when the weapon that we found – and many others like it – would have been held at the ready. Captain Murray might put the safety of the wounded as his first priority, but many members of his crew might feel their own skins as their prime consideration. Those were grim moments when the injured men, crying out against the gale in the pain of being inevitably roughly jolted as they were hauled up on deck, were lashed into place. The watching officers would have held their pistols in their right hands – kept tilted so that the locks were uppermost and the gunpowder grains could be retained in the vents – but thrust deep in the left sleeves of their greatcoats to protect the firing mechanism from rain and spray. The menace none the less real for being so concealed.

It would have been a long five hours, waiting for the tide to drop sufficiently for everyone to be able to leave the rigging, and proof of the terrible conditions which kept them unable to do anything other than cling on for dear life came with our later finds – the fittings of two quadrants, the eye-piece of a spyglass, and the battered casing of a splendid gold watch. These were not merely valuable but vital equipment in the performance of an officer's duties, and were the first things anyone would save if he could.

Captain Murray, however, makes light – in traditional naval fashion – of the sufferings they all endured from the severe weather conditions during the period of high water on the morning of 11 December 1798. Lying on the sea-bed stern-on to the reef, with her rudder broken off and her bow facing the wind and the sea, *Colossus* was still at that stage fortunately upright. There would otherwise have been little hope for her people, since the sea was running through her from bow to stern, with giant combers sweeping along the length of the upper deck and into the space below the quarter deck. The strength of the gale can be measured by Murray's revealing comment: 'the water . . . as the Ship rolled, struck with so much violence against the quarter deck, as to break several of the beams it gave me reason to apprehend every moment, that it would blow up . . .'. In other words, he was fearful that the sea would lift the quarter-deck by the very weight of water surging into the tween decks below.

However,

About 8 o'Clock in the Morning, I had the pleasure to see several boats coming to our assistance, and on their arrival, I directed the Sick & Invalids to go in the first Boats and the People by Divisions, into the others, as they came to us. Thus by the exertions of the People of the Islands in bringing, and the great activity of Major Bowen, the Commanding Officer of the Fort, in despatching those Boats from the Shore, I am happy to say, that, before three o'clock in the afternoon, with the exception of one, who had fallen overboard in the Night – I had the pleasure to see the last man go safely out of the Ship, and then, quitted her myself.

The unfortunate odd man out was the quartermaster, Richard King, who had been taking soundings round the ship.

4
Wreckage

HMS *Colossus* met her end on the Southward Well Reef, a weed-smothered rock outcrop which lies south of the island of Samson and indicates its position from time to time by the appearance above the surface of its tidal highest point, the jagged point of the Southward Well Rock. She hadn't a chance of escape, for the rocks, reefs and ledges lying athwart her path stretch from Broad Sound Ledge in the west, right through the Great Minalto Ledges, running up in a nor'easterly direction to Vincent's Ledges: in all a great barrier some 3500 metres long.

Samson is a strange-looking island, consisting of two hills joined by a low belt of land. Today there are only a few ruined houses surviving, but on that morning in 1798 there were some fifty people making a living there by growing potatoes, and every one of them would have been out, chilled and soaked by the screaming spindrift from the sea, but peering excitedly from the shelter of hastily erected windbreaks on the island's bleak, southern slopes. The looming, murk-enshrouded vessel was for them a gift from heaven, and their guarantee of good cheer that coming Christmas.

Shipwreck – any shipwreck – was welcome, for it brought at least timber for burning and rope for their boats. But this enormous ship, stranding right on their doorstep, offered the possibility of clothing, and footwear and provisions, and the certainty of tallow, pitch and candles. On the previous evening there would have been barrels, timber-hatches and other buoyant material washing in on the rocky, foam-creamed coastline below.

Even as they scrambled to reach it while the day was dying, they would have looked out to see the preparations being made on board the doomed vessel to lodge its complement of six hundred in the masts and rigging to escape the rising tide.

The Samson men would know, as soon as it happened, that *Colossus* had gone aground for ever. The Scillonian boatman has an instinct for a mortally wounded ship, and I remember when I was at Scilly many years ago and a wooden-hulled ship came ashore, a voice from the knot of onlookers: 'She's there for good, boy! They'll nivver get 'er off! No, nivver! Not en this world, nor the next!' It didn't look as bad as that at the time, but he was right.

Now, at first light, though there had been no let-up in the gale, every boat on the islands that could stand up to the storm was on its way to the rescue. Those from St Mary's came up from the south, sailing and rowing out before the fearsome wind and hence suffering greatly on the beat back to safety. Those from Samson, on the other hand, came in from the north, beating out of the shelter of their puny pier, and calling on every shred of their skill to put their craft alongside the wreck.

By the time the last of the survivors, the captain himself, had been rescued, the conditions had so worsened that the St Mary's boats abandoned the attempt to return to their own island, and accompanied the men from Samson back to their meagre harbour.

Ashore heads were being scratched at the thought of all those extra mouths to feed, especially if the storm continued and hindered the delivery of fresh supplies from the mainland. Overnight, beer, bread and potatoes were running out.

Out at sea the crazy, overworked old man-o'-war was abandoned at last to the mercy of the wind and the waves, the elements against which she had pitted her wits for all of her eleven years of existence.

Colossus, like the other great ships of her time, had her outer planking fastened to her rib timbers by 'treenails', spikes of hardwood, such as oak or green heart, which were driven into auger-bored holes one and a half inch or one and three-quarter in diameter. They were made 'full' or slightly oversize in order to ensure a tight fit, and were often split lengthwise so that a fine wedge could be inserted after they were driven home, and the holdfast made extra stiff. A ship built like this was a splendid structure so long as she was well maintained, but if these thousands of timber fastenings were allowed to 'work' or 'give' for any length of time, the vessel would become as gimcrack and spineless as a sack of maize. As the huge combers battered the hull of the cranky *Colossus*, she would have soon begun to break up.

On 17 December, a week after she had gone aground, the Samson men saw, through salt-grimed, slitted eyes, the ship's mainmast go by the board. The southerly wind and its following sea had forced the hull broadside on to the shore, so that her stern now faced west and her bow pointed east. With the ship listing towards the land, her starboard guns fell inboard; by the night of the following day her bowsprit had gone. With the next couple of days, as the storm subsided, *Colossus* was left on her beam ends, lying on her larboard side with her fore- and mizzenmasts flat on the sea's surface.

In that wind-free, storm-cleansed atmosphere which, in Scilly, follows a spell of really bad weather; in that tranquil anti-climax which allows the sound of the seabirds crying to be heard once again, the Scillonian boatmen would have gone out, to a man, to view the remains of *Colossus*. Lying on her side like a sick whale, she would have revealed at dead low water some three-quarters of her copper-sheathed, weed-grown hull. The great keel would have been fully visible along its whole length.

Within the wide expanse of water between the wreck and the shore, the sea surface would be chock-a-block with splintered timbers, tangled frayed rope, fractured spars and knotted sail-cloth, all undulating sluggishly with the slow movement of the swells. And, over all, the unforgettable tang of disintegrated seaweed interlaced with the gum-laden scent of pulverized timbers, such as white-pine and pitchpine. More than once in my lifetime I've seen such a disembowelment of a timber-built ship, and it is a terrible reminder of the incredible power of the sea, its frightening ferocity and cruelty.

For the people of Scilly all this jumble of flotsam was treasure trove. For the past ten years there had been a surprising dearth of shipwreck: a small vessel with a cargo of tobacco seven years back, another with timber five years ago, but, since then, nothing. It was high time matters were evened up, and they surveyed the scene with quiet satisfaction.

The first fine weather would also have brought out the St Mary's Revenue Cutter, no doubt with Captain Murray and his officers aboard to make their final assessment of the wreck and ascertain if any of their personal possessions might yet be saved. The ship's carpenter would also take a last look at his late charge, who had given him so much trouble and worry over the past twelve months. Of especial interest to him would be the stump of the fractured mainmast, that great spar he had reported as having 'complained much', and in which the skill of his calling would now enable him to diagnose the exact cause of its long-drawn-out sickness.

Another passenger could well have been Major Bowen, the commanding officer of the fort, supported by his aides, and all of them looking as uncomfortably out of place aboard the cutter as soldiers usually do in a ship. For him *Colossus* would have meant a great deal of extra work, and it would be natural for him to want to take a closer look at the culprit. In fact, everybody who amounted to anybody would have been out in the anchorage on that first fine day after the storm, and a majority of the lesser folk, too. There's a fascination in inspecting storm damage immediately after it has happened, let alone a wrecked ship, and such a ship! It was the sight of a lifetime to see a giant man-o'-war heeled over on its side.

Many of the islanders would be looking at the wreckage with a professional eye. The St Mary's blacksmith would be envious of the ship's great wrought-iron channel brackets, beautiful bar-iron, something like two inches in diameter. What wouldn't he give for a few of those fine fittings to which the shrouds were made fast? Then there were the eye-bolts, the iron straps and stays, the iron rigging fittings, the rails, the knees and the like. . . . If he could only get his hands on a 'jaffle' of those. . . . Such an assortment would be the making of him.

Scilly's carpenters and shipwrights would have been there, too. They wouldn't have known which way to turn when their eyes lit on the scores of handy-sized running-rigging blocks, the hundreds of fathoms of rope, the thousands of square yards of sailcloth, the plates of copper-sheathing – they beggared belief. And when it came to timber, the size of the wreck was awesome, for by their calculations there must have been not tens of tons, but hundreds of tons of wood in the ship, some of the timbers being three feet square in section.

The great seas, which Captain Murray reported as having swept along the length of the open upper deck, would assuredly have smashed through the bulkhead under the quarter deck. This forward bulkhead, and another aft of it again, led to his great cabin and the captain would have found his personal quarters were a shambles. It is extremely doubtful whether he ever re-covered any of his possessions, for the ship's log – the dossier of the ship's course throughout her voyage, entered up daily with a record of every happening aboard, including the coming and going of passengers and crew, and the onloading and offloading of cargo – is missing. In case of shipwreck this is normally the first thing that any commander thinks to save, and it would have been expected that Captain Murray should have wrapped it up in oiled silk (to protect it as much as possible from sea water) and buttoned it inside his greatcoat. His next thoughts would be for his quadrant and navigational dividers and then, possibly, his spyglass.

No amount of searching through the shelves of the Public Records Office or of museums has brought to light the log, and since the remains of Murray's quadrants and 'glass' were one day to be located on the sea-bed, this all suggests that the captain had no time for anything, other than his ship and his people, during the hours of crisis.

Meanwhile, the officers and crew of His Majesty's Late Ship *Colossus* were being shipped out of the islands by every available vessel. Food was getting so short that the shipwrecked jack-tars were becoming an embarrassment to the local people. On 16 December George Murray wrote to the Admiralty:

I beg to inform you that Lieut. Burleton of the *Hecare* Gun-Brig has this morning taken on board – in order to their being conveyed to Plymouth – 80 of the *Colossus*'s Crew – The *Hearlep* Gun-Brig will sail this afternoon with 106 more – I much fear few stores will be saved from *Colossus* except Anchors and Cables and in calm weather perhaps her Guns – as the Gale continued so long that she's gone to pieces – The getting the rest of the Crew from Hence becomes a great object on account of the additional Consumption of Provisions which will shortly distress the Inhabitants much.

During the few days before Christmas 1798, and taking scant heed of a public notice issued by the commander of the fort, the Scillonians would have presented themselves with many seasonable gifts from the wreck. The notice had stated hopefully:

1798 – HIS MAJESTY'S LATE SHIP COLOSSUS

Salvage will be Paid by the Navy Board for Any
Stores which might be Saved from the Said Wreck
and Which are Delivered at the Garrison at St Mary's.

However, the prize 'find' at that time of the year would have been provisions, and the 'salvage' paid by the Navy Board would be a fraction of what the goods were worth to the islanders.

Daytime raids on the hulk of the ship were out of the question, since it lay in clear view of the fort, unless there happened to be a sea-fog. But night raids would undoubtedly have been made on what remained of the ten weeks' supply of food, taken on at Lisbon, which would have been stacked in a locked store adjoining the galley on the forepart of the upper deck, below the forecastle. The well-known island skill of 'wrecking' would have been tried to the utmost, for *Colossus* had the tide flowing over her at every high water, and since she was on her side there were no decks to walk on. It would have needed the skill of a mountaineer, or a potholer, to move from one part of the ship to another, and it all had to be done in the dark.

By the week before Christmas, with all the officers and men of *Colossus* now gone, the islanders would have relaxed and settled to their normal lives of long-distance piloting, fishing and farming. Not that they would ever relax to the extent of taking both eyes off the sea at any one time, not merely in the hope of a wreck, but in fear of invasion by the French. This had been an imminent threat for four war-torn years past, and two years later a 74-gun man-o'-war flying the colours of Revolutionary France came over the horizon, together with an escorting frigate. It was intended to land troops, but fortunately for the islanders the larger vessel got so entangled with the rocks to the west of St Agnes that she sank with all hands. The loss entirely demoralized the crew of the frigate and it sailed away without a shot fired.

Over the Christmas of 1798, however, all was peace in the islands and the wreck-wood fires were bigger and brighter than for many a long year. Sitting round their open hearths, the cottagers would turn their talk inevitably to their favourite topic of shipwreck. Not necessarily of *Colossus*, but yarns of days gone by, handed down by word of mouth over generations. What I like about these tales is that they don't suffer exaggeration in the process. On Scilly a wreck-yarn has to be strictly accurate or not told at all.

I've got wonderful memories of long stays on St Martin's, my favourite among the islands. I always enjoyed the late evening trips in the 'bo-at' – as they say the word down there – to 'pull' the crab-pots, for one never knew what the catch might be. Often enough we caught more than crabs or lobsters in the withy-made cages, for French 'crabbers', grateful for the use of a freshwater well, would pay their dues in cognac. To see a pot coming up through the clear water with a lobster's huge paws embracing the straw-wrapped bottles was a very encouraging sight!

Back on land, after sluicing down and storing the gear, we'd be in to supper by a fire of sun- and sea-bleached timbers which would last beyond our protracted supper, well into the small hours. I shall for ever remember our wreck-yarns told then, laced with cognac and richly told by the very men who'd taken part in them. It would have been just the same in that Christmas of 1798, I could lay to that, for that's something that never changes.

The children would have huddled into their elders while they listened enthralled, and not a little scared, as they heard tales of drowning men and the great fire roared and cracked, devouring the salty, pitch-streaked timber. There would be tall, fluttering shadows on the rough walls behind, dumb figures playing out their agitated pantomime – menacing and jostling, threatening and bullying, stumbling and falling, and shrinking only to rise again. Every once in a while, as the heat scorched a copper nail in the glowing embers, the orange flames would flush with a brilliant green light turning the dark shadows to misty blue. And all the time there would be the reek of the hot oak-smoke as it wreathed to the low, blackened beams above.

'Ded 'ee ever 'ear tell of th' man-o'-war that struck th' Crow? Why, must be all o' twenty-year since, but 'ess, she struck th' Crow by God, an' with such might she left part of 'er oaken stem in the rock.'

'Ess, I mind that, they got 'er off of th' rock tho', she was the *Glasgow* if I mind right, back in 1778 it was.'

'HMS *Glasgow*! that's 'er! It was told that when she docked at Plymouth they found a brae' lump of th' rock still 'anging fast of 'er.'

'Talkin' of battleships, there was th' frigate – er, I forgets 'er name now, French she was, thirty-six guns if I'm correct. I mind she was lost on Pednathise Head? Mind that, does 'e? Not a blind soul was saved off 'er.'

'Wot was that wan with the wine, baccy and sugar? A brig she was . . . way back in 1780, out of Plymouth bound for Dublin. . . .'

'Why the brig *Glory*! 'Ess it was the *Glory* a'right, glory-be most like! Wine an' baccy, we blessed our stars th' day she came in!'

'There was another brig round about the same time, went ashore on St Helen's. . . .'

'Laden with Portland stone?'

'Portland stone! 'oo wants Portland stone! No, that was the brig *Charming Molly* bound fer Dublin an' nivver got there, she was lost to the back of Bryher. Th' wan I'm tellin' of was th' brig . . . an' this is 1780, mind, when six brigs were lost. . . .'

' 'Twere five to my way o' thinkin'.'

'Was it now! Five, was it? Come to think on it so t'was, anyway th' wan I'm tellin' of went ashore in . . . 'ess 1781, that's it, she was the *Endeavour*, a brig out of Teignmouth, but on this trip she was from Liverpool bound out fer Portsmouth. . . .'

'Wa' did she 'ave up?'

'You'd know as well as I do! She 'ad coal, herrin' and spirrots, remember th' spirrots? Brandy an' rum, fer land's sake! No wan could ivver forget that!'

'Remember the schemozzle we 'ad over th' *St Antonio de Lisboa?* Can 'ee mind the ruccus we 'ad with th' Customs?'

'By golly it were like the devil at prayers! Mind, I'll say truth, if it were not fer Abraham Leggatt – ye mind th' surgeon up at th' garrison? 'e that took to us like pitch? – if 'e 'ad not spoke up plucky to the Excise like 'e did we'd 'ave lain in a clove-hitch, it would 'ave bin alls up with us an' no mistake.'

'Take an' tell th' children wot 'twas all about, tell 'em.'

'Well, it was like this, the *Antonio* was a ship-rigged vessel bound from Oporto to London with wines, oils, skins an' sich-like and she foundered with all hands round about the back of Tresco. A brae' parcel of 'er cargo of wine came ashore in large casks, beautiful casks they were, and beautiful was th' wine within. Well, the long an' shot of it was we, an' lots of others, got the casks to a safe place an' covered it up with gorse an' bracken. Maybe 'twas a foolish, overbold act, but that is wot we did.'

'The next thing was th' 'ide-away was rummaged by the Excise an' they demanded that we should car' th' 'ole lot to th' Customs warehouse.'

'Which we defied 'em not to do, so they threatened to take it by force. Anyways, not 'aving no ch'ice we cast about for some way of gainin' time an' in that we we all agreed to go up to the Fort for a parley.'

'At the Fort th' surgeon, Abraham Leggatt, piped up staunch an' pretty for us, saying that all aboard the *Antonio* was dead as bilge and, being dead, could not claim the cargo and that we 'ad a right to the halves of it.'

'Not the alls of us 'ad gone up to th' Fort mind, so whiles they were up there talkin', th' rest of us moved a brae' many of the casks an' hid them in lots of places. They were never found so fortune favoured us in the end.'

'Wot about the Venetian vessel – I forgets 'er name – she broke up on the Crim. Ever so many people were saved off 'er. She was laden with cotton, cocoa, coffee, sugar and rum, most of it was saved, but there was cocoa in the islands for years after.'

'Another time we 'ad a scat-off with the Customs was in 1782, sixteen years back, her people had abandoned her and she was found floating off the islands – *Maria Charlotta* she was called – a Dutch-built galley of about 200 tons. She was loaded with French wines which was mostly saved by the islanders. We carr'd half the number of casks to the King's warehouse an' 'eld back on t'other 'arf in loo of salvage, which, in our way o' thinkin' was fair enow. But not the Customs, oh no! They wanted to give us a third. There agin we were saved by Surgeon Leggatt 'oo declared 'e wanted to know what's what, like the staunch gentleman 'e was.'

' 'Ess, 'e 'ad a head on 'is shoulders 'e did! Were 'ud we be, I ask 'e, where 'ud we be effen it weren't for men with notions like 'is?'

'Let's see now, in th' summer of 'eighty-two there were two wrecks within a matter of three or four weeks. Both foreigners they were, wan was the *Providentia Divina* on 'er way from Marseilles to Ostend with brandy an' sich. She was lost out on the Western Rocks with most of 'er people saved. Ever so many of 'er cases of brandy was salvaged but I speak fair when I say we 'ad no trouble with the Excise on that one.'

'Wan ship we did 'ave trouble over was *La Bona Resolution*, she was a fine Swedish square-rigged ship on voyage from . . . Batavia I reckon it was, bound for Rotterdam. She 'ad a mixed cargo with coffee and pepper; and I remember the pepper for the reason that some of the islanders were charged with stealing a large amount of this.

'The ups and downs of it were that th' pepper had been put into th' King's warehouse. The islanders broke into the bonded store and 'ad 'elped themselves to some of this. Th' joke was that when they were put on trial at th' Assizes they were acquitted because the captain couldn't tell if th' pepper was 'is or no!'

So it would have been during that far-off Christmas-tide, with that great ship lying stranded for ever in the middle of the islands. Deserted during the daytime, perhaps not so deserted during the hours of darkness.

Unfortunately for the islanders, those exciting night raids were dramatically brought to a halt by the appearance, in St Mary's Pool, of a small squadron of ominous-looking vessels. These consisted of a small gaff-rigged cutter, two transports and an Admiralty armed brig. The news quickly flashed round the islands that the ships had been sent to salvage the stores, guns and accoutrements from His Majesty's Late Ship *Colossus*.

These were precisely the orders that had been passed to Lieutenant Pardoe, officer in command of the gun-brig *Fearless*, from the Lords Commissioners to the Admiralty.

These gun-brigs, or armed sloops of war, were interesting vessels. The *Fearless*, of 149 tons burthen, would have had a single deck 75 feet in length, with a beam of 21 feet. She was armed with ten 9-pounder guns and four carronades, the guns being carried on the open deck. In addition to her gun-ports, she would have been pierced by eight row-ports aside. The advantages of being able to manoeuvre under oars were many for these small vessels, leaving or entering harbour under conditions adverse to sailing being just one of these. She would have carried a crew of twenty-five. With a draught of but seven feet, she was an ideal craft for donkey-work at Scilly.

Leaving Plymouth Sound on 26 December 1798, *Fearless* was at Falmouth by the next day where, during the last few days of the old year, certainly on New Year's Eve, the waterfront beer-houses would have seen something of her crew. On 5 January 1799 she anchored in the shadow of St Michael's Mount in Mount's Bay, Cornwall, and left the bay at three o'clock on the following morning. 'Strong gales' were reported in her log, but she came safely to anchor in St Mary's Pool at two in the afternoon.

Her zealous commander, Lieutenant Pardoe, had no sooner dropped his anchor than he boarded his cutter and, as he entered in his log, 'went on shore to see after the Stores of HM Late Ship *Colossus*'. The next day's entry showed that he meant business:

7.1.1799 Light breezes inclinable to rain, sail'd several merchant ships for the Eastward. People Employ'd getting the *Colossus* stores on board the Transports. Rec'd by Boat 114 lbs cheese, 85 lbs butter.

Progress was so rapid that by the 14th of the month the stores had all been shifted, and the log recorded instead, 'People employed Breaking up the Wreck.' The tally of recovered provisions included some 648 lbs of prime beef and over forty gallons of brandy. His superiors would have known that Lieutenant Pardoe had shown commendable promptitude and energy to rescue that amount of brandy from the clutches of the islanders.

All the same, the voluminous, closely written ship's log makes me feel a little sorry for the commander of the *Fearless*. He endured the same long spells of heavy, soul-destroying rain – day after day, and week after week – which I have myself known at Scilly, and he also had the nagging worry of keeping his vessel seaworthy. The log details at length the repairs that were found necessary. It is also informative on the way the wreck was broken up, and since this has an important bearing on the Hamilton vases, I'll be returning to it later.

5
Court Martial

The loss of a naval ship invariably involves a court martial to inquire into the conduct of the commander. At one time the high-ranking officers seated in judgment, under their even higher-ranking president, could also include interested civilians. Samuel Pepys was once granted a temporary commission as a captain for this purpose, and delightedly recorded the event in his diary. Writing on 13 March 1669, he says:

That which put me in good humour, both at noon and night, is the fancy that I am this day made a captain of one of the King's ships, Mr Wren having this day sent me the Duke of York's commission to be captain of the *Jerzy*, in order to my being of a court-martial for examining the loss of the *Defyance* and other things.

The system was later discontinued, as it could obviously lead to much malpractice.

Courts martial are always solemn occasions, and Captain Murray's would have duly impressed the 'audience' of midshipmen and others in attendance. However, the proceedings also had various intriguing features. The inquiry was held aboard His Majesty's Ship *Gladiator* in Portsmouth Harbour on 19 January 1799, in the wide, sternmost great cabin. It would have been sparsely furnished, with a long oaken table athwart its width, and the floor covered with canvas painted in chequered squares of black and white. Behind the polished table, with their backs to the steeply sloping square-paned stern windows, the twelve naval captains of 'good standing' would take their places. Dress uniform would be worn – blue coats with white lapels, white waistcoats and breeches, and the glint of gold in a plain gold-tassellated epaulette on each shoulder and gilt buttons with the naval emblem of an anchor in each oval.

The president, seated in the centre, would be even more resplendent. As a vice-admiral he would wear a coat of thick blue cloth with a stand-up collar, adorned with a gold-laced button-hole at each side, and lapels of a lighter blue which buttoned back. The coat sleeves – made short to allow the laced sleeves of his white kerseymere waistcoat to be displayed – had broad white cuffs bearing two rows of gold lace, and these together with the two silver stars on his gold epaulettes were the indication of his rank. His buttons, too, had a laurel wreath surrounding their embossed anchors. To the president's left sat the judge advocate, the civil officer in supreme control, his face cradled in the two upright wings of his large collar and his periwig on his head.

Reflected in the table surface would have been the white gloves and cockaded, gold-braided tricorn hats lying in a long neat row before them as the officers chatted before the session of the past deeds and doings of the man they were about to try, and of those under his command who would be sharing with him in the ordeal. Towards the front of the table Captain Murray's sword would have been placed lengthwise, and its position when the court reassembled at the conclusion of the hearing would have given him advance warning of the verdict. The point towards him would mean a verdict of negligence, whereas the hilt ready to hand would show that he had been acquitted and, after the announcement of the verdict, could step forward and return it to its scabbard in honour.

Leaning towards each other, with faces graven and lips pursed, the officers would have conversed in undertones of confidentiality, merging into a soft chanted prayer. They would be in partial silhouette against the filtered daylight coming through the panes of the windows behind them, moving in a ritual of slow, gentle nodding or shaking of heads, and patting the table with out-spread hands in emphasis of a salient point. As a friend of Nelson, Captain Murray would be likely to come favourably through this preliminary ordeal, for the admiral had on occasion spoken highly of him.

Yes, yes, a good man – that would have been agreed – quiet, unassuming, a splendid seaman, and likeable, too. It was in 1779 he'd been second lieutenant in *Arethusa* – beautiful craft that, by the way, 32 guns – when she had sighted a Frenchman off Ushant. Ah! let's see now, that would have been *L'Aigrette* – a frigate, too, but of superior force. True, the pursuit had ended with *Arethusa* entangled in the tricky rocks and islets there, so that her ship's company were taken prisoner one and all, but at least Murray hadn't wasted his time in captivity, but had acquired an excellent command of French by the time he was eventually exchanged and returned to England.

By 1781 Murray was first lieutenant aboard the 64-gun *Monmouth*, and by the age of twenty-three had fought his way up from midshipman to post-captain, all by his own merit and exertions in active service in America as well as European waters. As soon as hostilities with France resumed in 1793, Murray was appointed to command first *Triton*, and then *La Nymphe* – a French prize – before being appointed captain of *Colossus*.

More relaxed now, as they became better acquainted, the officers would run a finger round their high collars, or stretch their arms towards the huge, dark beams of the low ceiling above them. Their voices would be slightly raised now, and they would smile and nod more easily, while at his separate table a clerk would be busy with papers, quill and pewter sand-pot. With tottering, gyrating goose feather, the record of those present would be made with scratching, flourishing determination:

Sir Alan Gardner, Bart., Vice Admiral of the White and Second Officer in the Command of His Majesty's Ships and Vessels at Portsmouth and Spithead. – President

Captains – James Brine	Captains – John Packenham
Sampson Edwards	James Vashon
William Domett	Edward Bowater
James Mins	Herbert Sawyer
Richard Goodwin Keats	Francis Pickmore
Francis Fayerman	Frank Sotheron

Conscious of the fleetingness of human glory, the clerk appended the name of Mr Greetham Junior as judge advocate 'for the time being'.

At a sign from the president, a messenger would then have been despatched to the adjoining wardroom, where Captain Murray and his ship's company waited, to warn them that the court hour was imminent. The firing of a gun from the quarter-deck, and the simultaneous hoisting of the Union Flag to the head of the mizzenpeak, followed and the court was declared open.

The court record shows that the proceedings opened with a reading of the order from the Lords Commissioners of the Admiralty as to the purpose of the inquiry – 'the cause and circumstances of the loss of His Majesty's Late Ship *Colossus*' and the bearing thereon of the conduct of Captain Murray, his officers and the ship's company. Their Lordships quoted the letter written to them by Murray, and after the necessary oaths had been taken by the members of the court, the letter itself was read. At this point the court was cleared of all the people from the ship, who were then recalled individually for examination, beginning with Captain Murray himself.

'Have you any complaint to make against any of your Officers and Ship's Company respecting the Loss of the Ship?' asked the president.

'Not any,' answered Murray succinctly.

'Was their Conduct on Shore equally good as before the Loss of the Ship?'

'Yes, it was.'

'Have you any other narrative respecting the Loss of the Ship more than has been read?'

'Yes, I have,' and Murray handed over his more detailed account to the court, which was read out by the judge advocate and annexed to the record of the proceedings.

It was now the turn of the officers and ship's company to be recalled in a body to give an answer to the same vital general question which had just been put to Murray:

'Have you any Complaint to make against Captain Murray respecting the Loss of the Ship?'

'None at all.'

They then all filed out again, and the individual examinations began. First to be called was the first lieutenant, Richard Cheeseman, who was asked if he had heard the letter and narrative read, and whether the contents were true.

'Yes, certainly,' he replied firmly.

'What do you think was the State of the best bower Cable?'

'I think it must have been dry rotten, it was a new cable, we took it from England with us.'

'Was everything done that could be done for the preservation of the Ship and Stores?'

'It was.' Like his captain, the lieutenant was a man of few words on this occasion.

The next witness, the second lieutenant, George Marriott, also agreed that Murray's accounts were 'perfectly' true, that 'every exertion' had been made to save the ship and her stores, and that the general opinion of the 'best bower cable' had been that, though new, 'it was dry rotten'.

Examination of the next witness, the master, David Wallace, took a little longer. The master was the officer, ranking next below a lieutenant, who was in charge of the navigation of a warship – his title was later changed to 'navigation officer' – as opposed to Murray, whose primary task was the handling of the ship during battle operations. He agreed with the truth of Murray's account as stoutly as the others.

'Have you ever been to Scilly in a large ship before?' continued the president.

'Never, but I have in a small ship.'

'Did you think the pilot carried you into a good berth?'

'Yes, an exceeding good one.' In saying as much as this the master was exaggerating a little. St Mary's Pool is hardly 'exceeding good' in such a gale as *Colossus* had encountered – merely the best one available in the Scillies.

'Had you sounded?' continued the president, without examining the point further.

'Yes, I had.'

'What do you suppose was the state of the best bower cable?'

'I think it was dry rotten, it had been a long time in the ship.'

'Do you think there was a possibility of carrying the Ship to

Sea before the Accident happened?' This was a vital question. If the gale had increased gradually, rather than the wind having veered suddenly as had been the case, then Murray could have been accused of negligence in not getting his ship out into the open sea in time.

'I do not.' Those three words meant a very great deal.

'After the Ship was on shore was every Exertion made to heave her off?'

'It was.'

'From the State of the Weather do you think any Stores could have been saved out of the ship?'

'I do not.'

'Did you conceive any danger might arise from Anchoring where you did?'

'Not in the least, there was hardly ever an Instance a Ship's driving in that Situation.' A rather less laconic reply, for such instances had been known in the Pool.

'To what do you attribute the Loss of the Ship?' went on the president.

'To the badness of the cables.'

The court was now cleared, and the president and his captains having conferred, they came to an agreed verdict that the loss of *Colossus* had been due solely to the badness of the weather and the rottenness of the best bower cable, and that all concerned had done their best for the preservation of the ship and her stores. The hearing resumed and Captain Murray and his officers and the ship's company were fully acquitted, the large flourishing signature of the judge advocate completing the court record.

As the forefinger and thumb of Captain Murray's left hand guided the point of his sword back into its scabbard, and he sheathed it with a quick impulsive thrust of his right, he must surely have smiled to himself. Maybe less with relief than with satisfaction that his confidence in the outcome had been justified.

On the surface the inquiry had been about the loss of a ship through anchor and cable failure, but the notorious unreliability of such equipment was a pressing reason for extra precautions to be taken, and there could have been some very awkward questions. Supposing the president had pressed rather harder:

'As a good seaman, Captain Murray, you could surely have better anticipated the strengthening of the gale from a more dangerous direction, and have got her out to open water in time? Wasn't your real reason for staying where you were the fact that your ship was in such a cranky condition that she was practically unmanageable in gale conditions, and that she had been so cannibalized of gear that she lacked essential rigging and stays? Moreover, if you had in such circumstances to stay where you were, could you not have used the very good cable which had proved itself on the smaller bower to splice to the sheet anchor? In any case, why had you only one large bower cable, and indeed, why had you no spare anchor? Had you been put under such pressure by someone that you had parted with it against your better judgment, and so in the event brought about the loss of your ship? Only the compassion of divine providence has decreed that we are not here inquiring also into the loss of everyone aboard her!'

But these questions were not asked, either of Murray, who would have found them very difficult to answer, or of his officers and crew, who would have been bound to give the game away. There also seems to have been no inquiry into the whereabouts of the ship's log, which if kept in proper detail would have made such questions unnecessary anyway. Maybe it was lost with the ship, but it is puzzling that this should have been so. From half past five in the afternoon of the day the ship was wrecked, which was the time the anchors became untrustworthy, right up till midnight when the flood-tide had flowed for two hours, Murray's chartroom and private quarters would have been dry. Surely this would have given him, or his officers, ample time and opportunity to save the log? Perhaps this was done, and it was lost later, when the ship became a shambles of breaking seas and near-panic-stricken humanity.

If no extraordinary effort was made to save the log, was it that its loss was 'good riddance'? Captain Murray may have welcomed the opportunity to get rid of the damning record of how his ship had become so gimcrack and weakened that it had been criminal folly to risk bringing her back from Italy even in the face of a light breeze, let alone a full gale.

Whatever the truth, there is now no controverting the honourable acquittal the court gave Captain Murray, and which he justified by years of loyal service in time to come. Almost immediately he was given command of *Achille*, and after being employed some time in the Channel service, was selected by the Admiralty to 'sound the belts' when it became obvious that Denmark was about to come into the war on the side of Napoleon. This was a reconnoitring operation in the shallow waters off the Danish shores.

Having acquitted himself in this greatly to their Lordships' satisfaction, Murray was removed into the *Edgar*, a ship of lighter draught more suitable for offshore work, and in the ensuing Battle of Copenhagen, in which Nelson appointed him to lead the fleet into action, behaved with the utmost gallantry. His conduct cemented their friendly relationship, and Murray became Nelson's captain of the fleet in 1803 to 1805, became first Admiral of the Blue in 1804, and of the White in 1805, and finally collected a knighthood in 1815.

Meanwhile, in happy ignorance, Sir William Hamilton and Emma were in Palermo, Sicily, where the Royal Court and everyone else of note in Naples had fled in consequence of Napoleon's increasing victories by land. The Hamiltons made the voyage in Nelson's *Vanguard*, and the admiral stayed with them in their new home, as he had formerly done in Naples.

The news of the loss of *Colossus* was naturally first known in London where it soon reached Hamilton's nephew, the Honourable Charles Greville, who – in the intervals of his career as an heiress-hunting dandy – was looking after his uncle's interests in Britain.

The report of the shipwreck intrigued everyone in England, since the names of Hamilton, Emma and Nelson sounded like bugles wherever they were spoken, and interest concentrated on the loss of the Hamilton 'boxes' rather than the vessel itself. However, a report in the newspaper *The Star* merely recorded her as 'lost on Southward Well, a spit of submerged rock south of Samson', and mentioned nothing of the Hamilton treasures aboard.

On 9 January 1799 Greville wrote urgently to his uncle with the news of the disaster:

I am just told by Ld Spencer that an officer on board the *Colossus* has told him there were four large boxes belonging to you, what they were I know not, but I dread the result of enquiry lest some of your invaluable collections may have been in those cases. The ship you have possibly heard arrived with a convoy safe to Scilly, where she drove from her anchor on a rock, and foundered in the midst of the other ships. I am still in hopes that the cases were not such as I augur.

Fresh information was obviously arriving by the minute, for he sent off a second letter by the same post:

I find your boxes were deep in the hold; therefore till the ship is to pieces, they will remain there, &, even if they withstand the shocks of the ship, whose timbers, &c. give way to their force, it is a hope but a forlorne one.

He added the gruesome anecdote which, over the years, became legendary in the Scillies:

. . . the Lieutenant told the Scilly people there was great treasure in a box, describing it, & when the guns, &c. had broken all before them, & the ship was on its side, they got the box, & you may suppose their disappointment when their prize proved a dead admiral.

Poor old Admiral Shuldham thus managed to find a resting-place on land at last, but Hamilton undoubtedly skipped such paragraphs in his overwhelming anxiety to know the fate of his Second Collection. He already owed his bankers £15,000, had lost many of his other possessions and much property when he fled from Naples, besides having incurred great expense in setting Emma up in Palermo in the style to which she had become accustomed. He had been relying on the proceeds of the sale of the vases to restore his finances, and now all that the lieutenant's ruse had brought to light was the pickled corpse.

'Damn his body,' he wrote back to Greville on 22 March,

it can be of no Use but to the Wormes, but my Collection would have given information to the most learned & have convinced every

Intelligent Being that there is but one Truth & that God Almighty has never made himself known to the miserable Atoms that inhabit this globe otherwise than bidding them to increase & multiply & to leave the rest to Him – So thought the wise Ancients when the Mysteries of Bacchus & Eleusis were established – never will there be collected such a Number of Clear monuments to prove the truth of what I say again – Yet I hope some of the eight cases on board the *Colossus* may be saved – but come to the worst I have had the precaution of publishing the best that are supposed to be lost – & I have many living witnesses that the originals existed – I am sorry you did not receive a letter I wrote you when I embarked the eight cases on board, and in which I begged you to keep the *Colossus* in your eye & secure my cases at least in the Custom House untill I arrived – I have the rest of my vases here on board of a Transport, and most of my best pictures – and I hope they may get home safe. . . .

Hamilton's 'precaution' had been magnificently realized a few years earlier when volumes of engravings by Tischbein had been published, illustrating the paintings and drawings on the best of the vases life-size. These showed me, long before I was able to handle the remains of the vases themselves, the philosophy which governed the thought of the ageing ambassador, who was certainly no pillar of the established religion of his day. More important for the moment, however, was the confirmation of the actual number of cases which he had onloaded into *Colossus*. Other accounts are contradictory.

In a later letter of 8 April 1799, he again mentioned the number as having been eight, and went on to elaborate on how the vases had been packed:

As to my eight cases, all the best vases in my Collection that were on board the *Colossus*, I fear none will be Recovered, & it is a pity, for never in this world will such a Collection be made again. The Cases are so well made & Vases so well packed, that I dare say they may Float when the Ship goes to Pieces, and they are all cover'd with Tow and Strong Canvas, & Rope on the outside, so that they may not Break against the rocks; most of my Pictures & some few Vases are on board a British transport in this port, but the French have taken most of my furniture at Naples, Caserta, & Pausilippo, which I had not time to carry off, having left Naples in such a hurry.

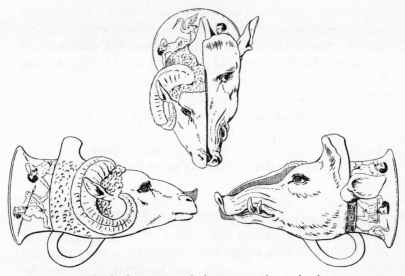

The drinking cup 'with the Boar & Sheep's head'

He added a final plea: 'I know you will, without my having given you the Commission, have given directions to watch the wreck of *Colossus*.'

Hamilton must have watched the incoming post with frantic anxiety in the coming weeks, but it was not until 8 June 1799 that any further news came, and then far from good.

I am sorry to inform you [wrote Greville], that only about ten Vases and Pateras, of which one only is of Consequence, has been preserved from the Wreck. That a box was opened is most certain, but what I recover'd was obtain'd from the people by one of the many Employed to watch the Landing of any Cases by the Sea. I was assured by Major Bowen that these were thrown on the beach by the Sea. The one I mention as of Consequence is the Drinking Cup with the Boar & Sheep's Head. I am still in hopes more may be thrown up.

The 'pateras' referred to, by the way, were the shallow pottery dishes used by the ancient Greeks in making libations to the gods.

How these items came ashore we don't know. Possibly a whole case of pottery surfaced, for if a number of the vases were upside down they would hold pockets of air which would give it buoyancy or, as divers say, 'air-lift', so that it could have struggled up through the jumble of submerged wreckage. In view of the reference to 'pateras', this seems more likely than that individual pieces – with sufficient air inside them and the right balance – escaped from a damaged case under water. No saucer-shaped patera would be likely to hold enough air to let it float for long in the sea.

There is no other contemporary record of vases having been recovered, or of anyone but Greville being interested in their salvage. Any seaman, such as Lieutenant Pardoe of *Fearless*, would assume that the vases were in a thousand pieces on the sea-bed, even if he had time to think of items such as pottery in the midst of his concern with the recovery of government stores.

His salvage work went on day after day, month in, month out. Spring came and went, the plankton increased in the sea, clouding the waters of the anchorage and swirling about the great wrecked ship. Its warped form would have become overgrown with fine brilliant green weed. At low tide, with any kind of a breeze, this would flutter from the soaked carcase like ribbons of glistening wet silk, though as the tide fell in warmer weather, it would form a dulled, mushy skin over the timbers, with a characteristic rotten smell, until the rising water again restored it to life. During the summer the masts, sails, yards and rigging would have been brought ashore, as well as many of the guns, blocks and other heavy gear.

Then came autumn, winter and another new year – a new century, too – and still Hamilton had not given up hope of his vases. On 25 January 1800 he wrote once again to Greville:

As to my cases . . . have you no good news of them? they were excellently packed up, & the Cases will not easily go to pieces, & the Sea Water will not hurt the Vases. All the Cream of my Collection were in those eight cases on board *Colossus*, & I can't bear to look at the Remaining Cases here in which I know there are only Black Vases without Figures.

Lieutenant Pardoe's problems were different ones that spring, as the calmer weather brought increasing raids on the wreck by 'outsiders'. On the night of 8 May he noticed a deal of small-boat activity around her, and that an Irish sloop, the *Tarmon*, had anchored alongside. She further appeared to be lying more unduly low in the water than would be expected from her 'manifest'

ABOVE: Mark and Mike at work, with the island of St Mary's behind them. The anchorage point of *Colossus* would have been near the coast of St Mary's, at a spot directly 'above' Mark's head, and from there she dragged her anchors right across to where the whaler is moored.

BELOW: A corner of my laboratory. Behind me are a collection of non-ferrous nautifacts polished clean of corrosion, and carefully sorted sherds after they had been cleaned and dried. To my left, as I mark each sherd with its identification number, are chunks of clib ready to be cracked open.

LEFT: The base of a Hamilton vase, as found on the sea-bed. To the right are the cut stems of two huge weed holdfasts.

BELOW LEFT: Mike, Mark and Slim working on the site with the air-lift.

RIGHT: One haunting little face among the many thousands of sherds, a decorative mascaroon from a vase handle.

BELOW: Detail of the Tischbein drawing of a satyr head, and the corresponding sherd. Note the differences in detail and the liveliness of the Greek original.

ABOVE: Glinting like gems, 'pieces of wine glasses and the like'.

LEFT and BELOW: Mementoes of the life of Nelson's sailors: a hand-sewn leather shoe, preserved by emulsified olive oil, a domino and an officer's button, 'an anchor in an oval'.

of beef, pork, soap, tallow, candles, pitch, etc., so the lieutenant ordered his people to make a search or – as the expression went – 'rummage' her. His suspicions had been warranted.

Reporting to the authorities, he wrote:

We . . . found two Tons of Iron Ballast in her Hold which had been taken up from the Wreck of His Majesty's Late Ship *Colossus*, and nearly an equal Quantity in the Boats alongside of her. I have Therefore detained the Sloop and the Boats at this Place until their Lordships pleasure is known and beg leave to add that Considerable Quantities of Iron Ballast and other Stores have been secretly conveyed from these Islands to different Parts notwithstanding the Public Notice, given by the Commandant that Salvage would be paid. . . .

Scilly was then a busy port of call for shipping of all kinds, so that it is no surprise to find the log of *Fearless* filled with incidents of looting from *Colossus* during 1800. Pardoe was kept busy boarding ships whose masters had, rightly or wrongly, come under suspicion of interfering with the wreck, to such an extent that he had time for little else. The Scillonians themselves were no longer a major worry to him for he had realized the skill of the islanders, not only at shipbuilding, but of ship dismantling, and they were now working to good effect on his behalf.

Archimedes once said, 'Give me but one firm spot on which to stand, and I will move the earth'; in other words, give him a fulcrum, some point against which he could place a lever – and a lever long enough – and he could move or prize apart anything. The Scillonians knew all about fulcrums, as does any salvage worker, but they devised their own special tools for this particular wreck. Most ingenious they were, too, and a number survive to this day. More than likely they were made from ironwork out of the very ship which they were to pull apart, timber from timber.

These levers, known in salvage as 'wrecking-bars' or 'pinch-bars', are usually simply narrow pieces of tempered steel and eight feet long. At the lower end they are drawn out to a tapering chisel shape, similar to that of a burglar's jemmy. The Scillonians added the refinement of a swivelling fulcrum to their bars, so that they didn't have to wait to be given a fulcrum, they just swung it into place whenever they needed it.

Taking into consideration the combined ruthless 'Breacking of the Wreack' by the *Fearless* people and the efforts of the Scillonians with their special tools, backed up by the tireless grapnel work of the illicit 'wreckers', the underwater scene at the wreck site would have resembled a submerged shipbreaker's yard.

During the dead-low spring-tides of summer, when the water would have been as still, and as clear, as gin, and the depth but two fathoms, the wreckage would have been clearly visible down below, more especially so if the weed was kept clear by chains being scuffed over the timbers.

As late as 1829 and 1831 guns were still reported visible on the site, amongst the last surviving massive timbers. These latter would have included the keel and keelson with the deadwood at the fore end and a similar, much larger amount of rising-wood at the after or sternpost end. Riveted together as these very large baulks of timber were, with long large-diameter copper bars, they would have delayed any salvage of the guns which had fallen down amongst them. I can imagine the great timber knees, the remains of the lower oaken main-frames, the hefty 12-inch-wide by 5-inch-thick garboard strakes (the outer planking of the ship next to the keel), the enormous stem, the great knee of the head which held the figurehead – all tethered together by twisted, contorted copper fastenings, sprawled across the weed and boulders of the sea-floor.

The Admiralty engaged a diver, John Deane, to recover what he could. Deane was the actual inventor of the first practical helmet diving apparatus, later refined by Siebe, which for the first time enabled a diver to pay attention to small finds in wrecks. He used his 'Patent portable and highly approved Diving Apparatus' to such good purpose that he rescued many of the big cast-iron cannon. Deane had the mind of a modern archaeologist and employed an artist to record to scale in delicate watercolours the precise condition in which his finds were discovered, and those of two cannon and a carronade recovered from *Colossus* have the patches of concretion and specimens of marine life shown adhering to them in scrupulous detail. He also recovered an impressive quantity of rigging blocks, tackle and accoutrements.

With Deane's departure to work on bigger and, at the time,

more rewarding projects, the grave of *Colossus* slipped into obscurity. Human effort had saved every particle of the ship itself which could be salvaged, which – to my way of thinking – is splendid. The remainder settled into the silt, sand and giant weed of Southward Well Reef. Not, as some would have us believe, that it lay there static and at peace, for in the Atlantean underworld of Scilly and south-west Cornwall there is nothing static and no such thing as peace.

So, the great wooden-walled battleship had gone at last, and in the years that saw its break-up the other characters in the story disappeared, too. Sir William Hamilton died in 1803, and who shall say that his death was not hastened by the loss of his beloved vases? Admiral Lord Horatio Nelson was killed at Trafalgar in 1805, and his 'poor Emma' died in abject poverty in 1815.

In Scilly all that remained to remind the locals of the demise of *Colossus* were the many treenail-studded door lintels, many staunch and upright timber pillars and many word-of-mouth wreck-yarns of near brushes with Lieutenant Pardoe and his crew of the gun-brig *Fearless*. Legend has it that the anchor preserved on the beach at Tresco came from *Colossus* – if so, it was the one she was lying to and which was salvaged by Lieutenant Pardoe – and also the two guns embedded in St Mary's quay, but I am none so certain myself.

PART TWO

The Legend Comes to Life

6

A Dive on Colossus

My love of wooden sailing ships grew with me from an early age. I remember, when I was four or five years old, playing with friends among the trestles and iron 'G-cramps' of a gang of shipwrights who were building a beautiful new boat on the harbour sands at St Ives. Sand castles, tick-tag or hopscotch were ignored by me every time the men applied a steaming hot plank to the bare ribs of that embryo lugger. I saw the birth of that ship and, much later, was to see her borne down to the sea on the strong backs and shoulders of a hundred men.

My interest in ships owed much to my mother. She came from a seafaring family and, in the days when masters took their wives and children with them, had spent two years of her childhood sailing round the world in her father's barquentine *Marguerite*. My bedtime stories, as far back as I can remember, were all of the sea; of sailing ships and far-away foreign ports-of-call.

Mother loved ships, but I knew she had no affection for the sea. This was understandable for, while she remained at home to finish her schooling, her parents and her younger brothers and sisters sailed for the Mediterranean, and the *Marguerite* was lost with all hands in the Bay of Biscay.

Even as a toddler I would be taken in my mother's arms to see the lifeboat launched, so I have early memories of my breath being snatched from my lips by the clawing of strong winds, of rain splattering down on my outsize sou'wester. I can recall the lifeboat's oiler-clad crew sitting motionless with large, fat, cork lifejackets round their bodies, with long oars upright, like a miniature copse of trees, while they awaited launching. The huge iron-shod, wooden-spoked wheels of the launching platform would be bogged down in watery sand, the big horses straining and hauling, rain-drenched men and women shouting, screaming and labouring, as they fought to manoeuvre that enormous contraption to the water's edge.

And then there are memories of storm-scrubbed, brilliantly sunny days standing on cliff tops, steadied by grown-ups from the sporadic buffeting of gale-force winds, and looking down on tall ships being picked to pieces by frothing, soft-looking, white water. Memories of sails ripping to tatters, of masts teetering and finally toppling in a tangled web of ropes and canvas. Of giant breaking seas tumbling over the lifeless hulls, tearing, wrenching, smashing until the ship's boats, galleys, deckhouses, fife-rails, wheels, binnacles, were swept away as if by a giant's hand.

The live ships and the dead ships that I saw most of in my younger days were of timber. I was taken to see them built – fashioned by master shipwrights and carpenters from oak, teak, mahogany, greenheart and pitchpine. Shaped by bow-saw and adze, chisel and gouge, draw-knife and plane. Fastened by tree-nails, copper bolts and bronze spikes; caulked with oakum-tails, Stockholm tar and pitch. Rigged with hempen line and lignum-vitae blocks and deadeyes.

What magnificent vessels they were! When I grew older I was privileged to go on board several of the larger sailing ships while they waited for orders off Falmouth – the *Pamir*, the *Archibald Russell*, the *Herzogin Cecilie* and others. Beautiful creatures they were, from the rounding curves of their gilded stern carvings right through to the charming figureheads at their prows. How I loved those figureheads! The graceful lines of those fine ships flowed smoothly from the exquisitely carved draperies of those serenely brave and resplendent beings.

Soon I became my own apprentice in the happy art of miniature boat-building. To my delight I discovered that, with a razor-sharp penknife and a chunk of soft-grained wood, I could carve myself pleasurable models of small craft as I walked about.

To discover an ability to carve is a thrill indeed, and in my keen-
ness I progressed by leaps and bounds. It was not long before I
was selling decorative Spanish galleons to the big stores of
London. As I grew up into my teens I went on to making really
accurate scale models – not of galleons, ornate and beautiful
though they were – but of British men-o'-war of that most
fascinating of all periods, the eighteenth century.

Though I was later to witness the death of many an iron vessel,
it was watching the wrecking of the timber ships which wrung
my juvenile heart, arousing a salvor's urge in me to recover
something of what the sea had stolen over the centuries. I made
a schoolboy's solemn vow to become a diver and do my best to
rescue those lost figureheads, those gilded scrolls and carvings,
those fine brass-bound teak wheels, and all those other splendid
relics, from bulbously intriguing copper lanterns and giant
bronze ship's bells to the fretted stair treads up which the sailors'
feet had fearfully fled for the last time.

Needless to say, I read every book I could find which dealt with
shipwreck. The libraries were full of them, and it became a
marvel to me, when so many ships had come to grief, that
shipbuilders could keep pace with the losses. But, of the many
tales that came my way, none intrigued me more than those of
the great wooden battleships which had foundered in sou'western
waters.

In the year 1707, for instance, four large men-o'-war had been
lost in the space of a single night among the Western Rocks of
the Isles of Scilly. They were members of the wayward squadron
under the command of Admiral Sir Cloudesley Shovell, 96-gun
flagship *Association*, the 70-gun *Eagle*, 50-gun *Romney* and fireship
Firebrand. Another famous name was that of 44-gun *Anson*,
engulfed in 1807 in the ever-moving sands of Looe Bar within
Mount's Bay. And, to complete the half-dozen, there was
Colossus, lying like the rest beneath the waters within a cormor-
ant's flight of my own home.

Although their names were constantly on my mind, I shared
my interest in these ships with very few, for in those days hardly
a soul took much count of old, sunken ships. Nevertheless, as I
came up to twenty, I was busy fostering my friendships with the

local salvage men of Penzance, and wheedling them into letting me take diving lessons. Yet it was at this very period that my enthusiasm to become a professional diver received a disconcerting setback.

I was then a learner-mechanic, working for Colonel C. H. Paynter on his very lovely estate of Boskenna, and during the three years I was with him Guglielmo Marconi, the pioneer of wireless telegraphy, was the colonel's guest. It was rumoured, and the story made the headlines of the London press, that the great inventor had become engaged to the colonel's daughter, Betty.

Finishing work late one evening – it must have been past midnight – I found myself with a seven-mile ride home and a motorcycle with a flat tyre. In emergency I had sometimes stayed the night, but when I spoke to the butler, he had a better idea. Marconi's Rolls was about to leave for Poldhu, a few miles the other side of my home town of Penzance, and he would ask the great man if I could have a lift.

I was already known to Marconi, for had not I, under his instructions, erected the aerial for the magnificent Marconi Marine Wireless Receiver which he had presented to the charming Miss Betty? This was an impressive unit with dozens of dials and switches, encased in its own polished teak cabinet. On the night of the gala ball at the colonel's home to which the élite of the western counties had been invited, I had been placed in charge of it, and the Marine Receiver and I were the sole providers of music into the small hours, but that is another story.

I sat on the front seat, next to the Italian chauffeur, and Marconi and a friend of his – both in bowler hats, I remember – sat in the dim rear of the car behind a glass screen. All went well as we swished through the pitch-black night; that is, until we came to the fishing village of Newlyn, a mile from Penzance. As we reached the cross-roads, at the bottom of a steep hill, the driver – crying out in loud and urgent Italian – collapsed over the wheel, clutching his hands to his abdomen in agony.

After a hurried consultation with Marconi, I took over the wheel, first of all to take the unfortunate man to hospital, and then – after some more mature consideration – I was once more behind the wheel bound post-haste for Poldhu. Marconi and his friend had an appointment at their experimental beam-wireless station which could not be missed, even if it meant that a comparative whipper-snapper such as myself should be allowed control of that strange, sleek, superbly sprung limousine. Marconi's friend moved in beside me on the front seat, the better to keep an eye on me, and as we went on our never-to-be-forgotten journey down the dark narrow Cornish lanes, I was given a lecture of an unexpected kind.

The man at my side, his bowler hat still firmly in place, began by asking me what I intended to make of myself.

'A salvage diver,' I replied, without hesitation and rather proudly.

Without replying, he slid back the glass panel behind us: 'This young gentleman intends to become a deep-sea diver.'

It was as if he were resuming a conversation, and I can only assume they had been discussing me earlier to while away the journey. Marconi's reply to this laconic statement was inaudible to me, but was relayed by his friend: 'The Signor wishes to know on what you will be diving.'

'Underwater shipwreck of all kinds,' I said, with all the boastful inexperience of youth. 'I hope to dive and bring back some of the thousands of beautiful and valuable things the sea has taken over the centuries.'

My response was relayed to the dim recesses of the back seat. Even though I was concentrating intensely on guiding that giant automobile through lanes which seemed to become even narrower, ever rougher and more dusty, I thought my lyric reply was taking some time in being conveyed. Eventually, while I was still holding my breath for fear of touching as much as a cow-parsley head with the gleaming front wings of the Rolls, my companion straightened up.

'The Signor,' he said simply, 'wishes you to drive very much faster. There is a danger of our being late.'

I felt tempted to reply that there was an even greater danger of our ending in a ditch. It wasn't merely that the roads were narrow and inadequate for so giant a car, but the radiator cap was fitted with a silver model wireless mast and antenna with a tiny white light at the top. It was a beautiful ornament, but shone in my eyes in the most infuriatingly distracting way, in spite of the most powerful headlights I had ever driven behind. In addition – and how I wished I had taken the main Lizard road – there was a stream in full spate ahead of us. At least my companion remained kindly and wisely silent while we negotiated that, but he then launched into the remainder of the advice he had to pass on to me. In a nutshell it was to the effect that, with so many live and beautiful ships sailing the oceans, it was foolishness to devote my life to ships that were dead. Dead ships never benefited anyone: 'It will be a great waste of time for you, and the Signor does not recommend it in any way.'

As we crunched down a rough and very steep hill, as we swung round its sharp right-hand bend with the car's headlight beams sweeping out and over the dark valley below, as I slipped into a lower gear and steadied the car with both foot and hand brakes, disappointment came over me like a great wave. My father had died some years previously, and, not having him to turn to, I felt grateful for the interest the two men obviously took in me, but their opinion of my eager plans saddened me.

I was looking for no reward from my share in the night's adventure, but I was given one just the same. I was invited aboard Marconi's steam yacht, *Electra*, then resting in the inner harbour of Penzance. The vessel was crammed with electrical gadgetry, and a live and beautiful ship if ever I saw one. With hindsight, I can say that diving has added sparkle, variety, and adventure to my life, which has been most full and enjoyable. But I often think back to that dark night, and that hectic drive to those wooden sheds on the Poldhu cliffs. Signor Marconi was right, and looking back in time from my home in the far reaches of south-west Cornwall, I now know full well that diving, as a full-time profession, would never have provided me with the way of life I really wanted and which I eventually found.

All the same, despite Marconi's advice, my obsession with work under the sea continued. In my earlier book, *Island Treasure*, I've told the story of my early diving lessons, and it wasn't long before I was a shareholder – a very junior shareholder – in a small salvage firm. We went in for undersea scrap: non-ferrous, ferrous, the lot. We weren't fussy, we couldn't afford to be!

One day we were working in Falmouth Bay, searching for wrecks, anchors – anything. As the sea-bed was relatively level, I had resorted to the method of lying prone on an iron grating, which was slung underwater to within a few feet of the bottom. Usually in this sort of work, for reasons of manoeuvrability, the grating was suspended from a small boat, but this was not necessary with our kind of skipper, who was the very same Cap'n Phil Nicholls who had put on my weights and helmet when I slipped under water for the first time to take a walk on the bottom of Penzance harbour. He could stop, start, reverse or make his cranky old converted trawler go sideways with such agility that small boats were out: we used the salvage vessel herself.

Usually, with good visibility, I could turn over on my back on the grating and look up at the wide, comforting, barnacle-clad buttocks of the trawler above me. But not this day. I could hear her, but not see her. The water was like milk. In Falmouth Bay at that time we were pestered by the presence of a dredger, and this day was no exception. The harbour was being cleaned out, the mud and refuse being taken well out to sea, but no matter how far it was taken the waters of the bay became clouded with the stuff. Why it should turn the sea a milky white I never did discover, maybe it had something to do with china clay, of which there are famous great deposits in Cornwall.

Anyway, there I was being wafted over the sea-bed what time the salvage vessel glistered her serene way across the calm blue sea, her tall thin stack held high, a diving flag fluttering at her truck, a whisper of steam at her vent pipe and, for that matter, from most of the pipes that writhed about her superstructure.

Presently I noticed ahead of me in the murky depths a mysterious lump on the sea-bed. For all the world it looked like a fat roll of muddy, crunchy, linoleum sticking out from another shapeless mass of corrosion.

'A bronze cannon!' I yelled, in the crazy, compressed Donald Duck voice to which all divers are reduced under water. I was always an optimist – well, it makes a change: most divers would have opted for, 'Looks like a bloomin' tree stump!', or something equally depressing.

Tree stump or bronze cannon, I had to find out, so I yanked

at my breast-rope. One sharp pull, meaning 'Belay!' – 'Stop!'
The flop-flop of the propeller overhead ceased immediately,
then started up again for a few revolutions only, this time for a
'kick' astern. And there, below me, was the large, fat, bewhiskered
sausage with its accompanying bulge of mystery.

I slithered down from my grating and attacked the hard, sharp,
gritty sea-growth of crud with the point of my knife. Underneath
there was neither timber nor yet my hoped-for, precious bronze,
but I was right that my find was a cannon. It was of iron, and
about eight feet long. Ah well, it was all grist to the mill; I
signalled for the derrick wire and down it came with its big
shackle landing on the sea-bed with a little eruption of fine
sediment. As I hacked a tunnel beneath the gun, large enough to
pass the wire through, I became aware, through the haze that I
was creating, that I was pulling out what looked like splintery,
ancient bones. I closely examined one or two pieces through my
front-glass. Yes, they were bones all right.

I shackled the wire to the gun and signalled for the lift. The
noise of the winch came down to me, transmitted by the vibra-
tion of the wire. 'Chutter-chutter-chutter', the wire tightened
and the muzzle of the cannon began to rise. I sat nearby on the
sea-bed, legs outspread, and resting back on my arms so that I
could tilt my great helmet back and have a better view of the
cannon as it went up. As the big bulk of it broke free from the
sea-bed there was a great flurry of smoky debris. The gun rose
into the milky heights above me, trailing a dusty wake as it
disappeared, while I listened to the noises from above. I imagined
the crew examining the thing, and waited and wondered if it
would be returned as not worth salvage. The drill in such cases
was that I stayed put and waited until either the thing reappeared
or there were two satisfactory pulls on my breast-rope to indicate
my offering was acceptable.

I lay back with my 40-lb. front weight just lifting comfortably
off my chest. My air, warmed by compression, was coming down
to me via a Siebe-Gorman two-cylinder double-acting pump
driven by steam power. The sound of the air entering my helmet
by way of an outlet over each of the three glass 'windows'
never varied, 'seep-seep' 'seep-seep'. Behind my right ear my

excess air rumbled and bubbled from my 'relief' valve in sporadic bursts. I looked at my hands; they were white and cold, but I was warm and dry. This was the life, I thought, as I watched some fish examining the hole in the sea-bed from which the encrusted lump had been plucked.

Then I became aware that bits and pieces were coming down from above. They were trying to clean the thing as it hung overside. There were small bits, then large lumps, and then some more of those things which looked suspiciously like bones. And then again, some obvious bones. Human bones, surely? And finally – 'Oh no!' – a human skull! This mottled white and brown thing came slowly down, rolling and twisting with powdery silt spilling from its eye-sockets. Then another! And, above that again, another! And a fourth! Following each other, they came floating down, appearing at first ghost-like, but becoming ever more distinct as they slowly, ever so slowly, came nearer – twisting and cavorting in the fog of water with ribs, femurs and tibias spiralling down with them.

I watched fascinated, not frightened, but certainly upset. I was young and for the first time I sensed that the sea was spooky. I was alone. Very much alone, for the nearest man under the sea was probably many miles away. I looked again at the hole in the sea-bed. It must have been a grave. Just at that moment a fish wriggled in the debris there, then darted out – my front-glass frosted over with perspiration.

One cannon may obviously mean many more on a wreck site, but although I searched the area round and about that lone find, there was nothing.

'The bones was tied fast of the gun,' said one of the crew, when I at last reached topsides.

'How d'you mean?' I asked, my imagination running ahead of me.

'Well, look, see here! Made fast with this – whatever 'tes.' He handed me several strips of material which felt like gelatine.

'It's leather!' said I, 'with a wire in it.'

' 'Twas leather – once. We da reckon the wire is selver.'

'Silver! Well, blow me!' I said.

The leather strap or belt had at one time been interwoven or inlaid with silver wire. Without that wire there would have been no story; the leather thong would have survived for but a short time only. Because of the wire, the bodies had been retained, and a snippet of history had been preserved but, mark you, only a snippet.

Centuries ago, in the middle of Falmouth Bay, four people had been secured by their necks to a piece of ordnance and cast into the sea. The questions come thick and fast. Why? And exactly when? Who could they have been? Were they men or women? Had they been already dead, or thrown alive into the sea? How old were they, of what nationality? What sort of a gun was it?

Today, if I had those same nautifacts, just as they came from the sea – the scraps of leather, the gun, those wire-trapped vertebrae, the skulls, and a goodly sample of the debris from under the gun, I could have used my knowledge of archaeological research to build that snippet of history into a fuller story.

In my boyhood dreams of diving as a career, I had not envisaged problems of this complexity, and another factor I didn't take into account was the law of salvage. The young diver has to make himself conversant with every aspect of the law of salvage, for every item of wreck on the sea-bed, whether it be large or small – a complete ship or merely a ship's bell – belongs to someone. According to law, it must be either reported or, if small enough, taken to the Customs House. There is one in every seaport, and here is located the all-powerful official known as HM Receiver of Wreck. The intriguing word 'wreck' is both singular and plural, and means wreckage of any kind.

If wreck is found and handed to the receiver, he will give a receipt and keep it for a year and a day in bond, during which period he makes every effort to trace its owner. If, as most often happens, no owner can be traced, the wreck is either put up for tender, or is sold by public auction, and the finder-diver is rewarded by a proportion of the value. In my day the diver was then given a third of the proceeds, but today, thanks to the new salvage laws, he will get close on one hundred per cent.

Having negotiated the legal and all the other difficulties of my chosen profession, I was by the summer of 1939 a partner in the

same salvage firm, which had by now grown to sizeable proportions. We had landed a Government salvage contract, locating
and overhauling various anchors and their 'trots', or lengths, of
chain cable, using the *Lady of the Isles*, an ex-Scillonian passenger
packet, as our base on the Scilly station.

We had chartered the trim little Scillonian launch *Mab* as our
diving boat, and, having completed the contract ahead of schedule,
found to our delight that we had a whole free day ahead of us. It
had actually been with the *Colossus* wreck-site in mind that I
had inveigled Algy Guy into letting me hire the *Mab*, for she was
the ideal little craft for what I was planning. Our 'free' day happened to be a Sunday, I remember, and I had to be very persuasive
in getting his co-operation. With a promise of providing an
evening's liquid sustenance, I cajoled two salvage friends, Percy
and Alvin Williams, to 'man' my pump, and 'spoke nicely' to
Cap'n Phil Nicholls, who agreed to 'tend' my air-pipe and breast-
rope. In those days, it took all of five men, including the diver,
to put one man on the sea-bed.

We motored sweetly out of the harbour at St Mary's, rounded
the weather-bleached pier head, the anchorage opening up before
us, and headed north. As we went, and St Martin's opened up on
our nor'easterly horizon, with the dark trees and white beaches
of Tresco over our starb'd bow, I explained that I wanted to
carry out a 'reckey' – a reconnoitre – of the Southward Well
Reef.

As we crossed the anchorage towards it, its enormous length
stretching out ahead of us, I could have wished for a more
precise location.

'Trouble is,' I said, 'that's all the records say – "lost on the
S'uth'rd Well" –'

'An' that's quite a stretch of water,' Algy answered reflectively.

'In other words you want to find out where she's lying,' said
Phil.

'That would be a miracle.' I pointed to the weed-tops already
showing further in towards the reef, and began to feel the day
was lost before it had begun.

'There's no sayin' she's weeded,' said Phil. 'If she drew twenty-
three feet, as you say she did, then she probably struck further

out, specially if she was takin' in water.' He was busy with a hastily made sounding-line fashioned from a heavy shackle bent to a heaving-line. ''Ere you are,' he said, plunging the line up and down and feeling the sea-bottom, 'twenty-five feet allowin' for the water in 'er.' He pumped his arm up and down: 'twenty-five feet, or nears-'nuff anyway.'

In no time at all I was over the side. I found myself in a boulder-strewn terrain with areas of bedrock divided by gullies of deep sand, typical of what I now call the 'Atlantic fringe' type of diving, to which I was then only just becoming accustomed. The sea was like vegetable soup, with plankton and tiny shreds of weed flowing steadily past me in slow motion. In some places the bedrock had been colonized by giant kelp, the massed palm-shaped heads, supported on long spindly stalks, drooping and weaving. I realized at once that any organized search of the site would mean clearing large areas of this weed, but there were clear spaces, boulder-strewn plateaux, sandy patches and gullies. These are least I could explore.

Quite early in my 'reckey' I saw a symmetrically oval object lying to the side of a sandy gully. At first sight it looked like a large wooden ship's rigging block. There was a groove round its centre where a pulley wheel would be, and my pulse beat a little faster, for this would be a clue indeed.

I started forward excitedly. To do this in my type of helmeted diving gear meant leaning against the water like a man walking into a force eight gale. By the time I got near enough to drop on my knees and examine it closely, I found that it was a 'stone-killick'. Clean, smooth sand-scoured granite, it was an excellent example of a stone anchor of long ago, and the groove round its middle would have held a twisted iron bar, which would have formed not only the flukes, but also the ring. It wasn't a rarity, for there are many of these stone anchors to be found – sometimes just holed stones – but they are well worth keeping an eye open for.

I gave three pulls on my breast rope and, after some delay, down came a line with a shackle in its eye-splice. It took only a few seconds to slip a rope round the groove and watch the smooth stone hauled away, to become merged in the shadowy, distorted silhouette of the launch above me. I have it still, complete with renewed twisted iron bar, lying in my nautical museum as a memento of my first, and last, personal dive on *Colossus*.

When I came to tackle the weed, I had to push my way through its slippery growth of undulating foliage, its maze of chest-high upright stems. Some were round-sectioned, the size of broomsticks and covered in warts, and others oval-sectioned like three-inch wide plastic straps, bending and weaving. All were surmounted by a luxuriant growth of madly cavorting fronds and tendrils, which rose many feet above me. Every now and again I stopped to get my breath, walking against the current was hard work, and got down on my hands and knees to search among the twisting roots.

On my first ascent from the shallows – the water was barely five fathom deep – I asked that my pipe and rope be lashed together, to make my forages through the weed-covered reef less frustrating. While this was being done, I stood on the diving ladder without my helmet, and Algy Guy took the opportunity to ask me: 'What interests you in *Colossus*, Roland, what did she have aboard?'

'Well . . .' I had purposely kept off this subject, for the hearsay stories of the wreck had long ago died down. 'Er, furniture and, you know, loot from the Battle of the Nile, you never know what you might find.'

Algy pushed his white-topped peaked cap further back on his head, sucked his teeth and looked earnestly at the far western horizon, where the stalk of the Bishop Light stood clear-cut against the sky.

'Wasn't there some kind of valuable pottery, belonging to some gent or other . . . ?' he asked.

There was no denying it. 'You're right,' I said, managing to avoid a guilty pause in my reply, 'but what's the betting you'll find any of that down there now?'

'No!' Algy laughed. 'That's for sure. That's been flattened long ago, and anyways I can't see you spending money and time just lookin' for pottery!'

'It's the ship's fittings I'd like to find,' I said truthfully, 'anything from the nautical past would give me a big thrill.'

Algy was man of the sea enough to understand that, and my secret was safe.

Down again, I pottered about in the shallows, taking my time as I crawled or walked over the colourless sea-bed. I could imagine the scene topsides: Phil holding my pipe and rope in his hands, looking down at the sea as if playing a sluggish fish, and Percy and Alvin slowly winding away at the single-cylinder double-acting Siebe-Gorman pump, endlessly smoking their cigarettes.

It was quite pleasant down there I remember, particularly with the thrill of knowing I was down on the site of my first man-o'-war. I plunged my hands into the gritty, sandy gullies, I hacked off with my knife many of the weed holdfasts themselves, but I found nothing. It was all clean rock, sand, boulders and weed – not a musket ball or a copper nail in sight.

Some twenty-eight years were to elapse before I again visited the *Colossus* site. By that time Algy Guy had met a violent death in a quarry accident at Scilly, and the other three men with me on the dive – like the old seamen that they were – had just faded away.

Over that same period, too, my old-time diving methods and equipment had been superseded by Jacques Cousteau's invention of the aqualung. With a back-pack of oxygen bottles and webs on his feet, the diver was set free to move like a fish under the sea, and at very low cost, so that the way was opened for thousands of amateur divers to explore the undersea world for pleasure.

I put in an exciting lifetime of diving during those years, and my team visited every one of the sunken men-o'-war on my list, except *Colossus*. I thought of my work on her as the crowning glory of my career.

I chose *Anson*, the nearest of the ships to Penzance, as the one to start training my newly assembled, modern diving team. She presented a tremendous challenge in that she was completely submerged in gravelly sand. There were few intervals of calm in the series of giant Atlantic combers which expelled their in-built energy in great surging eruptions of boiling surf over her grave, where she had lain since a sou'westerly gale had driven her ashore from an at-anchor position in Mount's Bay. She broke to pieces quickly in the surf, her keel, garboard strakes and bilges sinking into the sandbar under the great weight of her guns and iron ballast blocks.

She was a strange wreck, and it was a strange place in which she lay. Mount's Bay is the only place in Britain where a river has been permanently and completely blocked by a sandbar. Many years ago the River Cober flowed freely from its source at Carmenellis, past Helston, and on to the sea. Then successive storms threw up a great sandbar across its mouth, and Looe Pool was formed by the dammed waters of the choked river. It is a singularly eerie place, and the local people are convinced that it inspired Tennyson in his description of the lake into which Excalibur, the sword of King Arthur, was cast:

> On one side lay the Ocean and on one
> Lay a great water.

Anyone seeing the bar for the first time cannot fail to be impressed by the enormous mass of sand which the tides keep for ever on the move.

When diving on the *Anson* during the Second World War, I found it gave the kind of sensation you'd expect if you were working in a cauldron of agitated soda-water. On a windy day in desert lands you get 'dust-devils'. Here there were 'sand-devils', ribbons of sand scurrying across the sea-bed, weaving to and fro as they went. They were really something to remember.

Our salvage vessel was anchored right in the surf, and we managed to raise four grotesquely mutilated cast-iron guns, weighing in all about twelve tons, which went – with other cannon from local public parks – as scrap metal to make weapons for newer campaigns. We had found them lying half in and half out of the sea bottom, and the interminable 'run' of the sands had twisted them into bizarre, Henry Moore shapes.

As a warship, *Anson* was naturally the property of the Admiralty and after the war I successfully applied to them to buy the remains of the wreck outright. She was probably the last man-o'-war to be disposed of in this way, and we worked on her for four years.

Sand is always a salvor's bugbear, but there are not many sites where the volume of ever-shifting sand is so great and the overhead surf runs on such a giant scale. All the same we found a great pyramid of iron guns and ballast blocks bound together by the mysterious material I call 'clib'. Marine archaeologists call it 'concretion', lumping it together with another mystery material which is really something very different, and which I call 'crud'. They also manage to give the impression that it materializes from nowhere, rather like ectoplasm at a seance.

Clib is actually an old Cornish word, and when I was a child, and my mother told me that my hands were 'full of clib', as she very often did, it meant that they were very dirty, or 'clibby'. As I have mentioned, undersea clib occurs on iron guns as a gritty growth, and I did find one writer who attempted to explain it as the result of electrolytic action. The trouble with this theory is that clib doesn't occur on bronze guns found underwater, and bronze is a far superior conductor of electricity to iron.

Clib is primarily made up of rust. On land this is usually in the form of a fine deep-red powder, but under the sea it is naturally liquid. When given off by deteriorating wrought-iron, this liquid rust sinks into the sand, gravel or silt of the sea-bed, since it is heavier than the sea-water. It is also a *powerful binding agent* and thus forms an aggregate with whatever it comes into contact: the resultant 'mix' is *clib*.

Clib can be a great hindrance to salvage work, for it is found spread over the sea-bed in large densely packed plateaux, which usually have to be blasted apart. Yet it does have the redeeming feature of imparting long-lasting protection – sometimes for centuries – to any non-corroding items which happen to get imprisoned inside it, and even restoring a kind of ghostly life to ferrous items which have totally disappeared. For example, the divers on *Colossus* found a large nodule of clib which had obviously formed round some quite unidentifiable article, enclosing it like a nut-shell. Such a coating must never be hammered away, because of the danger of ruining whatever is inside. The usual method of dealing with it is by carefully calculated pressure, first one way and then the other, just as the expert will use a nutcracker to extract the kernel of a nut without bruising it.

In this case, however, I suspected that rather more special care was needed, and an examination by X-ray proved me right. I cut it in half with a diamond-tipped saw, and found I had a perfect mould of a flintlock steel pistol decorated with silver stars, just as it must have dropped from the hand of someone on board the ship at the moment of shipwreck. The wooden stock of the weapon, which the sea-water would obviously not corrode, had been beautifully preserved *in situ* by the formation of clib over it as the steel parts turned to rust, and although the steel parts themselves had completely disappeared, the clib had formed a perfect mould of them. How perfect a mould it was could be judged by the way the carving on the surviving stock of the weapon had been thus duplicated in 'reverse'. The hammer or 'frizzen' – the steel part of the lock against which the flint strikes – was found to be closed over the pan, and a hard pellet of gunpowder still remained inside. The cock – the part holding the flint – was in the half-cock position, and there in the mould of the barrel was a lead-ball shot. For some reason best known to Captain Murray and his officers, the pistol had been loaded and ready to fire when the ship was wrecked. The clib had not only preserved the vital means of 'reconstituting' the weapon, but encapsulated a little mystery of the past.

Now we come to 'crud', the other element in the portmanteau compound known to marine archaeologists as concretion. This is another word with a long pedigree, and which, like many old English words, has crossed the Atlantic: there it has come down in the world, and is not a word to be used in polite society, but in Cornwall it's another story. When I was a boy a 'crud-loaf' was a mouth-watering crusty loaf, and undersea 'crud' is just that in the crusty, crunchy sense, though far from edible. Handle it without care and it'll have the skin off your hands like the rough tongue of a tiger.

Solving the problem of exactly how crud is formed took me many years. It 'grows' on and around submerged cast-iron guns, and on very little else, and is mainly composed of colonies of minute sea-animals, which build little calciferous cells for themselves, very like those which make up the wax combs of honey-bees, but – in comparison – on a minute scale. Living in colonies of hundreds of thousands, they constitute a spreading grey-coloured growth – hence their popular name of 'sea-mats'.

Their natural habitat is the large, smooth blades of kelp, where they will live happily throughout the life of their host. However, like other animals, they do their best to live in conjunction with man and the artifacts he leaves in his wake. Leather, timber and rope defeat them, and they don't like metals such as lead, bronze, copper or brass which give off immediately toxic salts. Wrought iron, too, is a non-starter as a potential site for a home for them, simply because it rusts too quickly to give them a chance of a foothold, but they are fascinated by the possibilities of cast-iron, which – in the initial attraction of its smooth surfaces – must seem to them like some superior species of seaweed. It is a fatal fascination, however, for the rust from the iron insidiously forms a poisonous solution beneath them, and slowly but surely kills them off. Undeterred, as one layer of mats dies, another is built up over the bodies of the dead. This happens time and again, with layer after layer forming until the crunchy crud is 20–30 mm ($\frac{3}{4}$–$1\frac{1}{4}$ in.) thick.

Enshrouded like this by crud, a cannon resembles a giant sausage tightly encased in an equally giant skin. However, unlike clib, crud is porous and so does not have the same merit as a preservative. Under the crud-skin the products of corrosion form an ever-growing inner layer, made up of ferrous oxide, carbon and graphite, and looking like intensely black butter. This miniature world of inner space, therefore, is one of pressure and counter-pressure, and hereby hangs a tale – or, rather, fins.

When marine archaeologists examined the crud layers taken from ancient cannon found under the sea, they were much exercised and excited by the presence of what had 'obviously' been excrescences on the barrels of the guns. Of the many theories advanced, the favourite was that they were cast-iron fins, cast integral with the gun-barrel. The scale drawings that were produced, showing these 'fins' as square-edged oblongs, were something to wonder at, and the old-time gun-founders must have turned in their graves. Their wretched lives had been shortened enough by worry over the number of 'misses' they scored in casting plain barrels incorporating only trunnions: with numerous fins to be included as well, there would never have been enough guns even for a mini-battle. There were also the most ingenious speculations as to their purpose, and I sometimes think the whole craze was inadvertently started by the brilliant lady who discovered the flying bombs – Hitler's secret weapon – at Peenemunde, by picking up the give-away shape and tail-fins from aerial photographs. The marine archaeologists had visions of early marine secret weapons, gun barrels which took off like flying fish at sea!

The real explanation is delightfully simple, once processes actually at work under the sea are carefully studied. The pressure from the build-up of the corrosion layer beneath the layer of crud may at times become greater than that of the sea outside. The crud then splits longitudinally, like an unpricked frying sausage, allowing the pressures to equalize. The result is that the corrosion material is then forced out through these cracks, itself hardens under the action of its liquid rust content, and is preserved in varying rupture shapes within the final crud layer which constitute the famous 'fins'.

Which all goes to show that a dry-land archaeologist cannot just wave a magic wand and turn himself into a nautical archaeologist. Not that many land archaeologists realize that they even need a magic wand! My favourite story in this connection is of the land archaeologist to whom I was trying to explain some aspect of work under the sea without much success. 'But then,' I said at last, in some exasperation, 'you don't know anything about underwater archaeology, do you?'

I should have known better. 'Of course I do,' came the unhesitating reply, 'I've often excavated in heavy rain!'

This response has become a by-word in our little group, and when we have a particularly tricky underwater salvage problem, we tend to speak of it as a 'heavy-rain job'. I should add, by the way, that a *nautical* archaeologist is a very different animal from a *marine* archaeologist. The latter will often describe nautical gear in a way which shows he would be shipwrecked in no time at all if he ever put to sea in a real ship. Once a marine archaeologist has cottoned on to a nautical term, however, he runs it to death. Scupper-pipes are a case in point.

Old-time ships of the line certainly had a few major scupper-pipes for draining away water when the sea broke over the vessel, usually about four inches in diameter, and some having soldered-on spouts. Once this was grasped, every pipe to be found with a lead plate attached at an angle was described in reports of wrecks of armed vessels as a scupper-pipe. The majority were of such small dimensions and incorporated such acute angles that, to be scupper-pipes, they would need to be designed by a mad plumber for a child's toy submarine, for no surface ship would need that amount of scupper-pipes. They were actually guides for the lines which raised and lowered the gunport lids. There would have been at least sixty-six of these on a 74-gun ship, which explains the number that are found.

But, to return to that pyramid of clib on the *Anson* site. From that we recovered many iron 24-pounder guns, including a 42-pounder carronade (a swivelling gun) in near perfect condition. There were also all kinds of ship's fittings, some shipwright's tools, flintlock guns for use against the enemy when it came to fighting at close quarters, and a collection of the ship surgeon's instruments and medicines, including a bottle of hand-made camphor pills. All these were conserved and retained for my marine museum.

I was ready to go on to greater things, now that I had my diving team in trim, and I obtained Admiralty permission to dive on and salvage the remains of Admiral Sir Cloudesley Shovell's flagship *Association*, and her fighting sister ships *Romney*, *Eagle* and *Firebrand*, as well as *Colossus*.

During our salvage work on *Association* we rescued many hundreds of the ship's nautifacts, of which the most important was a fine solid silver dinner plate bearing the admiral's personal coat of arms. This was the one and only nautifact which clinched the identity and history of the wreck for all time, and one which – had we been so inclined – would, in a court of law, have given us prior claim to salvage the wreck. It was the vital clue, such as I might nowadays have had the skill to find at the site of the Falmouth Bay skulls, and one which opened up the whole story.

Talking of skulls, and the clues they can give. . . . There was, amongst the hundreds of crushed skulls and bones we discovered on the *Association* site, one which was splendidly preserved. Such human remains are usually better left undisturbed, but this was a unique find. Located three feet deep in the granite sediment of the sea-bed, and being itself completely packed with the same material, it had escaped the fracture and disintegration which had befallen the hundreds of others and was worthy of investigation.

Through my friend, the late H. Lee Duncan, a fellow of the Edinburgh Royal College of Surgeons, it was sent to Mr C. E. Renson, a dental specialist, who described it at length in the *British Dental Journal* (Vol. 128, No. 2, pp. 95–6, 20 January 1970). 'A search of the relevant literature,' he wrote, 'has revealed no mention of a skull of greater antiquity, in a similar state of preservation, having been brought up from the depths of the ocean.' He went on to conclude, from the abundant evidence provided by the teeth in the skull, that it was that of a boy of thirteen to fifteen years of age, and so possibly of a midshipman or cabin-boy.

Unlike that 'lone ranger' of a gun in Falmouth Bay, those on the *Association* site came in all shapes and sizes, ranging from specimens just tipping the scale over the 10 lb mark to giant cannon of three tons and more. So varied were they that I came to the conclusion that the admiral must have been an avid collector of firearms. The smallest item we located was a brass handgun, an antique even in the admiral's own day. The wooden stock of this most unusual gun was missing – a great pity, for it was this which was the peculiarity of the type in that it would have been four to five feet long. The method of firing was by placing the butt end of the stock on the ground, or against a bulkhead, or some other immovable surface, and then holding the gun at the desired elevation with one hand while setting a match to it with the other. These guns were muzzle-loading and fired a one-inch stone or lead ball. They originated in northern or central Europe in the late fifteenth century, and I had found two similar weapons on the *Romney* site, so that the oddity of these fifteenth-century weapons being carried on an eighteenth-century warship would seem to be not entirely due to Admiral Sir Cloudesley

Shovell's collector's instinct. In my opinion they were used for launching smoke-balls and signal flares of various kinds, for which they would have been ideal.

Another intriguing discovery was the brass after-half of a small 'take-down' gun, two feet long and complete with trunnions, pan and vent. The missing half was the cast-iron muzzle which was made to screw into the brass breech. The idea of this design was to produce a small cannon which could be unscrewed into two halves and packed away in a ship's boat, and for even easier transportability they were made with a gun carriage which was a light, wooden, spindly wheeled affair, rather like a baby's perambulator of that period.

We also recovered several brass breech-loading cannon from *Association*. Their barrels weighed a handsome 140 lb, but the design and casting were poor, so that they were notorious for blowing off their breech-blocks to the detriment of their long-suffering crews. In fact, they had a reputation for having killed more men to the rear of them than in front of them.

Our proudest discoveries, however, were the three magnificent bronze cannon which the admiral had apparently captured in some engagement with the French, for they were ornately decorated and bore the names of the great personages at the Court of France in whose honour they had been cast. I took these trophies, which we had in turn 'captured' from the wreck, to my workshop and, in the course of cleaning the largest of the beauties, found the clue to the problem to which I wanted to know the answer every time I touched them: in which of the famous battles of the time had they changed hands? There, crudely but deeply cut into the metal of the breech-ring, was the hitherto hidden word 'VIGO'. The suggestion which I offered in *Island Treasure*, that these majestic culverins had been taken in the Battle of Vigo Bay in 1702 – when the combined English and Dutch fleets captured or destroyed seventeen French galleons – had been confirmed. That is the thrill of submarine nautifacts, the world under the sea abounds with intriguing questions to which they provide fascinating clues leading to the answers.

There was also, in the case of our team, a special advantage in our having located and worked on British naval wrecks which foundered at varying intervals over a period of time. It was in 1707 that *Association, Romney* and *Eagle* sank; *Anson* came to grief exactly a hundred years later in 1807, and *Colossus* went down in 1798. This provided me with a heaven-sent opportunity to compare the nautifacts and fittings of one wreck against those of the others, and although the time difference between the last two wrecks was small, it was found to be of considerable significance.

To take even such a minor detail as the non-ferrous metal screw-threads of *Association*, for example, these are crude indeed compared with those found on both *Anson* and *Colossus*. The difference that a hundred years makes is quite startling, the threads on *Association* being poorly cast and then clumsily touched up with a three-cornered file, whereas those on *Anson* and *Colossus* had obviously been cut from solid metal with a die.

On a larger scale, other fittings which changed greatly over the period were the giant sheaves, or pulley wheels, from the equally giant rigging blocks which, at one time, had raised and lowered *Association*'s yards. These sheaves were cast in bronze and weighed some seventy-two pounds each, so that the trio fitted in a three-fold block would have weighed close on two hundredweight. When we came to *Anson* and *Colossus* a century later, they had even larger sheaves from similar blocks, but these were now made from lignum vitae and weighed only twenty-seven pounds each. However, there were also significant differences between the sheaves of the two later ships, those from the *Anson* having bronze spindles on which the timber pulley wheels turned, but both the rigging blocks and the sheaves from *Colossus* being patently experimental. In every case they are stamped with the month and year of manufacture, many having a new type of triangular bronze bearing with an iron axle.

While working on these sunken warships we have brought to the surface several cast-iron guns for experimental purposes. One fact was instantly apparent: the shallower the water from which the guns came, the more deteriorated they were. This was proof, if indeed proof were needed, that shallow water, with its constant turbulence, is very much more oxygenated than deep water which is untouched by atmospheric storms. Best preserved of all were guns excavated from below the surface of the sea-bed, encased as they invariably were in clib.

In the study of ancient seacraft there are always secrets within secrets, and as an example of how one discovery leads on to another, I can't do better than re-tell, a little more fully than I did in *Island Treasure*, the way I found out how the old-time gunners kept their guns free from rust when they were out of action. At first I was merely intrigued by the fact that every gun was sealed at the muzzle by an oaken tampion or plug. I assumed that this has been done to keep salt spray from the bore, and even when I found that the vents, or 'touch-holes', had all been plugged with a tapering spile of oak, I merely assumed that this was a prudent move to keep rain from filtering into the breech. What I had still to discover was that the bore of each gun that I examined contained a bright, new round-shot and a gallon of olive oil.

Each of those apparently simple oak tampions had a staple on the inner side, to which one end of a two-foot plaited coir lanyard was attached. At the other end of the lanyard was a woven ball, also of coir, which was designed to be a slack fit to the bore. I had never heard or read about this procedure, but I saw at once how it worked. With the gun-barrel lined up in the *horizontal* position, every roll of the ship would set the round-shot running, in its oil bath, from breech to muzzle and back again. The coir ball would cushion the impact of the shot against the tampion, and the oil would act similarly at the breech end of the bore. It was an ingenious system, and one that really worked, for all the guns that I have seen which were prepared in this way were in excellent condition. In every case the round-shot rolling out of the oily barrel glistered like silver under its own coating of lubricant.

As with the skull from *Association*, found at the Gilstone, I have often needed to call on the aid of experts in other fields. I knew nothing of metallurgy, so that in 1970 I sent samples of every kind of metal we had recovered from the 1707 wrecks to the British Non-Ferrous Metals Technology Centre. I asked if they would kindly examine them, and give me as much information as they could on their composition, possible methods of manufacture, and the nature of the corrosion products on them.

My request met with a most enthusiastic response. The director, Dr Alfred James Kennedy, obtained a grant-in-aid from the Royal Society to enable an investigation to be carried out, and the result was a splendid treatise, illustrated in both black-and-white and colour, produced by Hector S. Campbell and Douglas J. Mills, and full of fascinating information. When I mention that I sent them fragments from the larger nautifacts, such as the various bronze guns, the bronze sheaves, a bronze mortar and two bells; and also some individual small nautifacts, including a pair of brass dividers, a cutlass hilt, a copper sheet and rivets, a copper fastening in oak, a sounding lead, several lead shot, a lead scupper pipe and solder joint, a pewter platter and spoon, several silver pieces of eight and an English silver crown, and that each and every item received a chapter in the report, it will readily be appreciated that space forbids me to quote.

The report was as wide-ranging as it was thorough, and even went into a comparison between the composition of the big French bronze guns we had recovered from *Association*, and those from the Swedish warship *Wasa*, which sank in Stockholm harbour in 1628. They turned out to be remarkably similar, both being made of a bronze or gunmetal, with 4–4·5% tin, 0·5–1% lead, and 1–1·5% zinc.

The authors adduced further evidence to support my own thesis that 'Atlantic' wreck sites are anything but static. Having expected galvanic action to occur on such old-time locations, where metals of different kinds have long lain in close proximity to one another, and yet finding none, they suggest: 'The reason for this lies in the frequent changes in position [of the metals] that have taken place over the years.'

Another problem was raised by the rope we salvaged, and a laboratory report was obtained through the kindness of British Ropes Limited on the basis of samples I sent them. After a submergence of 264 years, the material – flax – had a fibre strength which was 'found to be still surprisingly high'.

Modern marine archaeologists, most of whom have served their apprenticeship in the sun-drenched Mediterranean, have a highly coloured and idyllic picture of conditions on the sea bottom. In the Atlantic area conditions are very different, and I went down as a young man into an underwater world which was rugged, colourless and strange. It wasn't merely that vision was very limited in northern waters, even in rare calm conditions I slowly became aware, in the course of my work, of mysterious sea-forces at work which left me completely perplexed and which no one seemed to have written about. A helmeted diver, who has to walk slowly over the sea-bed, rather than skim over it like a fish, has far greater opportunity to pick up the ominous clues of their existence.

Even as a teenager, I had been puzzled by the enormous mounds of seaweed which came ashore on our beaches, much to the delight of farmers in need of fertilizer. I knew that it grew at depths of thirty to fifty feet down, but how was it torn from the sea-bed? Breaking seas could easily slash large growths from low-tide rocks, but there are no breaking seas forty feet below the surface, just solid compressed water. It's impossible for a diver to wrench the weed off the rocks himself manually: he has to cut it stem by stem, and its slippery streamlined shape makes it even harder for the sea to get a grip. The only way to shift it in quantity from wrecks is by explosives, and some such explosive force might be exerted by the sea itself to bring ashore the amount which I used to see carted off for manuring the farmers' fields.

There are abundant other clues to the mysterious forces at work, if the diver takes the trouble to look for them, as I did. Right from the start of my diving career it struck me that the ocean floor – and I am talking now of the clear open spaces that become visible on the rare occasions of complete calm – has the windswept appearance of a prairie. There may be no tumble-weed, but there are rounded boulders, free of growth and obviously not static. Some may be the size of a haystack, but still owe their rounded appearance to their having been mobile for centuries, driven here and there by the gigantic forces.

Trapped under huge rock piles are to be found rusted girders and iron plates, with their serried rows of rivets and their serrations of rivet-holes. At first I used to think that this ironwork from old-time wrecks had been forced into crevices under the rock face, but I soon discovered that many of the rocks had been deposited *on top of the iron*. I'd have given a good deal to see it happen, provided – of course – it didn't mean being *physically* present under water at the time! I got my wish in an unexpected way.

During the Second World War we recovered 'wet scrap'. This consisted of ferrous and non-ferrous metals from wrecks, either submerged or half-submerged on the coastline. Once I was working with my team at Lowland Point, Coverack, just inshore from the Manacles, on a ship called the *Ocklinge*. We had been driven from the site by atrocious weather when we were phoned by a nearby farmer who told us our large and heavy personnel shed had just been blown across the field in which it had been 'anchored', and totally destroyed.

When we reached the cliff-head there was a hundred-knot wind blowing, and it was difficult to keep our feet. Sure enough, there was our beautiful, snug wooden shed lying flattened in one corner of the field, so down we went to investigate, which brought us within a couple of hundred yards of the wreck on which we were working. She had been an old tramp steamer, and we had cut her down to her inner, false bottom which had left her looking like a gigantic dais, standing flat and even among the jagged rocks of the shore.

We cowered behind a low hedge, and, covering our faces with our hands, we peered through the cracks between our fingers. The wreck was shrouded in spray and spume, giant seas completely hiding her at times.

'What the hell has happened to her?' asked one of the men.

'There's a ginormous rock on top of her,' I said. And so there was, a rock as big as a two-storeyed house. It was moving about on the flat plates of the ship's false bottom, and the screech and groan of it shunting up and down rose high above the sound of the storm. As we watched, we saw the biggest seas we had ever seen come rumbling in, with great high-flung heads of water tossing and leaping, as if a dam had burst. The sea-level looked as if it was higher than the land on which we stood.

We saw that rock taken up and tilted over the wreck's stern, and slid over the length of the propeller shafting in a welter of solid water. We turned and looked at each other in blank astonishment. When we were later able to inspect it, we decided, from its appearance and its covering of small weed-scrub, that it had been driven up from the sea-bed. We also found that, as it was punched over the wreck's stern, it had actually bent the 18-inch diameter propeller-shaft and had sheared off the two upstanding blades of the 6-ton cast-iron propeller itself.

Many books will tell you that all remains tranquil at the sea bottom during a storm, but I doubt whether that is true, at all but the greatest depths. During the time I was making a film with my team for *Paris Match*, to be shown by the French Radio and Television Organization ORTF, I was lucky enough to go aboard the Bishop Rock Lighthouse. Chatting with the men who tend the light, I heard the story of the biggest sea ever to be logged.

One late afternoon the keeper on watch saw, down in the sou'west quarter, a line of white water: it stretched from the southern to the western horizon, and it was moving fast. He called up his two mates, and the three of them watched in awed horror as the foaming, leaping wall of water raced towards them.

'They reckon'd they were done for,' said the keeper, as he sat on the edge of his bunk, small and curved to fit into the lighthouse wall. 'They reckoned it would topple the light, and it very near did. When it struck, cups were jerked off their hooks, plates slid off shelves and the lantern in its mercury bath was upskud, so that the mercury splashed all over and ran down the stairs.'

Sir James Douglass, the celebrated engineer who built the Bishop Light, recorded that coarse sand from the sea-bed, 150 feet below the Rock, was constantly thrown up to the gallery 120 feet above sea-level. That means – for it could have come from nowhere else – that the sand was scooped up and hurled a total height of 270 feet.

I had one narrow squeak in the aftermath of such a storm myself, when I was diving near the Lizard Point. The reverberations of a fierce Atlantic storm were coming into Mount's Bay in great oily swells – silent, slow-moving, unbroken hills of water. We were working under some towering rocks, and, with the salvage vessel lifting and dipping right over me, I had to hang on to the cliff-face every now and again as the surges came. Granite formation is very convenient for this sort of cliff-hanging, as there are numerous horizontal crevices. I had happily put my fingers in one of these half a dozen times, when, suddenly, in attempting to use it again I found it had disappeared. Puzzled, I placed my front-glass nearer the rock-face to have a closer look. To my surprise and horror, I suddenly saw it open and then – it seemed an age as I watched – it closed with such force that granitic grit spurted from its jagged lips. The weight of those incoming sea-swells was so enormous that it was tilting the whole rock-pile, by ever so little, but tilting it nevertheless, like an outsize logan-stone.

I slumped against that rock-face, helmet resting hard against it, as I clawed its barnacled surface in my efforts to retain my position against the flow of the tide. During those long minutes I thanked God that I still had eight fingers intact, and as I collected my thoughts I could hear through the copper of my helmet, and above the soft incoming gulps of air from my pump, the harsh lamentations, the growls and groans, given out by that enormous, cathedral-like pile, as it continued its ceaseless, age-old struggle against the sea.

The effects of gales, however, though impressive in their power, are expected. Even the visitor to the seaside is familiar with coastal roads and promenades being totally demolished, though it may actually have happened during the winter storms between his holidays. More frightening are the freak waves which pluck people from beaches or cliff paths, and overwhelm ships when the sea is otherwise comparatively calm. As lately as 1978 the *Boston Sea Ranger*, a 90-foot trawler of 170 tons, was engulfed by a giant wave off Land's End with the wind at only force three to four, and only a little before that a similar fate overtook the coaster *Union Crystal*.

Such waves may be caused by earthquakes or, according to a more recent theory, by the escape of enormous quantities of methane gas which may lie in an immense reservoir within the earth, being left over from the time of its creation. These causes may also account for the less-known stupendous releases of power which take place at indeterminate periods of time in the underwater world and never reach the surface at all. They are not always accompanied by a gale, though a surface storm may precede them. The sun may be shining and the day may be wind-free.

The only signs of any submarine turmoil may be the truly impressive, slow up-and-down breathing of the sea and the darkening of the water by the silt-storms below. Maybe a stray slipstream of current may coil to the surface, or the gulls will wheel and dip into the huge swells to filch titbits of crushed marine-life that have come up from the sea floor, but these are the only signs.

The only visible signs, that is, but the audible signals are something never to be forgotten. They take the form of a submerged roar, a bombilation of sound coming up from the bottom of the sea; a thunderous pandemonium born of the rumbling and tumbling of hundreds of boulders being agitated by turbulent forces – like a herd of bison being attacked by ravening wolves. The crew of the *Scillonian*, the ferry ship that plies to and from Scilly, have told me that they have heard the rolling boulders reverberating through the plating of the ship as she has passed through the islands.

Our name for these phenomena in our part of the world is '*ground*-seas', and what could be more apt than that? I have lain awake on many a silent night in Higher Town on St Martin's Isle, and have heard the roaring of Golden Ball Bar some two miles to the nor'east'ard. It is then that the tumult of the undersea world comes home to the imagination, the fury and bedlam of the water and rocks below the surface, with not a breath of wind, nor any other sound to disturb the night other than the calling of the curlew on the beach below me.

By the time I had become an experienced diver, I had become accustomed to the startling fact that 'our' sea-bed moved, something that seems impossible for marine archaeologists to grasp. In their writing and thinking they persist in trying to extend their land-dig techniques to the undersea world with an earnestness that recalls early missionaries trying to impose European dress on the natives of tropical climates.

On land it is standard practice to take a 'pre-disturbance survey' of the site of an intended dig before anything whatever is touched. I doubt whether even Sir James Douglass could convince archaeologists that, when it comes to the sea-bed of south-west Cornwall, there is no such thing as a pre-disturbance period. The survey of any wreck site on the Atlantic fringe off south-west Cornwall and the Scillies would merely show the latest rearrangement of the debris by the most recent ground-sea disturbance, for debris is all that remains of any wreck more than a century and a half old in that part of the world.

I am always reminded of the holidaymaker who stopped me in the main street of Hugh Town on St Mary's Island to ask: 'Have you broken into her after-cabin yet?' This was when we were working on a particularly interesting historic wreck, and I tried to explain to this bewildered visitor from the Midlands that there was no 'wreck', not by way of the semblance of a ship. In fact, I said, an amateur diver could well swim over the very spot without realizing any vessel had ever foundered there.

'It's like searching through the twisted, broken debris after a house has burned down,' I went on desperately, as his expression grew increasingly blank.

'Under the sea?' he asked, incredulously. He put his spectacles on to take a closer look at such an idiot as I must be.

'Yes, well, sort of . . . only, in this case, it's not a fire but the sea that's done the damage. The tides and currents, you know.'

He snapped his spectacles back into their case, and slowly shook his head. Looking me slowly up and down with a set face, he said: 'You must all be bloomin' mad!' And he walked away.

7
Emma's Vases and the Big C

A typical sou'wester was howling over Penzance one evening in November 1973 and, as I looked out of the window of my Admiral Benbow Inn over the eastern curving sands of Mount's Bay, the sea-girt castle of St Michael's Mount itself was shrouded in spume. I had been watching the antics of the waves, breaking in great slow-motion explosions over the harbour wall. The *Scillonian* passenger packet was lying against the 'south arm', the granite pier which points directly to the east across the Bay and lies broadside-on to the incoming rollers. Both the ship herself, and the gang of men offloading her, were lost for minutes at a time in white, high-flung clouds of flying spray. Outside the harbour mouth a never-ending succession of prancing 'sea-horses', with foaming manes blowing and tossing ahead of them, raced each other to the sandy shore.

Heavy rain showers, with scarce an interval between them, brought the short-lived twilight earlier than usual, and as darkness fell I went down to the warmth, light and snuggery of the Shipwreck Bar. Here I was surprised and glad to find two dishevelled figures discarding their drenched outer garments. Mark Horobin and Slim Macdonnell were members of our diving team, both about the same height, but otherwise as different as chalk and cheese.

Mark was the lean one. He had trained as a surveyor, a most suitable occupation for a married man with two children, but decided that diving was very much more exciting. Mind you, he got off to a flying start, for he joined us first when we were diving on the remains of Sir Cloudesley Shovell's *Association*, and a very fine diver he turned out to be. When there's no treasure about, he does his level best to satisfy the Parisian gourmet's lust for lobster.

Slim, as his name suggests, has twice the girth of Mark – and it suits him. For years I've known him as one of the world's top underwater cameramen. As his letterhead declares, he'll undertake the most hazardous of projects anywhere in the world, and he has proved it to be true. I am quite certain he would agree to be tipped over Niagara Falls in a barrel, provided he could poke his camera lens through the bung-hole – and was paid in advance!

'Got a moment to spare?' said Mark.

'The whole evening's in front of us,' I replied.

'Sure?' put in Slim. 'We can come some other time. . . .'

'You couldn't have come at a better time,' I said. 'Mike Hicks is across the road at the Georgian House, and doesn't go back to Scilly till tomorrow, so we can have a real get-together. I'll send over for him. He'll be as surprised and pleased to see you on a night like this as I am.'

'Well, that's fine.' Mark rubbed his chilled hands together energetically. 'By golly, it's lovely and warm in here!'

'It's the Big C,' began Slim, moving to the heart of the matter. 'We thought we ought to get something moving for next season.'

This was our nickname for the *Colossus* wreck. Search the weed forest and sandy gullies in the region of Southward Well as we might, our efforts had always been in vain, and though our failure didn't deter us at all, for it was only a matter of time and patience before she was found, we were anxious about the appalling risk that someone else might get there first.

At that moment Mike Hicks appeared, grinning all over his face. With his ample build and his rolling gait, he rounded the bar-head like a ship coming into harbour under full sail.

'You should have given warning of approach!' said Mark.

'You should at least have slackened your way,' I added. 'What will the harbour-master say?'

Powerful and thickset, Mike is a black-bearded, dark-eyed Scillonian, born and bred from a long line of hardy men and women steeped in the ways of the sea – and of the beautiful islands in which they are so happily marooned.

'What's on, then!' he asked, drawing a chair up to our table.

'I'll give you three guesses.'

'Well, I reckon I won't be far wrong if I hazard a guess at the Big C.'

'Right you are,' I said, and while the gale roared over the roof-tops, and shook the four corners of my old inn, we sipped our half-pints of lager and our tots of rum and shrub, and talked of the priceless vases lying shattered on the sea-swept reef of Southward Well.

I was quite a bit relieved for a start that the vases we were in search of bore no resemblance to the large, plain, unglazed and – to me – unshapely storage amphorae which have been brought up in their hundreds from the Mediterranean. These can be seen on show in every museum in Italy, set in closely packed rows and as gloomy a ceramic sight as you could wish for. The vases we were on the trail of were painted with figures of men and women, animals and birds, and a world of other things, in two distinct styles – the 'black figure' and the 'red figure'. In the black-figure vases the figures are like black silhouettes on the base clay, which can be grey, red or white, and in the red-figure vases all is black except the figures and decoration, which are red. There would also be a number of plain, unfigured black vases, which owe their appeal to their perfection of finish and simple grace of form.

The basic method of producing the vases themselves was no mystery. The preparation of the clay, its moulding on a foot-operated wheel, and its firing in the kiln, followed the simple universal rules. Large vases were built up in horizontal sections – the foot, lower body, upper body and neck being thrown separately – and the whole being joined together by the use of clay 'slip', a fine solution of clay and water. The entire vase was then pared down, while rotating on the wheel, to its final exquisite profile. There are thus no two vases exactly alike in shape and size.

The intriguing process is the finishing of the vases. In days gone by I had had a well-found pottery in the cellars of the Admiral

Benbow, and we turned out all our own pots, bowls, coffee mugs and the like. I never got round to doing the 'throwing' myself, leaving that to others, but I was fascinated by the firing and glazing processes, and did a prodigious amount. And it is in the final painting and firing that the mystery and wonder of Greek pottery lies.

I had often admired the specimens in the Department of Greek and Roman Antiquities at the British Museum – many of them, of course, having been part of Sir William's First Collection – but I now studied them with added interest. I was especially struck by the beautiful and unusual glow of the red-figure pottery – an orange-red with a slight sheen, this being the colour of the fired clay, which has a high content of oxide of iron. The black areas of these pots have a high polish akin to that of black patent leather, and I was to find when I came to have the pleasure of handling it for myself that it had the hard, smooth feeling of plate glass. It was entirely different from the thick, liquid appearance of modern glazes.

This surface sheen seems to have been achieved by preparing a 'slip' for the surface preparation made of clay of the finest possible consistency. Chemicals, such as potash, were mixed into it to break it up thoroughly, any tendency to resume a lumpy condition being prevented by further additives, such as urine. At this stage, the assembled vase, thrown as I have described, would have been timed to reach the right leathery consistency for the painting to begin. An initial thin, quick-drying coat of the special slip was then applied to the pot. Then the artist might make a preliminary sketch of the design to guide himself, and these outline sketches are sometimes still visible where the artist has not painted exactly over the lines, or when he changed his mind and the final design differs from his first thoughts.

The parts of the pot intended to be black were now painted in with a thicker solution of the fine clay, and touches of white or purple paint or incised lines might be added to emphasize particular details. Since the design only became fixed on firing, the artist could make erasures with a wet sponge, but he did face the problem that the design areas covered with thick slip, eventually black, and the background areas of fine slip, eventually red, were at this stage so similar in colour that it was difficult to distinguish between them. The delicate detail and fine lines were in no danger of being lost by their fusing or running together because the firing temperature was low. The final touch might be the addition of the artist's signature, and the value that was attached to the work of individual artists is illustrated by the fact that signatures on some vases that have survived are suspected of being forgeries – the art world was as nefarious then as now!

Once the design was dry the tricky process of firing began. The intense orange-red ground colour of Attic pottery results from the normal action of fire when air is freely admitted to the kiln. (Attic, by the way, means 'made in Attica', the area around Athens, so that some scholars prefer to call it Athenian, and pottery of similar technique and even style made elsewhere is not Attic.) Within the kiln the oxygen contained in the air combined with the carbon being released by the fuel to form carbon dioxide, and the iron naturally present in the clay became ferric oxide (red), so that during this first oxidizing phase the vases became wholly red, with the areas where the thicker solution of the clay had been applied turning the deepest colour. Next, during the second period of firing, ventilation was restricted, so that there was less oxygen to combine with the carbon, and carbon monoxide was formed instead. Carbon monoxide is chemically hungry for oxygen, and if it can't obtain it from the reduced air supply, it will take it from the clay of the pots themselves, converting the ferric oxide in the clay into ferrous oxide or magnetic oxide of iron. Both these oxides are intensely black. Then, in the third period of the firing, ventilation was again restored within the kiln and the pots would begin to revert to red again. However, the areas where the thicker clay solution had been applied would be less easily capable of being permeated and re-oxidized, so that these would remain black, whereas those covered by the thinner solution would once more be orange-red. Halting the firing process at the precise moment when the contrast between red and black had reached its apogee must have been a matter of fine judgment, and when the moment was not precisely caught, the language of the potters must have been as colourful as the pots.

'How many pots were there in *Colossus*?' asked Slim.

'Unfortunately,' said I, 'there's no record of the number. All we know is that all those sent back to England in her were packed in eight cases – size unknown, though they would probably be pretty hefty.'

'Not knowing the size of the case, and taking into consideration there'd be large and small pots, makes it pretty much pure guess-work, eh, Rowley?' said Mark.

'We have got a few other facts and figures that might help,' I said.

In 1796 Hamilton's great ambition was to sell his Second Collection as a whole, rather than break it up into lots, and the most promising customer for such a deal seemed to be the King of Prussia, Frederick William II, who himself owned a porcelain works. As a go-between, Hamilton enlisted his friend the Countess of Lichtenau, Frederick William's acknowledged mistress and the 'adorable friend' of the Earl-Bishop of Derry:

I think my object [of keeping the vases together] will be attained by placing my Collection, with my name attached to it, at Berlin. And I am persuaded that, in a few years, the profit which the arts will derive from such models will greatly exceed the price of the Collection. The King's manufactory would do well to profit by it.

For a long time past I have had an unlimited commission from the Grand Duke of Russia but, between ourselves, I should think my Collection lost in Russia; whilst in Berlin it would be in the midst of men of learning and literary academies.

There are more than a thousand vases, and one half of them figured. If the King listens to your proposals, he may be sure of having the whole Collection, and I would further undertake to go, at the end of the war, to Berlin to arrange them.

On reckoning up my accounts – I must speak frankly – I find that I shall needs be a loser unless I receive Seven thousand pounds sterling for this collection. That is the exact sum I received from the English Parliament for my first collection. As respects the vases, the second [collection] is far more beautiful and complete than the series in London, but the latter included also bronzes, gems and medals.

Poor Hamilton! Although his Second Collection was then at its peak of perfection and he was desperate for funds, he refused to sell it piecemeal, but was quite unable to find a buyer for the whole. It was consequently destined to diminish through the fortunes of war and shipwreck in a far worse way, and bring infinite distress to its creator, who had expended so much money and care in assembling it.

'A thousand pots couldn't go into eight cases of any manageable size,' said Mike, 'so what happened to the rest, after he had picked out the best to be sent home in *Colossus*?'

'Well, he had to leave quite a few behind in the Palazzo Sessa, when he fled from Naples to Palermo,' I said.

'Yes, but hold on,' said Mike. 'I can't remember why he had to go to Palermo, tell us again about the ins-and-outs of it.'

'It's quite a long story,' I said, and had all our glasses recharged before launching into the details.

In November 1798 Nelson had returned to Naples from Malta to find news of his creation as Lord Nelson of the Nile, and busied himself – in typical Nelson style – in urging the reluctant Neapolitan monarch to attack the French rather than wait for them to attack him. Ferdinand, nerved to the attempt, made a triumphal entry into the newly established 'Roman Republic', but the French had merely made a strategic withdrawal before making a concentrated attack on his troops. Ferdinand was swiftly driven out in a headlong retreat back to Naples, which he reached on 13 December, Nelson having preceded him in the *Vanguard* on 5 December. The French were expected almost hourly, and plans were put into operation by Nelson for the evacuation of British residents, and of the royal family.

By now the political situation in Naples was explosive; the city was a powder-keg of intrigue and rumour. Many of the nobility were disloyal to the King, having been carried away by the new revolutionary doctrines, and were impatiently awaiting their chance to switch their allegiance to Napoleon. The King's supporters among the lower classes, on the other hand, the so-called *lazzaroni* or 'beggars', displayed a frenzied loyalty which was almost more embarrassing to Ferdinand. They were often more anti-French than pro-King and were bent on making him fight the advancing French armies.

There was a period of cloak-and-dagger preparation for flight, because neither the King's adherents nor his opponents must guess what was happening. The British residents and their possessions, as well as Hamilton's pictures and other antiques, were smuggled out to Nelson's ships in small boats, the warships having prudently withdrawn out of range of the guns in the Neapolitan forts. The harried diplomat had to leave enough in the Palazzo Sessa, of course, to make it look as if no flight was intended.

Matters were even more difficult for the royal family, who dared send nothing direct to the ships, but channelled their gold and their jewels, and their clothes and other belongings through Emma's hands at the Palazzo Sessa. Hamilton estimated the royal treasure taken out to the British fleet as worth some two and a half million pounds. On 21 December Sir William told his servants that they could have some time off, while he – in company with Emma and his mother-in-law – paid a visit to friends. Instead, the three of them hurried down to the beach and after two fearful hours in a small boat found themselves safely aboard *Vanguard*. Nelson himself went to the quayside, where a secret tunnel emerged which led to the royal palace, and took the King and Queen and eight other members of the royal family out to his flagship.

Bad weather prevented the departure of the ships the next day, but they slipped out to sea on 23 December, when the wind eased, only to find themselves caught on Christmas Eve in the worst gale that Nelson had experienced in all his years at sea. The three topsails of *Vanguard* were split from top to bottom. In the emergency Emma's real worth shone out like a star, and she tended the Queen and her little ones throughout the long-drawn-out storm without a thought for her own comfort or safety. Little six-year-old Prince Carlo Alberto suffered even more terribly from seasickness than the rest, and when he at last went into convulsion, it was in her arms that he died.

Sir William, fearing the worst, loaded two pistols and awaited the foundering of the ship with one in each hand. Rather than hear the 'guggle-guggle-guggle' of sea-water in his throat, he declared he would shoot himself. Another passenger, the Imperial Ambassador, Count Esterhazy, was also convinced the end was nigh, and decided after much heart-searching that it would be prudent to throw his snuff-box overboard. It was decorated with a coloured miniature of his charming mistress in the nude!

His gesture was wasted, for the fleet arrived safely at Palermo, the second capital of King Ferdinand, in Sicily. Here, Sir William and Emma at first found indifferent accommodation, but later improved upon it, and the packing cases with the inferior quality vases and Hamilton's pictures arrived happily intact. In June Nelson acquired a new flagship, the newly built *Foudroyant*, and it was in her that Sir William's remaining treasures were eventually to be taken to England.

'So, how many pots do we have now?' repeated Slim patiently, looking from one to another of us, and patting his nattily shirted chest with open-fingered hands as he sat back in his chair.

'So far as I've been able to work it out, there were about seven hundred pots that Hamilton sent home, the larger number on *Colossus*. So, if we say three hundred in *Foudroyant* and four hundred in the Big C, I reckon that would be about it.'

'But even four hundred in eight cases!' Slim was a bit incredulous. 'Fifty per case seems a bit over the odds.'

'The smaller ones could have been packed inside the big ones,' suggested Mike, lighting up a small thin cheroot.

'What exactly do our lot look like?' said Slim.

'Well, Hamilton said he had packed his black vases in *Foudroyant*, those would be the ones without figures and therefore not so valuable,' I said. 'Later, when these cases were opened he had to admit that, after all, they contained some very good pots. They must have been okay, as he sold them to a Mr Thomas Hope for four thousand pounds, which in those days was a tidy sum.'

'So . . .' prompted Slim.

'So, if Sir William said his best pots were aboard the Big C, and that's exactly what he did say, it's the red-figure vases we'll be looking for, or rather, pieces of them.'

'What's the betting we'll find one or two intact?' said Mike.

'Not a chance.' Mark was definite.

So was I. 'No way at all,' I said. 'They'll have been mashed to fragments in the ground-seas.'

'You never know,' said Mike. 'Stranger things have happened on land!'

'The pots were packed in tow – the coarse, broken, hemp fibres unusable for rope-making – but even so I don't think they'd have survived unbroken.'

'Anyway, it's settled that we're looking for red-figure pottery, then,' said Slim, relaxing, pushing out his legs and tipping back his chair, 'a red-figure pottery just as it comes.'

'I keep thinking about those cases, though,' said Mike, 'trying to imagine exactly how the break-up would have come.'

'To get it right, you have to remember they'd have been surrounded by crated pictures and furniture,' I warned him, 'all that prize loot being brought back by the officers from the Battle of the Nile.'

'What's that got to do with it?'

'Make a world of difference, I'd say. Just imagine the sea bashing to and fro in the hold, which it would have done, especially when she hove over on her side. The two hold openings in her upper gun-deck would have looked like a couple of caves with the sea pounding in and out. . . .'

'I see what you mean,' said Mark. 'The sea alone would have been bad enough, but give it the pictures and furniture to add to the bashing, and the Hamilton cases would have been really in for it.'

'Don't forget, either,' I went on, 'that the wooden cases would have had no stability under water; they would have had negative buoyancy, certainly, but not much, especially if some of the pots were upside down and contained air. So, it's certain that they would have been flung about in the hold like one o'clock.'

'Then they must have broken apart within the first day or so of the Big C going ashore,' agreed Slim.

'I'm sure of that,' I said. 'I'm sure, too, that more pots than are known to have been washed ashore must actually have come to the surface. Some would have got clear of the wreck, and others would have been smashed as they floated on the surface amongst the wreckage.'

I turned to the copy of the beautifully executed builder's drawing which we had obtained from the Maritime Museum.

To spread it out flat we had to pull another table alongside. Across the top, written by quill in the usual flourishing hand, were the specifications:

Colossus of 74 guns – Launched at Gravesend 4th April 1787

As Contract:		*As Built:*
Length on the Gun Deck	– 172 ft 3 ins	172 ft 3 ins
of the Keel for tonnage	– 140 ft 5¼ ins	140 ft 4 ins
Breadth Extreme	– 47 ft 9 ins	48 ft 0 ins
Moulded	– 47 ft 4 ins	47 ft 4 ins
Depth in Hold	– 20 ft 9 ins	20 ft 8¼ ins
Burthen in Tons	– 1703 24/94	1716 74/94

'Where would the cases have been stowed?' asked someone.

I put my finger on the plan: 'About fifty to sixty feet for'ard of the stern-post,' I said.

'Just imagine that lot turning over,' said Mike in awe, nodding towards the drawing. 'Just think of the guns tumbling down into her lower quarters. . . .'

'And the barrels of gunpowder and lead-shot,' I added, 'not to mention the tons of round-shot. . . .'

'And the iron ballast-blocks . . .' put in Slim.

'The whole blinkin' interior of the ship would have been a maelstrom of water, chockablock with gunpowder, broken barrels, crates, rope and what have you,' reflected Mark.

I rolled up the drawing and snapped on its elastic bands: 'I reckon the Hamilton cases and the pottery inside them had just about had it even by the time they first started grapnelling for them. That case with the lead coffin in, which they did manage to salvage, was probably an Admiralty-stores case made of pretty hefty material.'

'So, where are we now?' said Slim.

'The pottery was broken up in the hold for the most part, barring the exceptions we know about and stayed there until the ship broke apart herself. If this were the Med,' I said, 'we'd probably find the stuff in one area, but since this is Atlantic diving, I'd think it would be well scattered.'

'All we have to do is find it!' Slim held his hands up high and

Rehberg's version of the Attitudes: Emma in the role of the Homeric hero Pylades (above), and in a more feminine pose, with a 'Greek' vase apparently decorated with a depiction of herself in a more dramatic stance.

wide, as if blessing us all. 'That's all we've got to do, it's so simple!'

'Hang on!' said Mark. 'We haven't found the blinkin' wreck site yet!'

'See what I mean?' answered Slim.

'Well, anyhow, here's to finding the Big C and the broken pots!' said Mike, and we all held our glasses high.

So we drank to our hoped-for success in finding the fabulous fragmented pots: pottery which had been fired and painted some three to four hundred years before the birth of Christ, and which had been thought lost for ever.

Then we turned again to the historical side of the project, more especially to the lady who had been the most prized of all Sir William Hamilton's fantastic collection of beautiful things – Emma herself. It was something quite new for us to be embarking on a project with a feminine touch. True, we had found among the remains of Sir Cloudesley Shovell's men-o'-war – the masculine litter of clasp-knives, clay-pipes and human bones – a few gold keepsake rings, given by girls to their sailor sweethearts. Running round the inside had been the sentimental inscriptions: 'In thy sight is my delight' and so on, which marked them as lovers' tokens given in parting. But now we were to search for Emma's 'baubles', those priceless vases which we knew she had toyed with in elaborating the celebrated attitudes.

'You know what puzzles me,' said Slim, 'is how anyone could make a proper "performance" out of "attitudes". I mean, I've read what the German poet Goethe said in that book of his, and I still can't get the hang of what was really going on.'

'Well, that's where we're lucky,' I said. 'Lots of people do have the idea that Emma just "emoted", as they used to say in Hollywood, but what she was really doing was rendering the high points in plays by the great French dramatist Racine, who used for his plots all the famous old classical stories, which everyone in Emma's sophisticated audience would have known. We know this because the artist Friedrich Rehberg produced a collection of twenty-two line drawings of *Mrs Hamilton's Attitudes*, dedicated to Sir William, in which he explains that she was "representing the principle characters in the plays of Racine in their proper costume". As usual, in any publication associated with Sir William, they had an educational purpose and were planned to form "a useful study for amateurs in drawing, from the most correct and chaste models of Grecian and Roman sculpture". Never missed a chance to teach somebody something, did Sir William!'

'Now that sounds more like it,' said Mark, 'puts more life into it.'

'They were pretty dramatic stories, all right. Emma is shown as the biblical heroine, Tamar, the daughter of King David, who was raped by her half-brother; as Agrippina, the mother of Nero, who poisoned her husband, the Emperor Claudius, so that her son should inherit the throne; as Medea, who killed her children when her husband, Jason, left her for another woman, and so on. In that last one, as Medea, she must even have had a young assistant, for the drawing shows her half carrying the body of a young girl under her arm.'

'No wonder she could hold an audience. . . .' Slim was no longer puzzled.

'The drawings also show us how she looked when she dressed as a young man. One attitude was her rendering of Pylades, one of Homer's minor heroes, and in that her dress is kilted well above the knee to reveal as shapely a pair of legs as ever graced the London stage. But,' I added severely, 'it's chief interest for us is the background "prop".'

'Pity about that,' said Slim.

'It shows,' I went on, 'a big bowl on a stand, filled with some sort of plant, and decorated round the side with figures enacting some kind of dramatic scene. The artist could have been just inventing, but I'd guess it might have been an actual pot from the Palazzo Sessa, and there's always a chance it was on board *Colossus*, though it could have been too big and heavy. At least the drawing is clear enough for us to have a chance to recognize it if we ever find the bits.'

'Any other helpful pot clues?' asked Mark.

'Well, the one where she appears as Tamar shows her carrying a jug with fluted moulding in her right hand, and a big pottery cup on a stand in her left – rather like a giant champagne glass.

That's got a kind of repeated "v" mark decorations round the rim . . . and you never know.'

'Well, well, well. . . .'

I had really astonished them this time. 'And then Rehberg shows some furniture, too – a table and a stool, for example, in the one where Emma plays Agrippina. There's a little head set on one of the legs of the stool she's sitting on – could be metal – and if Sir William managed to get a few bits of furniture aboard, too . . . Well, if we find something like that, it'll be an idea to think about.'

'You're right enough there,' said Mark.

'Mind you, I said, Emma's attitudes could have their comic as well as dramatic side. A darned funny thing happened once – after they had settled down in Palermo. The Hamiltons had a dinner guest who was a bit of a bore, and Emma decided to enliven the occasion by the impromptu execution of one of her most effective poses. She gracefully slipped to the floor, swept loose the comb confining her splendid waist-length hair, and kicked the folds of her gown into place. Then, eyes raised to heaven, she lay motionless on her side, the pose perfected. One of Rehberg's sketches shows exactly how she looked.

'Taking his cue, Hamilton leapt to the window to fling back the curtain to admit the sunset light, but the horrified guest, imagining that Emma was in the throes of a fit, thought only that her husband was opening the windows to give her air. Without hesitation, he made his own first-aid contribution. Grabbing the water carafe from the sideboard, he poured the contents over the astonished performer.'

'What did they say?' said Mark, laughing.

'Oh, Hamilton said: "You have spoiled, my good friend, one of the most perfect attitudes that Emma ever executed – how unlucky!" '

'Yes, but what about Emma?'

'Ah, history leaves that to the imagination.

'It must have been while they were at Palermo that the news of the loss of *Colossus* reached poor old Hamilton,' said Mark.

'He was poor old Hamilton, all right, now,' I agreed. 'The voyage from Naples had been a terrible drain on his strength, and the climate in Sicily didn't agree with Nelson and Emma, let alone the ambassador himself. And when he got the news of the loss of his greatest treasures, it was the last straw. He suffered from bilious attacks and rheumatism, and a wider division began to develop between Emma, in the full robustness of her early thirties, and the man whom she could now see only as a querulous invalid, obsessed by concerns she could not share.'

'You'd have thought Hamilton would have come back to England,' said Mark.

'Actually, that was what he planned, but there was now a chance that Ferdinand might be restored to the throne of Naples, and he not only saw his duty as being that of diplomatic adviser to Nelson in helping in that restoration, but hoped to return to Naples as ambassador himself. To him it was now more home than England.'

'Surely,' intervened Slim, 'Nelson did do just that – restore the royal family, I mean. In rather short and bloody order, if I remember right. So, why didn't Hamilton go back?'

'For one thing, the short shrift the little admiral gave the rebels was much criticized at home, even in that undemocratic age, and, for another, neither George III nor his ministers appreciated the tales which had long been coming back to England of the *ménage à trois* at the Palazzo Sessa and at the Palazzo Palagonia in Palermo, and which had now climaxed in Emma joining Hamilton and Nelson aboard the *Foudroyant* to stage-manage the coup in Naples.'

'So he was given his cards,' said Mark.

'That was about the size of it. Nelson, too, for that matter. But before Nelson actually returned, he decided on a cruise to Malta – then in the hands of the French – to see how the blockade of Grand Harbour was going on. Despite the years of gossip, it had only been since 12 February of this year that Nelson and Emma had been lovers, and when *Foudroyant* sailed from Palermo on 23 April, with the Hamiltons and a number of their friends aboard, it was by way of a delayed honeymoon. The great British warship with six hundred officers and men was essentially being used as a pleasure yacht.'

Having visited the sights of Syracuse, where the party was

particularly impressed by the huge rock-hewn ancient Greek theatre, they crossed to Valletta, where *Foudroyant* took up her station with the British squadron. Once she came under French fire from the forts, and Nelson was infuriated by Emma's refusal to go below: in excitement at being involved in a real action, she insisted on staying with him on the quarter-deck. But he could never be angry with her for long. He later looked back on their three weeks at Malta as idyllic – 'those days of ease and nights of pleasure'. For Emma the pleasure was marred by her discovery during the trip that she was pregnant.

At the end of May *Foudroyant* was back at Palermo, and, after a farewell banquet for his friends, Sir William returned aboard the warship with Emma for their first stage of the journey back to England. Nelson also had on board the Queen of Naples and three of her daughters, all on their way to Vienna to visit yet another daughter, the Empress of Austria. At Leghorn the party went ashore and proceeded by coach to Ancona, with Emma enjoying hairbreadth escapes from being overtaken by French troops after Napoleon's victory at Marengo, rather more than her husband. At Ancona, they again took ship – a Russian rather than a British vessel this time – for Trieste, and proceeded in triumph to the Austrian capital. It was to be four months from their departure from Palermo before Sir William thankfully set foot in England once more, a time of excitement and exultation for Emma and Nelson, fêted everywhere the little admiral went because of his symbolic value as the only Allied commander to have trounced Napoleon.

After a few recuperative weeks in Vienna for Sir William, who had suffered much from the hazards of sea and land, which had included the overturning of the coach in which the trio were travelling, they crossed Europe and finally landed at Great Yarmouth. On the way they had passed through Prague, Dresden, Magdeburg and Hamburg, and despite the advanced stage of her pregnancy, Emma manipulated her draperies to such effect that she was able to continue performances of the Attitudes to select audiences en route. Some of the exhilaration she displayed possibly arose from a feeling of desperation at her situation. Sir William's reaction to it is not recorded, but his preoccupation seems rather to have been with the state of his own health and his feeling of grievance against the British Government for having replaced him in his diplomatic mission. The forms of discretion were still being nominally observed, with Emma writing to 'dear Lady Nelson', but the celebration dinner for the trio's return, held at a hotel in St James's in London, when Lord and Lady Nelson, and Sir William and Lady Hamilton, all put their feet under the same table, must have been quite an occasion. Nelson's clergyman father was also present at this first meeting of the two women, and maybe we owe it to his spiritual influence that no incident took place to hit the headlines.

Emma, with her husband and her lover, spent Christmas with the raffish William Beckford at his imitation medieval castle at Fonthill. The indomitable mother-to-be, due to give birth at the end of January, enlivened the celebrations with a song recital and even a rendering of the attitude of Agrippina, before returning to Sir William's house in Piccadilly to produce her daughter, Horatia. The baby was whisked away to be cared for by a nurse in rural Marylebone, where Emma and Nelson visited her. As a first-time father, Nelson was delighted with his child, which he believed was a divine blessing of his 'marriage' with Emma. He seems not to have known of the existence of her earlier daughter by Fetherstonhaugh: for once the voluble Emma had been discreet.

At the time of the unorthodox addition to his family, Sir William was deeply absorbed in preparing his best pictures from the Palazzo Sessa for auction at Christie's. In the course of unpacking his treasures, Hamilton had a pleasant surprise which was calculated to drive all thoughts of the unwanted infant from his mind. The degree to which he was the dedicated connoisseur rather than the outraged husband is shown by his letter to Nelson, obviously written in the happiest excitement. 'It is quite beyond all expectations,' he wrote, 'that I have found so many of my fine vases; fortunately some cases of the worst were taken on board *Colossus* by mistake, when I thought the eight best cases were gone.' These were the cases brought home by the *Foudroyant*, but the cases we were eventually to recover from the wreck site suggests that Sir William was seeking rather to console himself,

and encourage purchasers of the surviving part of his hoard of
vases, rather than recording the exact situation. For he was now
off to Christie, who had just handled two sales of his paintings,
brought home on *Foudroyant* also, with plans for a third auction
of the vases. In the event Christie was disappointed of handling
the deal, and Sir William came to an arrangement with a private
buyer, Mr Thomas Hope, who offered him £4000. In the belief
that these remains of his collection would thus still be kept together as a memorial to his name, Hamilton agreed, although the
price was a thousand below his asking figure. It was not to be,
and even this shrunken collection was later dispersed, although
some were happily acquired later by the British Museum. The
Hamilton First Collection, after being shown in Montagu House,
was displayed in the 'Hamilton Room' after the new wing of the
British Museum was opened in 1808, and even when merged with
the main collection in the early 1840s, both these vases and the
items acquired from the Second Collection were still identified
on their labels as 'Hamilton Collection' and have the initial 'H'
on their bases.

Following the excitement of the sales, Sir William, now with
less than three years to live, was beginning to find his situation
less and less enviable. Those who commiserated him on his
treatment by Nelson and Emma on the long European journey,
however, forgot that the near septuagenarian was not averse to
an attempt to join in a dance on the trip. He would complain
of strain, and then with human illogicality embrace situations
which caused it. Emma and Nelson must have come to regard
him as indestructible in his powers of recovery, and with something of a conscience about their own relationship reacted, as
people do, with a certain inconsiderateness. They were also all
three bound to be constantly together. Emma and Nelson
could not bear to be separated, and the thinning veil of
respectability could only be maintained by Sir William
being present also, so that he was dragged away from his
London friends when she had a whim for sea bathing, or any
other fancy.

All the same, it is hardly possible to take Nelson seriously
when, writing in the exaggerated high-flown way he commonly

used, he wished the old gentleman dead so that he might marry Emma. No one knew better than he that this would still leave the impediment of his legal wife, Fanny, with her chill nagging, her inefficiency in packing his kit, and her passion-extinguishing addiction to flannel underclothing. Shouting – very understandably – that she was 'sick of hearing of "dear Lady Hamilton" ', Fanny had rushed from home, but a divorce was a practical impossibility and she was still a youngish woman.

In his exasperation Sir William expressed himself forcibly more than once after the return to England, notably at about the time of Horatia's arrival. Nelson wrote in some anxiety to Emma as to the possibility of her 'uncle [their code word for Hamilton, in case the letters fell into other hands] being so hard-hearted as to oblige you to quit his house'. In the circumstances, 'hard-hearted' seems a curious wording, yet Nelson would later happily have organized his own 'Tria juncta in uno' – Emma, Fanny and himself – if Fanny had not objected! In the eighteenth-century days of no standard machinery for divorce, and families of the 'enlarged' type comprising often quite distant relatives and hangers-on, all living in huge houses, such arrangements were not unusual in the upper levels of society, and tended to be remarked on only when the parties were greatly in the public eye. The caricaturists of Nelson's time had a field day in depicting his domestic affairs, but it was with ribald enjoyment rather than the shock and consequent ostracism that would have ensued a few decades later.

At last, at ten minutes past ten on 6 April 1803, Sir William died in his wife's arms, with Nelson holding his hand. A later anecdote told by Sir William Gell relates that, as his coffin was carried down to the hearse, Emma was seen by the assembled crowd performing attitudes of wild grief, to the amusement of some and the sympathetic sorrow of others. One child is said to have gone to its mother and begged her not to cry 'for they say as how it's all a *sham*'. It was too harsh a judgment. Trained all her life to dramatic expression, it was second nature to her, and the expected death of the ailing Sir William was not an event to jolt her out of the line of her customary reactions. There were no 'attitudes' when Nelson died.

Sir William's preoccupation with the fate of his treasures was now over, but – not far short of two centuries later – ours was becoming as intense and anxious as his had ever been. And, as Mark, Slim, Mike and myself sat in the Admiral Benbow that convivial evening, chatting about the long-ago participants in the story, we came at last to the nub of the matter, for him as for us – hard cash.

Mark, with an earnest look in my direction, broached the fundamental question. 'Will you finance us?'

I was too experienced in the game to be in a hurry with my answer. I glanced round the low-ceilinged bar-lounge, at the many souvenirs of my previous encounters with wrecks. Leaning out from the centre of the bar, right opposite me, was the figure-head of the schooner, *Young Godolphin*, one of my trophies from the days of helmeted diving. He was a fine young gentleman, with beautiful dark curly hair running down in handsome side-boards to frame his sun-bronzed, clean-shaven face. Well kitted out he was, too, with a well-tied cravat and a snug-fitting blue-reefer jacket. One moment you looked at him, his face seemed grave and set, with maybe a glint of a tear in the corner of his eye, and at another you couldn't be sure he wasn't about to wink. I have never been able to make up my mind. Was he maybe winking in encouragement now?

'Will you do it?' Mark pressed me.

I pursed my lips and looked past him down the room to another of my favourites, a figurehead of a girl this time – from a French ship. One breast escapes from her otherwise tightly enfolding draperies, and for all the look of innocence in her dark eyes she knows it, but stares straight ahead, just as she had done in the days when she scanned the seven seas and knew them in all their moods. This handsome pair and all my other treasures had many a time cost me far more than I had bargained for when I recklessly embarked on the chase.

'Well, what do you think?' It was hardly more than a murmur, for Mark could guess what I was thinking, and was beginning to get discouraged.

'We'll carry on searching until the money runs out.' I said it and I meant it. At least with *Colossus*, I was on safer ground than

I'd ever been before. Shrouded in giant weed she might be, but she was there on that reef without a doubt.

So, we got out our charts and planned our moves for the summer of 1974.

'There's one thing,' said Slim, 'we'll be able to protect her legally when we do find her, and that'll make a change.'

He was right, for although the Protection of Wrecks Bill before the House in 1973 was not yet enacted, it was well on the way to being so. We had been among the first to lobby members in favour of such a measure being passed, and it seemed very fit and proper that we should be among the first to benefit.

8

Underwater 'Cowboys' and Modern 'Attitudes'

The one great hazard to our enterprise remained – 'foreigners'. Anyone who comes to Cornwall or the Scillies from beyond the River Tamar at Plymouth is called a 'foreigner' by old-time locals, and I had reason enough to know what might happen.

To cover the real-life adventure story of our treasure-hunting exploits on the site of the *Association* wreck, I had written in my earlier book of three wrecks still to be located. One area I mentioned as 'just crying out to be explored' was Silver Carn; I had also told at some length of a lost Dutch East Indiaman with a cargo of silver, which we had long searched for without success; and finally I had also referred to *Colossus*.

While I busied myself for two years building my Maritime Museum at Penzance, itself the realization of a long-treasured dream, I had two instalments of bad news. Silver Carn had been explored by someone else, and the flagons of mercury, or quicksilver, had been found which gave the rocks their name. In the early days of the wreck of the vessel carrying them, some had broken open and the rest had now been salvaged. Then I learnt that the East Indiaman had also been found. Two 'pocks' to be eliminated from our well-marked wreck chart of hopeful localities.

Almost hourly I expected to hear that *Colossus* had been found, too, for I had in my book given her position and told how I had applied to the Admiralty back in 1960 for permission to dive on her! Permission to dive on her . . . how honest can one get? Maybe someone else hadn't waited for permission, and the Big C was already stripped!

Within an hour of our arrival in the islands, the news was everywhere that the Morris team were looking for *Colossus* yet again, and that 'this time it's a find or bust effort'.

'Just another Roland Morris publicity stunt,' said one. 'Don't know what to be at next, if you ask me,' chimed in another. We ourselves paid no attention to this sort of comment, for what our ears were open for was any clues as to the operations of the 'foreign divers' who invade the place in the 'summer season'.

'She's not on S'uth'erd Well!' said a member of one such team complacently. 'We've searched scores of times; there's no sign of her.'

Our spirits rose. The Big C was safe.

'We've even swept the area with a magnetometer without any luck,' said another, 'so you can rest assured we've looked for her and – she's just not there!'

One of the team's leaders, however, was less sure that *Colossus* 'wasn't there'. 'She's under thirty feet of sand,' he opined knowledgeably, 'you'll never find her! But, I'll tell you what, if you ever do, I'll present you with five bottles of champagne!'

'If we do find her, and we do get the champagne, it might not be worth the drinking,' I retorted. 'It might taste of sour grapes!'

In the meantime I congratulated myself that I had never mentioned anything in *Island Treasure* of the Big C's cargo of priceless vases. The 'summer divers' might not have given up the hunt so easily had they known. The Protection of Wrecks Act had received the royal assent in the summer of 1973, but it could not take effect as far as we were concerned until we could discover the site of *Colossus* and have it covered by a special order under the Act.

After my own abortive dive in 1939, I did not resume my search for *Colossus* until 1968. In that and each of the following four seasons my team and I spent four or five weeks, all the time we could spare in the midst of other work, to look for her. Now, however, the team settled down to a whole season's serious search. At last came the day! Slim and Mark set off in the loaded whaler as usual, leaving the boat-cluttered quay and standing upright in the small craft as they steered their sinuous way through the throng of launches filling up with holiday sightseers. With outboard engine throttled down and a small, but dazzling white, bouquet of thrashed water at the stern, they rounded the quay-head and cleared the harbour. Then, the throttle opened wide, the little boat dug in her stern-quarters and, bow lifting and dipping over the swells, raced away towards Samson.

As they sped over the anchorage, leaving the island of St Mary's astern, the long yellow line of Par Beach on St Martin's Island showed on their sou'easterly horizon. Further north, and on their starboard bow, were the silver beaches of Tresco, with Tresco Abbey grey among the dark bank of trees. Right ahead the twin hills of Samson stood in hazy, hot silhouette, against the blue of the sky.

With knees flexed against the bumping ride, the wind in their faces, and the noise of the engine and the scudding water beneath the fibreglass bottom in their ears, the two divers shouted to each other as they closed in.

'What say we try for the anchors?'

'Suits me! Let's close the reef from the south!'

'From the gravel, you mean?'

'Yes! It'll make a change from the weed!'

A hand closed on the throttle and suddenly the boat became horizontal again. The near silence, with only the slop-slop-slop of water under the bow as the boat's way took her to the mooring buoy, was startling in its suddenness.

Up to now in this season of 1974 the two divers had been struggling to penetrate the maze of weed holdfasts which obviously camouflaged any trace of the Big C. We had often thought of locating *Colossus* by looking for the two small anchors she had dragged across the anchorage, but the drawback was that, in our experience of dragged anchors, the dragging process itself builds up such a mound of sand or gravel that, when it levels off, the whole anchor is concealed. We had tried it just the same in previous years, many times and without success, so that we had come to think of it as a very long shot indeed.

But, on this sunny day in August 1974, Mark and Slim decided to have another go, using a different method. This time they would work to and fro, from east to west, making long compass-guided swims on a series of fixed lines over the clear gravel of the anchorage, moving one step nearer the reef on each successive parallel.

Luck was with them. On their third swim, as they went down one of their imaginary fixed lines, swimming side by side the regulation two metres apart, they saw – not two – but three anchors. Mark wrote in his subsequent diver's report: 'two of these were unlikely to have come from any other vessel than *Colossus*'. He had recognized them as British naval anchors of the correct period, and close to the smaller of them was an irregular pile of iron scrap, coated in clib and partly buried in gravel. This was a vital detail, for I had noted that one historical record mentioned that one of the anchors used by *Colossus* had been weighted with iron to increase its holding ability.

The moment when the two divers spotted their target in the hazy green underwater world was marked by an increasing frequency in the bursts of ascending bubbles as their breathing quickened with excitement. Giving each other the age-old thumbs-up sign in mutual congratulation on their achievement, they swooped for a quick examination of their trophies, and noted that each had a broken 'arm'. This, as I mentioned earlier, was why they had dragged so disastrously.

Next came the taking of a bearing from their wrist compasses along the line of the shank, or central iron bar, of the anchors, rather as if they were golfers eyeing the lie of their ball before a tricky putt. Anchors offer very little resistance to water impulses, so that the ground seas should have left them very much in their original position, and they should point us exactly in the direction of the remains of the Big C. Comparing their calculations, Mark and Slim fixed on the angle as 60° west of north, and finned off hopefully, arms stretched forward, left wrists clasped in their own right hands, holding their compasses steady.

A straight swim of just ninety metres brought them over a gravel bottom, scattered with copper sheathing tacks and pieces of broken glass and domestic pottery. These were promising signs. Swimming on further towards the weed-covered reef, they came upon a large sand-filled gully, like a boulder-strewn river-bed. Such gullies are always likely places for wreck of all kinds, and

Mark and Slim swam down close to the bottom. Their trained eyes ready to spot the smallest detail, they swam in and out of the boulders like two inquisitive seals. The tally of their finds was:

one 12-lb round-shot with a naval broad arrow mark
ten 1¼-in.-diameter copper bars
one complete glass wine bottle of the late eighteenth century
one glass seal embossed with the letters GR
four 'interesting' pottery sherds.

The round-shot did not in itself signal the presence of a man-o'-war, for it could well have come hurtling over the anchorage from one of the Garrison guns. The broad arrow has been used to mark government stores since the days of Elizabeth I. Lord de L'Isle, as Commissioner of Ordnance, used his own device for the purpose, and his successors saw no reason to change it. Pepys never took kindly to it, though, for he rightly thought that an anchor would have been much more appropriate for the navy. All the same, it was a useful pointer, especially in combination with all those copper sheathing tacks. These were curved and bent, obviously having been used, so that they indicated a timber naval vessel had once been present. The matter was clinched by the big copper bars, actually five-foot-long rivets, thick as broom-handles, which showed by their red colour where they were broken that they were of good quality.

In building a wooden ship such rivets fasten heavy-section timbers together. For example in joining the ribs to the keel, or in building up the sections of the ribs themselves (the second, third and fourth futtocks), in way of 'the turn of the bilges' – the curve where the bottom unites with the sides of the ship. *Colossus* would have incorporated thousands of them.

Inserting them was a skilled operation. A hole had to be bored through the timbers being fastened together, using a large auger – an iron tool with a long twisting shank, a circular cutting edge and a screw point. The two holes had to coincide exactly in a straight line, and it was a disaster if they were out of true. In itself this was quite a feat of strength, the T-shaped handle of the auger having to be grasped with both hands. A copper bar was then driven through the hole, leaving an inch and a half protrud-

The Colossus Vase restored:
a product of Athens in its greatest period, under the rule of Pericles

TOP: Some of the 32,000 sherds in their passage through the cleansing process in my laboratory.

LEFT: A piece of the many tons of clib being squeezed and cracked apart by pressure from my 5-ton lifting jack.

ABOVE: A portion of one of the many species of sea-mat (*Flustra foliacea*) which form the encrustation we call crud.

A little lion's head of eighteenth-century Wedgwood, probably part of a pot lid.

RIGHT: A black-figure fragment, the oldest of the excavation, showing the incised decoration carried out while the pot was still only leather-hard which was practised by Corinthian painters of the early seventh century.

RIGHT: A lady of more than two thousand years ago, and (ABOVE) a little perfume pot such as she might have owned.

ABOVE: A flintlock pistol completely shrouded in a thick layer of silt-clib, and (RIGHT) a portion of clib coating showing the self-made mould of the carving on its stock.

BELOW: One of the two *Colossus* carronades being used as a temporary survey marker. Note the silt and loose-rock terrain.

ing on each side, and tight-fitting copper roves, or washers, were then slipped over the ends of the bar, and the soft metal riveted over the rove. This riveting action drew the timbers together, 'clenching' them tightly.

The rivets were our first, and most important, clue, for they told that a great naval vessel had lain here, and she could be no other than *Colossus*.

The wine bottle, which stands on my desk as I write, raised our hopes by its perfect condition that we might find one or two vases intact. Long immersion in the sea has robbed the glass of its original gloss, and replaced it with a slightly dull opalescent sheen. In colour it is a dark amber, almost black, and has a miniature growth of sea-mats and bristle-worms scattered over it, which are a joy to examine under a powerful magnifying glass. It is eight inches high and five and three-quarter inches in diameter, and was blown collarless, an 'applied' triangular section collar having been added at a later stage. Substantial collars were essential in those days as the corks were retained by a twine tied beneath them. The glass seal is the same very deep amber as the bottle, and must have broken from one of the many hundreds of similar ones which must have been carried aboard. We were to find many similar seals, all deeply embossed with the letters GR – Georgius Rex – referring to the reigning King George III.

Certain though they now were of their find, Mark and Slim never gave a sign of their triumphant discovery when they returned to base. In the evenings, after the daily diving stint, the very act of leaving the empty 'bottles' (compressed air cylinders) at the compressor yard had to be done with a lethargic air. And in the mornings, when the refills were picked up, there had to be no air of joyous anticipation, but a show of listlessness.

The other divers would eye them curiously.

'Found 'er yet, then?'

'No, not yet, the sea's a big place, isn't it?'

'Yeah, but she's nowhere on the reef.'

'We're beginning to think that ourselves, but we've got to make a show y'know.'

'Seems a waste of time....'

'Well, we are being paid for it. We promised Rowley we'd have a look an' . . .'

'See what you mean.' This was something any diver understands. 'Well, there's that about it, if you're being paid . . .'

' 'Tis a shame, though, we'd like to go back and tell him we've found her.'

'Yeah. Well, don't want to dishearten you,' this was always said with satisfaction, 'but she's definitely not on S'uthard Well.'

After a short drive in the mini-van down to the quay, my divers were 'on-stage' again. The unloading and lowering of the bottles to the Boston whaler loaned to us by a friend, Ken Hay, and the stowing of them into the restricted space aboard this efficient little diving craft, had to be carried out under the watchful eyes of many interested quay-loungers and holiday-makers.

After a while we all became as expert in our 'attitudes' as Emma herself. Fun might be bubbling inside, but laughter was cut to a minimum, as we must never appear otherwise than acutely dispirited. When we were out of earshot of the crowd, the boys would tell the funniest jokes, but we reacted with the gloomiest expressions and saddest of gestures: it was a hilarious pantomime. The same applied in the evenings when we went for a drink in the crowded bars – a crowded bar in Scilly meaning that you drink with someone standing on your feet.

After another week's diving on the site, the strain of keeping the glad tidings a secret from the rest of Scilly began to tell on all of us. The time had been spent mainly in recovering small objects near the reef which might have put other divers on the right track. In our display of dejected melancholy, as we left the islands bemoaning the way Lady Luck had let us down, we excelled ourselves, and also ensured that everybody was delighted to see such a collection of dismal jimmies depart.

Somehow we had to safeguard our claim on the *Colossus* wreck until it could be covered by the Wreck Protection Act. The correct legal procedure would have been for us to go to Her Majesty's Receiver of Wreck at St Mary's Custom House to report our discovery, but so far from 'protecting' our interest in the wreck, this would merely have served as an advertisement to everyone in the islands of our find. Simply the sight of us heading in the direction of the Custom House would have been enough.

Instead, we waited till we got back to Penzance and then visited the Commissioner of Oaths, whose offices were appropriately situated in a little terrace house which must have been built not far off the time the Big C met her end. We went up to the first floor to a room which would then have been a bedroom, I suppose, and I imagined how it would have looked with the glint of silver candlesticks on the elegant little mantelpiece over the cast-iron fireplace with its looped swags of fruit and grasses. Flower-decorated china bell-pulls also survived on either side.

There was also still exquisite cove-and-roll moulding where the walls and ceiling met, and the square-paned window retained its light and elegant sash bars. It had been a lovely little room, and in a curious way still was, for the leaning piles of fusty documents occupying every available space had their own atmosphere of old-time tranquillity. It would have been no surprise to any of us to hear the grind of carriage wheels and the clatter of hooves on the granite flags in the street below.

The lawyer smiled as he took a preliminary note of the purpose of our visit. 'HMS *Colossus* – the one-time property of George the Third, I presume?'

I laughed, and corrected him with the wording I had read so often in the old records: 'The late ship of His Late Majesty, George the Third.'

'Ah yes, of course.'

The statutory declaration 'relating to the discovery of the Wreck of HMS *Colossus*' was a yellow-coloured document, dated 3 September 1974, under which Mark David Horobin – on behalf of Roland Morris, Michael Hicks, Slim Macdonnell and himself – did solemnly and sincerely declare:

On Thursday 8th August 1974 at about 15.00 hours Greenwich mean time I discovered the wreck of HMS *Colossus* in the immediate vicinity of Southward Well Ledge in the Isles of Scilly. In the week following the discovery namely from the 9th to the 15th August 1974 in accordance with our agreement with the Ministry of Defence my colleagues and myself removed from the wreck and at present retain the following items, namely: 1 Complete bottle, 1 Sounding lead, 2 Pulley wheels, 2 Trigger guards, 1 Musket stock brass-plate, 1 Glass stopper, 1 Seal in glass with letters 'GR' (Georgius Rex), 1 Sail-maker's seam tool, 1 Brass ornamental knob, 2 Copper sail roves, 1 Broken bottle-top, 1 Broken bottle-bottom, 1 Corner from white-glass bottle, 1 wine-glass bottom with broken stem, 6 Copper nails, 1 Small fixing nail, 1 Large copper fixing nail, 1 Miscellaneous copper catch with hole, 1 Copper spike, 6 Pieces of miscellaneous pottery, 4 Pieces of miscellaneous coloured glass, 1 Piece of crud and wood, 1 Copper bar 8″, 1 Piece of copper sheet, 1 Cannon-ball with arrow, 10 Copper fixing bars, numerous pieces of broken glass and pottery, numerous copper pins, nails, rings etcetera. AND I make this solemn declaration conscientiously believing the same to be true and by virtue of the Statutory Declarations Act 1835.

With that, Mark signed his name, and the commissioner added his own flourishing signature: the document was complete and we had done the best we could to comply with legal requirements and keep our secret.

Nature would also help us keep the secret, for the end of the diving season in Scilly was in sight. It is never economic to dive after the second week in October, and we went into the winter of 1974–5 content with the knowledge that the remains of the Big C and her cargo were safeguarded till spring.

My original application to work on *Colossus* and her sister ships had been made to the Admiralty in 1960, but the Admiralty ceased to exist in 1964, and it was the Secretary of State for Defence who succeeded to the Admiralty's 'powers, rights and titles', and who drew up the agreement under which we were to operate. This included clauses which showed very clearly that the 'men from the Ministry' had not the slightest idea of the conditions under which underwater salvage is carried out.

In particular:

THE SALVOR is not given any exclusive right to dive and carry out underwater salvage operations . . . and the Secretary of State for Defence hereby reserves the right to grant similar rights to any other salvor and salvors.

Ask any salvage man if two *or more* salvage teams can work, at the same time, on the same sunken vessel, and he will suspect that you are not in your right mind, even to ask such a ridiculous question.

Scarcely less ridiculous was the provision concerning the finding of any actual treasure:

The Secretary of State for Defence shall be absolutely entitled to one half of, or one half of the market value of, any of the aforesaid objects [i.e. those belonging to the five ships covered by the agreement – *Association, Eagle, Romney, Firebrand* and *Colossus*] which prove to be made of, or to include, gold, silver, jewellery, precious stones or other objects of unusual intrinsic value.

This had most serious consequences for me. For example, when I recovered Admiral Sir Cloudesley Shovell's silver plate, bearing his coat of arms – the only nautifact which confirmed the identity of this particular wreck – I estimated that it had cost me £600 to find it, the search period having been particularly long. When it came up at Sotheby's (all treasure items have to be sold at auction to establish the value), I desperately wanted it for my museum, and bid £2100 for it. As my 'reward' for recovering it I received £1050 – 'one half of the market value' – so that, deducting also the £600 it had cost me in the first place, the beautiful, battered solid silver plate stood me in at £1650. The transaction was not an economic proposition for a non-profit-making museum such as mine, and so I was forced to sell the plate again.

The Protection of Wrecks Act of 1973 altered all that, so that such iniquitous arrangements will never be enforced again, and divers can now expect, if not 100 per cent of the value of salvaged goods, something very near that figure. Slowly, very slowly, the salvage laws are being sorted out.

One thing the agreement did give me, however, was the right to retain what ship's gear, equipment and accoutrements I salvaged. This, of course, was a great advantage to my museum, for it meant that practically every item from Sir Cloudesley Shovell's ships could be exhibited there, and has been seen by scores of thousands of visitors. When it came to *Colossus*, the same clause still applied to her, so that we were quite in order to *remove* and *retain* nautifacts from the site of the Big C, too. So, insane as its conditions had been, that old agreement came in handy after all.

On top of my troubles with officialdom, I had had endless difficulties with 'cowboy' divers. I have a file among my salvage records labelled 'BELAY' – a nautical word meaning 'Stop!' – which includes letters and documents running into thousands of words dealing with our expensive court cases, protests, appeals and injunctions.

'Cowboy' divers are the ones too lazy to research and explore for their own wrecks, something I find incomprehensible, for this is one of the most exciting pursuits I know. Instead, they wait until someone else locates a wreck, and then calmly dive and help themselves to anything they can find. Needless to say, the Receiver of Wreck sees very little that they manage to pocket. In my 'hard-top' diving days such a thing would have been unheard of, for helmeted divers were professionals for whom salvage was a whole way of life with its own code. The new scuba technique brought its blessings, but it also brought the 'cowboy', and there was no legal way to put an end to his activities. I tried claiming that I was 'the diver in possession' – no such right was recognized; and even when I tried asserting that the intruders were using 'dangerous tactics' and putting my divers at risk – which was certainly true enough – it was all to no avail. Only in the long term was there hope that something might be done.

My file bulges with letters, especially to that steadfast and dedicated lady marine archaeologist, Miss Joan du Plat Taylor, and the clever and patient Member of Parliament for St Ives, Mr John Nott. Under the Ten-Minute Rule, which allows Members of Parliament to introduce private Bills on any subject of their choice, he tried to get the matter covered by a separate new Act – and failed. At the time salvage law was governed by various clauses of the Merchant Shipping Act of 1894, and when a new Merchant Shipping Bill was under consideration by Parliament, he tried again, this time to get the problem solved by inserting new clauses dealing with wrecks in the larger Bill.

In a debate in March 1970 he told the House: 'It is the date which indicates why the law needs amending now. In 1894 diving was a difficult, if not extremely hazardous, occupation. Those responsible for that Act could not have foreseen the huge advances in diving techniques which have occurred since the Act became law and which now frequently lead to the discovery of many fascinating relics of the past.

'There is nothing in the law stemming from the 1894 Act to prevent anyone from removing any object from an historic wreck or causing serious damage to items of great historical and archaeological interest, as long as the person reports his finds to the local Receiver of Wreck. . . .'

He pinpointed the two respects in which the law was deficient: 'First, the black market sale of recovered material at an immediate hundred per cent of value is much more attractive to the diver than the official declaration for a normal maximum of thirty per cent of its value after protracted and lengthy negotiations. In other words, the present rewards are too low for the diver.

'Second . . . the destruction of property is not prevented, as there is not a law of underwater trespass in Britain, nor has the Receiver any instructions to do other than accept material, irrespective of its intrinsic or historic worth and irrespective of its ownership or contract.'

Having detailed the eight new clauses he wished to have incorporated in the new Bill, he went on to say: 'This is an urgent matter. Many people feel very strongly about it and there is a need to revise the law.'

He was supported in this by Dr Reginald Bennett, member for Gosport and Fareham, who had also backed his earlier Ten-Minute Rule Bill. I had naturally been keenly interested in all this and had sent Dr Bennett, and some others, copies of my book *Island Treasure*. He now referred to this in his speech:

'I have read with great interest the history of the salvage works on *Association*, on the Gilstone Ledge off the Scillies, as reported by one of the best-known Cornish wreckers – with all respect to my Honourable Friend – and I have also met some of those who took part in salvage on the same wreck on behalf of the Fleet Air Arm at Culdrose, who had an operating unit of divers who were working not simultaneously with, but certainly in close succession to, the others on this wreck.

'It is inescapable that the rivalry and somewhat competitive efforts of these two salvage groups on this particularly valuable

wreck from which so much of intrinsic value and so much knowledge has been derived, did a great deal of harm to the cause of
the recovery of the material and the synthesis or resynthesis of
the history.

'Therefore, I feel that it is most advantageous that it should be
known quite clearly who has the right to salvage a wreck when
it is of such value and that this legislation seems the most appropriate, most ready and the only convenient way to establish some
rights on this subject.'

Emanuel Shinwell, who hadn't quite understood the points
at issue here, then intervened to make a party thrust: 'It is significant that when the Opposition discover that there is an industry,
or something akin to an industry, which produces no profit, they
are ready to hand it over to the State. I must say that these are
strange speeches coming from the Tory Party. The Honourable
Member for St Ives suggested, in an excellent speech – and he
always makes excellent speeches – that there should be a mono-
poly by the State in the discovery and preservation of historic
wrecks.'

John Nott's riposte was effectively brief: 'No.'

'That is what I understood from the Honourable Gentleman's
speech,' rejoined Shinwell, 'but if he did not mean that perhaps
he will tell us what he did mean.'

'Anyone,' John Nott explained once more, 'can excavate an
historic wreck as long as he has the permission of the President of
the Board of Trade, and certainly there is no question of any
ancient wrecks reverting to the Crown which are not of great
national importance.'

And so the Parliamentary sparring continued, with Mr Cranley
Onslow – the Member for Woking – breaking in to support
John Nott 'in a capacity which a great many Honourable Mem-
bers could also claim – that of an armchair archaeologist'.

'And an armchair politician, too!' interjected a wit.

'Let the Honourable Member speak for the armchair politician,'
went on Cranley Onslow imperturbably. 'I am not concerned
with them at the moment.

'I wish to cut across the party lines and remind the House that
those of us who watch, as most of us do when we can, the tele-

vision programmes of Jacques Cousteau showing him discovering wrecks in the Caribbean, or wrecks which have been uncovered off Ceylon, off Florida, in the Mediterranean, and off the shores of these islands, must have seen the enormous advances which have been made in the techniques available to the archaeologists in this field over the last ten years and the way in which their work can now be brought into our own homes. No one should be in any doubt about the extent of public interest in this country: here we have something unique – a time capsule which we have only just begun to know how to open, the past locked up under-water round our shores.'

John Nott's gallant efforts to insert new clauses in the Merchant Shipping Bill failed, but in July 1973 a separate Protection of Wrecks Act received the Royal Assent, at which time Cranley Onslow was Under-Secretary of State at the Department of Trade and Industry.

When I read in the press of the passing into law of the new Act, I closed my BELAY file with a sigh of relief that we had at last shot down the 'cowboys' and hog-tied their methods. I was a bit premature in doing so, for the next thing I knew I read that one of 'our' wreck sites had already been designated at the instance of others. In other words, a rival team had applied for, and been granted, the protection of the *Romney* site which we, ourselves, had located! Even under the new Act, the actual finder of a wreck can discover that all his research, all his expenses, all his investment of planning and hard work, gives him no rights or standing in regard to the site whatsoever. This is quite wrong, since the discoverers of a site are surely as entitled to full credit for their achievement as the discoverers of anything else, other-wise it can be truly said that diving courtesy in this country has sunk to lower levels than shark's dung!

9

'Cannon to right of them . . .'

Natural difficulties of finding a wreck site having been overcome, and all the legal hazards negotiated, it might be thought that all was plain sailing – or rather plain diving – for the salvage operator fired with zeal to explore his dearly won historic ship. Not a bit of it!

Jealousy takes odd forms, but even I was astonished to read an article in a diving magazine which described me as 'the most hated man in the British diving world'. Curiosity impelled me to ask the author why, when I happened to run into him. 'Why?' he said, apparently even more surprised that I should be surprised. 'Well, you've been too successful, that's what. You've had more than your share of luck.'

Which was probably why, when we salvaged *Association* simultaneously with another very well-equipped team, it was not at them but at us that the accusing fingers pointed. We had not carried out a preliminary full-scale survey of the undisturbed site before starting work: we had broken the prime archaeological rule. I certainly had to plead guilty to not undertaking the impossible. The Gilstone site is composed of a moving pile of giant rocks, and just how many times the sea has broken that rule about not disturbing the site, I hesitate to calculate. Some disturbance, too. One of the large bronze cannon we salvaged from *Association* was rescued from underneath a rock the size of a bungalow, and it was *bent*. Even if the site had been undisturbed, no one ever seems to work out that, at the depth we were working, the diving time for each diver is restricted to an hour a day, and that sea conditions restrict diving operations to thirty days a year. To carry out a survey would take the better part of all that time, and the next year the sea would have rearranged everything again.

No matter how many times you point this out, the smears go on. During my work on *Association* the campaign reached its peak when one national newspaper virtually accused me of jackbooting through a valuable and historic wreck for the sake of the loot it might produce. This was so totally untrue that I sued for libel, though very much against the advice of my legal friends who frightened me to death with estimates of my costs if I lost. I claimed no cash, just an apology and an end to the innuendoes, and I am happy to say that these came to an abrupt halt, the newspaper concerned publishing a handsome apology and making a small donation to my maritime museum.

It wasn't finished yet, though. Someone else tried another tack, and there were banner headlines in the press that I had used explosives on an historic wreck site. This, at least, was fact, but a very necessary fact. Using explosives sounds emotive, whereas they are an essential tool for the salvor and properly employed can be graduated in force from the equivalent of tapping open an egg to destroying a fort at one go. I have used explosives all my life, and during the years of the Second World War handled very little else. I notice that those who were foremost in making these accusations against me – they were amateur divers at the time – have now learnt to use explosives in their own wreck projects.

Apart from being annoying in themselves, these attacks were unhelpful to my chances of being allowed to undertake further operations, and I was worried about the answer to my application for 'designation of the site of *Colossus* for protection from unauthorised interference', under the provisions of the Protection of Wrecks Act 1973. At last it came. My application, said the Department of Trade, was being put before their Advisory Committee at their next meeting on 19 March 1975.

An explanatory leaflet enclosed told me that the Committee, under the chairmanship of Lord Runciman of Doxford, had been appointed to assist the Secretary of State in the selection of sites to be designated, and the selection of persons to carry out salvage operations. Words such as salvor and salvage had hitherto been pretty well taboo in marine archaeological circles, and I was intrigued to see them here.

The membership of the Runciman Committee is eminent indeed. Included are: a solicitor, representing salvage interests; a member of the British Museum's Department of Coins and Medals; a professor of economic history from Leicester University; the Master of the Armouries; a representative from the British Sub Aqua Club; a director of the National Maritime Museum; the chairman of the Council of Nautical Archaeology – a professor from London University; the Hydrographer of the Navy – a Rear-Admiral from the Ministry of Defence; a professor of history, who formerly taught at the Royal Naval College; the Chief Inspector of Ancient Monuments and Historical Buildings from the Department of the Environment; a member of the British Museum's Research Laboratory; a director of the Science Museum; and – if required – representatives of the Museums of Wales, Scotland and Ulster.

A couple of butterflies fluttered in my stomach as I ran my eye down that list, but – although my reliable grapevine told that I didn't have the votes all in my favour by any means – I duly received the vital crested document (appropriately sea-green in colour):

WHEREAS by the Protection of Wrecks (Designation No 2) order 1975 the area (hereinafter called 'the restricted area') within a distance of 300 metres of the point where a vessel lies wrecked on the sea bed at Latitude 49°55' 15" North Longitude 06° 21' 02" West was designated a restricted area for the purpose of the Protection of Wrecks Act 1973; and WHEREAS by virtue of the operation of the said Act and Order diving and salvage operations otherwise than under the authority of a licence granted by the Secretary of State are prohibited in the restricted area: and WHEREAS Mr Roland Morris of the Museum of Nautical Art, Penzance, Cornwall (hereinafter called 'The Licensee') desires to survey the site of the said vessel lying wrecked in the restricted area;
NOW THE SECRETARY OF STATE, in exercise of his powers under section 1 (3) and (5) of the Protection of Wrecks Act 1973, HEREBY AUTHORISES the Licensee during the period 12 May to 31 September 1975 inclusive to carry out diving

operations in the restricted area for the purpose of surveying the site of the said vessel lying wrecked and to use in the restricted area all such equipment or expedient for that same purpose.

There were four conditions. Only named divers could dive in the restricted area; only small articles likely to facilitate identification of the wreck might be recovered; the operations were to be under the overall direction of the Department of Greek and Roman Antiquities of the British Museum; and a progress report was to be delivered to the Secretary of State by 31 July 1975.

The document was dated 12 May 1975, and in a covering letter from the Department of Trade, Mrs Pamela Vincent mentioned that the Advisory Committee had asked her to tell me that they attached great store to the protection of the site in view of the great archaeological importance of the main contents of *Colossus*, 'namely Sir William Hamilton's collection of Greek and Roman antiquities, and the possibility that some appreciable remains of the collection may have survived'.

Whether or not we were to be granted designation of the Big C site, we had to make preparations well in advance for our accommodation at Scilly, for it might be impossible to obtain once the holiday season got into its stride. Luckily, we found a large house in the later stages of completion where we could live while the builders and electricians put the finishing touches round us. The sound of hammering and the smell of paint were minor inconveniences, reminiscent of holidays abroad at the time of the hotel boom, and we had plenty of space. Mark, with his wife and two small sons, occupied one 'flat'; Slim and his mass of photographic cine gear were ensconced in another; and I took an upstairs 'suite', ideal for my drawing work and still photographs. There was still plenty of room to put up visiting officials and friends.

We were indescribably exuberant as we motored across the St Mary's Road anchorage the first day we started work. It was noontide on a day in May, with the sun astern of us, high in a cirrus cloud-flecked sky, striking warm on the back of our necks. Mike Hicks stood at the wheel of his graceful, powerful launch – the 66-foot-long *Sea King* – and we stood in a group near him, while Barry, the boatman, was up on the forepeak sorting out the mooring line. It could have held a hundred passengers, but we had it to ourselves, and needed every inch of the seats and floor-boards for our clutter of 'wet-suits', compressed-air bottles and all the conglomeration of modern-day diving.

As we motored sedately and leisurely towards Samson, the twin diesel engines, turning over at a mere half-throttle, sounded as quiet and as sweet running as a pair of electric turbines. The light breeze, set up by our progress over the glittering water, was cool. Slim and Mark were getting into their diving gear and our talk was of finding our 'marks' – landmarks on the surrounding islands which, when eyed up in line with each other, would tell when the launch was correctly positioned over the site.

'We'll just chuck our anchor over for a start,' said Mike, 'and fix up a permanent mooring later.'

A bucket of water had already been brought inboard, and the divers were dipping their face-masks into it, swashing them about and rubbing the glasses with their fingers so that they wouldn't mist up. Demand valves were tested with much blurping and blowing of released compressed air, and then, with the help of anyone at hand, the twin sets of cylinders were hefted on to the divers' backs. Mouth-pieces were inserted and tested for comfort, lines of spider-web-like spittle stretching and breaking – bright in the sun – as they were removed. Overboard went the galvanized anchor, the mooring rope flinging its coils from the forepeak-deck in hot pursuit. But not for long, the water was shallow, but six and a half fathoms.

'Hold her there!' called Mike. And Barry took a couple of half-hitches round the timber samson-post at his feet, making sure the mooring line was resting snugly in its bow-fairlead as he cried: 'All's fast!'

With the cutting of a boat's engines, a change comes. There's no need to speak with raised voices any longer, and every sound – drowned till now by the engines – is suddenly switched on. It is like the abrupt change of scene and sound which occurs in a television play. The massed sea-birds over on Samson were squabbling and screaming their heads off; the water wapped against the hull as the *Sea King* swung round into the tide; the boat's timbers creaked as she wallowed from side to side in the gentle swells; and the sound of our own feet on the floorboards, all became suddenly and clearly audible.

With a three- to four-hour stint ahead of them, the divers wasted no time. Face-masks pushed back on their heads, they clambered up on to the slatted seat running along the side of the launch. Perching on the gunnel – the upper edge of the boat's side – with their backs to the sea, they leant inboard against the weight of their twin-sets, and turned to look at each other.

'Now, don't start picking up everything you come across,' said Slim, eyes twinkling and a touch of banter in his voice.

Mark's reply was inaudible, as he pulled his mask down over his face, bit on his mouth-piece and, with a steadying hand against his glass, threw himself backwards into the sea.

Slim looked at us inquiringly, hunching his shoulders and holding his hands apart in a gesture of innocent perplexity: 'Did I say something wrong?' he asked, blandly.

The next minute he was gone, too, with a splash which sent globules of white water splattering into the boat.

'And what was all that about?' asked Mike, expertly applying a lighted match to the slim cheroot sticking out at an angle from his black curly beard.

'This business of being forbidden to recover any nautifacts, other than objects which may assist in the identification of the wreck,' I said, quoting the official wording.

'But aren't you sure that she's *Colossus*?' asked Barry in surprise, jerking his head in the direction the divers had disappeared.

'We're as sure as we'll ever be,' said Mike.

'So . . .?' Barry still couldn't get what we were on about.

'We're supposed to be making what they call a pre-disturbance survey,' I said, understanding his bewilderment only too well, for he knew the sea almost as well as I did. 'Essential on land, I grant you, when you're beginning a dig, and right enough in the Mediterranean where a wreck may lie static for centuries. But here . . . The trouble is that, if the right blow comes along, we can have silt sweeping over the whole site in a matter of a tide.'

'Could be from the east, or from the south – either way would do it,' nodded Mike.

'Too true,' I said. 'And I reckon the reason we took so long finding the site in the first place was not just the weed, but the build up of silt. An overlay of silt can come along gently, imperceptibly, an inch or two being enough to camouflage everything, and you'll never know it's happened. Granite silt is the same colour, whether it's one or five inches thick, and the sea-bed *looks* just the same.'

'And we just happened along when she was clear,' Mike gave a grin of satisfaction. 'No wonder the others couldn't find her.'

'It's always a hazard with a completely sandy site,' I said. 'At Looe Bar, where *Anson* lies, there's a very large naval anchor, complete with wooden stock. It has been seen standing among the breakers there half a dozen times in the past forty years. I saw it once myself, twelve feet high and leaning on its wooden stock. By the time I had rushed away and come back with a suitable tractor, it was half covered, and by the next tide it was gone.'

'How d'you mean, *gone?*' asked Barry.

'Well ... sanded over again,' explained Mike.

'Twelve feet of sand!' exclaimed Barry.

'That's nothing,' I said. 'On Looe Bar you can get a twenty-foot sweep of sand during the course of a sou'westerly gale.'

'So, there you are, Barry,' said Mike. 'The first thing you learn when you become a salvage diver is: never, ever, miss a chance, for it may never come again.'

'What kind of things shall we recover, then?' asked Barry.

'Things that could identify the wreck,' said Mike, with a glint in his eye.

'Which means just about everything,' I explained. 'Bottles can be dated, so can clay-pipes and cutlery; musket parts and buttons can provide valuable clues. The larger copper-spikes and nails were stamped with the broad-arrow, as were the sheaves – the pulley-sheels – from the running-rigging blocks. Even ordinary pins will give a clue.'

'Go on!' Barry began to think we were pulling his leg.

'Yes, indeed,' I told him. 'In the time of *Colossus* they were hand-made. The top half-inch of wire was flattened and rolled into a ball to form the head. We've found a fair number on other sites. Hand-made pins mean your wreck pre-dates the industrial revolution.'

By the end of an hour we were looking at our watches, and Barry – whose job it was to keep a look-out for the divers – was soon calling out: 'They're both up!'

Slim slipped his bottles off while still in the water, to get rid of the encumbrance before heaving his mighty frame into the boat, but Mark came aboard with his twin-set still strapped in position. Spluttering and sniffing, they sat in the welcome sunshine, their puffed and swollen faces showing the effect of pressure – a minimal 1·32 kilos per centimetre at the depth they had been working – reinforced by the tight-fitting surround of their hoods.

'Did we hit the right place?' asked Mike, eagerly.

'Right on,' said Mark. 'I located a nest of round-shot about seven metres off the sou'east edge of the rocks, in sand. The depth was some twelve metres, I should think.'

'There's a lot of random glass and two large bottle bases,' said Slim, adding with mock secrecy: 'I'll bring them up later if no one's looking.'

The first day's task, and indeed that of the week that followed, was to accustom the divers to the site, and try to reconnoitre a few large nautifacts to be used as survey points from which measurements could be started. In this we were not disappointed. By the end of the first ten days of the 1975 season, diving at the astonishing average rate of three hours a day for each of the three divers – Mark, Slim and Mike – some seven cast-iron cannon were located.

Using the guns as fixed survey spots, to which the survey lines were stretched, the site was measured and 'triangulated' – that is, the position of the guns was established, not only individually, but in relation to one another. The most westerly of them, for example, was found 270 metres sou'east by east of the Southward Well Rock, so that we could fix its position in relation to the Admiralty chart, and from this pinpoint the longitude and latitude of the centre of the site.

We found that two of the seven guns were carronades. This was a splendid and exciting discovery, not only because they were such impressive weapons but because they were an important clue as to the original location of the bow-portion of the wreck. Carronades were never counted in the overall armament of the ship. The Big C was a 74-gun warship, but she would have carried these two carronades in addition, mounted at the fore-end of the forecastle, one on either side, and in way of the inboard end of the catheads.

These guns were named from the place they were made – Carron, near Falkirk, in Scotland. They were short, powerful and large-bored, but their distinguishing feature was that they were swivelling guns, and hence not mounted on the usual four-wheeled carriage. They were placed instead on a heavy timber 'slide' which slid in a greased guide and thus enabled the recoil to be absorbed when they were fired. As swivelling guns, capable of a large arc of fire, they were obviously best sited in the bow, and the swivelling guides on which they moved were bolted to the forecastle deck. Finding these two together, within 7 metres of each other, suggested that they fell from the ship when she was on her side.

It is interesting to note that these short 'stuggy' guns were designed to fire 42-pound round-shot, but were more usually employed in letting off a heterogeneous collection of missiles, such as scrap-iron, horseshoes and the like, at point-blank range – much to the detriment of the sails and rigging of the ship at the receiving end.

Since carronades were not mounted in the usual type of gun-carriage, which had steps by which the barrel was raised or lowered, they had their own built-in mechanism for the purpose, rather like an ordinary car-jack with a threaded upright shaft.

It took a great deal of time for the three divers to measure and triangulate the survey points, and to understand why it is necessary to envisage the sort of *average* conditions they were working under. First of all, think of a golf course about 100 metres square, with the usual undulating terrain of mounds and bushes and sandy bunkers. In this case, there would also be a large gully, a copse or two of trees about four metres high – representing the weed – and a goodly scattering of weed-grown boulders and smaller rocks overall. Amidst all this, imagine the seven scattered cannon.

No great difficulty in plotting their position so far. But then suppose that the golf course has been flooded to a depth of 12 metres, and the water is so comparatively opaque that visibility is cut to 4, or at best, 8 metres, and the task becomes a time-consuming problem.

With the Big C, however, we were in luck. We might have had to wait twelve months for lasting, perfect conditions, but in that summer of 1975 we got them straightaway. The water was as clear and sparkling as champagne, and the site was a gem in itself. The anchorage was protected by rocks, islets and islands from all except gale conditions, and the actual sea-bed in St Mary's Road, though a very rough place indeed in certain conditions, has been guarded over the centuries from those most terrible of sea movements, those underwater waves which had devastated our previous wreck sites, by the phenomenally large, overlaying growths of weed of the locality.

The first thing that struck us about the site, however, was its astounding size. A wreck site, where the wreck itself has disappeared, is measured by the area over which nautifacts are found. The upper gundeck of *Colossus* was known to have been 172 feet 3 inches long, and we found nautifacts over an area three times that length, which was at least proof of the energy of the Scillonian 'wreckers' in their dragging operations of long ago. We had fully expected the Big C site to resemble that of an underwater ship-breaker's yard, never imagining that a vessel could have been spread so far afield by human effort.

The sandy, rock-strewn gully I have mentioned separated the site into two, and ran north and south. We called it Emma Gully, and referred to the two halves as the East Side and the West Side. We had located the carronades on the East Side.

As if to help us further in clinching our location of the ship's initial bow position, Lady Luck guided the team to the ship's galley. The clues consisted of a number of smoke-blackened marble fire-slabs, which were found 8·5 metres west of the carronades. Since the galley would have been situated below the forecastle deck of *Colossus*, and roughly 25 feet aft of the carronades on the deck above, the finding of the fire-slabs and the carronades in one area was ample confirmation of the original lie of the bow.

In addition to the seven cast-iron guns, now located and identified by affixing copper tags, the sea-bed which they surrounded bore 'a heavy scattering of nautifacts', according to the divers' reports. These included sheaves of lignum vitae – that hard, dense 'wood of life' – and also of bronze; many other bronze ship's fittings, and a large accumulation of round and bar-shot. The latter consisted of two half-spheres of cast-iron connected by an iron bar, so that when it was fired, it whirled through the air with a sound like a buzz-saw. Psychologically, it frightened the enemy to death, as well as taking a terrible toll of the spars or rigging at which it was aimed.

There were also many bronze musket parts, hardly surprising when it is remembered that each musket or flintlock pistol might have five or six different bronze components. There were also quantities of flints, for *Colossus* would have needed a large store of them. It is not generally known that the big naval guns of the period were fired by flintlock. At one time cannon had been fired by applying a slow-match and linstock to the touch-hole, or powder-primed pan, at the breech. The slow-match was a saltpetre-treated length of rope which acted as a slow-burning fuse, and the linstock was the small, spiral-shaped, metal rod round which the length of slow-match was twined.

However, slow-matches were crude, and each and every one constituted a fire hazard and had always to be kept in a protective container, so in 1755 the Admiralty adopted the flint-lock mechanism. A specially designed flintlock was attached to the breech of the guns by two bolts, and was operated by a lanyard. This lanyard was usually given two round-turns about the gun-captain's wrist, and held in his hand, so that the command went: 'On the order, Fire! No. 1 fires with a turn of his wrist.'

In our third week's diving we were still engaged on our 'pre-disturbance survey', and on most days were using Ken Hay's *Boston Whaler* as well as the *Sea King*.

On this particular day the two craft were moored alongside one another, and the sea was 'slight' in a nor'east wind. We had begun with a general 'sweep', or reconnaissance of the East Side, locating nothing more exciting than broken bottles, pieces of iron pipe, round-shot and a copper bar. The first hour's diving having been completed, we were all seated down in the after well of the *Sea King*, with the top of the *Whaler*'s windcheater occasionally bobbing into our view over the gunnel as we drank our steaming hot coffee.

It was still May, but the sun was hot enough to dry the splashes and wet footprints, and the dripping pools where the divers sat, in short order.

'Oh, by the way,' said Slim casually, 'we've found and tagged cannon number eight.'

'Well, well,' I said, delighted to hear the news. 'Thanks for telling us, aren't we getting blasé?'

Slim ignored my shaft of teasing sarcasm. 'I've a feeling,' he said, 'that – apart from that – the East Side isn't going to produce much.'

'I agree,' said Mike. 'The nautifacts seem more numerous the further west we go.'

Turning to me, Mark said: 'We have been working in way of cannon o-o-five, and we cleared the area below it to see what it was lying on. There's a shallow layer of silt covering fairly large rocks.'

'The rocks are movable with the aid of a wrecking-bar,' put in Slim.

'We dug down to 80 centimetres without reaching bedrock,' Mark went on, 'yet in the area south of the cannon we tried out the sand-probe and found – on average – that the silt was 25 centimetres deep.' The probe was one of our newer tools. It consists of a strong slender tube through which compressed air is fed and bubbled out at the other end. By inserting this into the sand, with suitable guidance and pressure, the operator works the tip straight down to the sea bottom, and the depth can be read on the scale printed on the side of the tube.

'Doesn't seem to be much buried in that silt, though,' said Slim. 'Just a few pieces of ship's pottery, some clib mixed with brass and leather – oh, and one of the bits of pottery has a handle.'

'You're sure it's ship's pottery?' I said hopefully.

'Yes, worse luck!' laughed Slim. 'It's heavily glazed and obviously domestic, and there's signs of more of the same kind further west.'

Underwater visibility was 'good' on this day, ranging from 8 to 12 metres, and the boys were in a genial mood. They were in luck, too, for in the next hour's dive, which took them to the West Side of Emma Gully, they found a second whole, quite undamaged, bottle, and three more cast-iron guns.

'The last cannon we found and tagged is 0-0-eleven,' said Slim, 'and running a line eastwards over to Cannon 0-0-six, we found the distance was 50 metres – spot on.'

'We also measured the carronades, as requested,' said Mark, looking at his waterproof notes. 'They both measure 1·35 metres long. The bore, not counting the crud growth, is just over 15 centimetres.'

'Hold on!' I hastily opened my battered brief-case and took out a slim, dilapidated book – one of my special treasures. It is a gunnery book, written with a quill pen in the meticulous hand of the period, and with the name of its compiler inscribed on the fly-leaf in faded ink: Lieutenant Richard Malone 1835. He little dreamt as he made his careful notes – 150 closely written pages of them – how useful his detailed information would be to me in my work as a salvor: I only hope it was as useful to him in enabling him to rise in the service! He has never let me down yet, and continues to give me priceless assistance.

'Let me see,' I murmured, '– 1·35 metres long – why the hell can't we have these measurements in feet and inches? After all, that's what the gun was made to! Well, that's near enough to 4 foot 6 inches long, and 15 centimetres bore – or thereabouts – is – ah, yes. . . .'

I fluttered the pages over, passing on the way Lieutenant Malone's information on carronades – '4 feet 6 inches long by 6·25 inches bore; weight of gun 22 hundredweight, takes a 42-pounder round-shot.' Then, a bit further on, came the invaluable lieutenant's details of the performance of the gun we had just found. 'Let me tell you,' I said, 'the charge would have weighed 3 lb 8 oz, and if the gun was fired P.B. – which, for your information is point-blank – the shot would have travelled 270 yards. On the other hand – only if you are interested, mind – with an elevation of five degrees, the shot would have gone 1350 yards, which, gentlemen, is – ah – just over three-quarters of a mile.'

'Mm–!' said Mike. 'Not bad! Not bad at all!'

'Oh! Any time . . .' I said, modestly basking in the lieutenant's borrowed laurels. 'Just ask, and I'll oblige.'

'I wasn't meaning you,' said Mike, 'I was talking about the gun.'

Within a very short time the divers had gone overboard once again for their third, and last, dive of the day. We had planned to fit in a fourth, but they had complained that the water was extraordinarily cold, which it can very well be at Scilly, so we cut it out.

With all the divers down, Barry and I were left to our own devices.

'That's eleven cannon they've located so far,' he said, swabbing down the seats where they had been sitting. 'Why do you reckon Fearless and John Deane, for that matter, left so many behind?'

'They must have been covered by wreckage,' I said, 'or they'd have had them sure enough. Guns were a *very* valuable commodity in those days.'

'Would they have been that valuable?' said Barry.

'Absolutely priceless. In those days a land army could fight in many ways, even without field guns if necessary, but a navy – no. Without its guns the British Navy would have been nothing; every ship was a floating fortress, and a fortress is useless without guns. In a vital naval battle every gun was worth its weight in gold.'

'Yes, I see what you mean.'

'For a long time,' I explained, 'the gun-founders were not all that clever. They had many disasters and failures in making cannon, and they never, ever, really produced a surfeit of cast-iron guns. In fact, the Ordnance Board, from way back in history, always seems to have been desperate for more artillery. The right kind of iron ore was scarce, and so any failed or suspect guns were never discarded but carefully brought back to base.'

'For re-casting?'

'That's right. There was quite a traffic to and fro from the Med during the Napoleonic wars. New guns were sent to Gib and Lisbon, or to specified ships in need of them, and all the old ones that could be got together were brought home. In October and the rest of the tail-end of the year, when bad weather meant there was no chance of encountering the enemy, many British ships came home with few, or even no, usable guns behind their gunport-lids. In fact the lids were caulked and sealed for the voyage.'

'But they'd have plenty of scrap guns in their holds?'

'Not always,' I said, 'it depended entirely on what was available. Having left most of her serviceable guns in store at Gib a ship could come home with but a few scrap guns, and her ballast trimmed – to make up for the loss of the weight of her cannon – by stones. Or her ballast-trim would be made up by cargo, for these warships were not above doing a fair trade in all kinds of goods.'

'But what about those divers who say they can identify an old-time wreck by counting the guns on the site?'

'Taking into account the varying sizes of the guns – twelve, twenty-four and thirty-two pounders – and also considering the endless permutations on the number of serviceable and non-serviceable guns a ship might have aboard. . . .'

'You'd say these gun counters couldn't prove anything?'

'I'd say they must be nut-cases to try,' I said, 'and hard-put for some way to occupy their time. For a start you'd have to be sure that you'd got all the wreck on the site, and, often enough, it isn't. There's only part of *Romney* on the site we found: the rest of her is somewhere else, and one day someone will find it. *Eagle* – another of our finds – was not only spread over three different sites, but was probably overlaid by a second, and even a third, wreck. Then, there's *Association*, which was a 96-gun ship of the line. In her case, there are 62 guns at the site, and five 12-pounders were salvaged from her soon after she sank. . . .'

'By the old-time divers,' said Barry. 'I remember reading about that.'

'Yes. And we could account for some of the rest by the fact that there's every evidence her fore part broke away and floated off to the nor'-east. But how do we know there are any to "account for"? Are they really "missing"? Who's to prove they were ever on board?'

'What I don't understand is how a bit of a ship could go off by itself,' said Barry.

'Why, being made of large-sectioned timber, they had positive buoyancy – even if they were badly damaged, they just didn't sink. I remember myself two cases of old-time men-o'-war which had been converted to training ships. When they got too old for further service, they were supposed to be scuttled and sunk. Well, they wouldn't sink. They had to be blasted apart before they did. It was obviously the same when Sir Cloudesley Shovell's ships were smashing about among the Westard Rocks. They broke apart as they wallowed half-seas under, and their parts were scattered.'

It was getting chilly now, and Barry looked at his watch. 'They should be up soon, and I bet they won't be sorry. It'll be a lot colder down there.'

'Cold can be the very devil,' I said, 'though in my time as a hard-top diver only my hands were affected. I could never wear gloves, so I suffered, and used to go about with lily-white hands all the time.'

There was a sound of snorting, coughing and sniffing, overside.

'Here they are,' said Barry. 'Guess who'll mention the cold first?'

'Slim?' I murmured slyly.

'You must be joking!' said Barry, laughing. 'He's well protected!'

'So's Mike, so it'll be Mark, right?'

Having handled his bottles to Barry, Mike came aboard, his suit glistening and dripping. The other two clambered into the *Whaler*, coming up its short metal steps. Standing close together, in the small space aft of the helmsman's seat, they slipped off their sets.

'By golly, it's simply *free-e-zing* down there!' Mark was too busy shivering to see Barry look at me and laugh at this confirmation of our guess, and went on: 'I remember, we drank all the coffee, too!'

'Never mind!' I said, 'it's rum and shrub on me tonight.'

'Can't bear the stuff!' said Slim.

'I bet if I offered you one right now, you'd take it!' retorted Mark.

'Wouldn't,' said Slim, hunching his shoulders and smiling.

'Start her up,' called Mike to Barry, who went amidships to the *Sea King's* engine-room. The electric starters whir-whirred and the two engines broke into life. Mike, still in his wet-suit, but minus his hood and fins, stood at the launch's wheel. He pushed the two gear-levers forward and eased the two throttle levers into full speed. The launch turned half-circle, away from the Island of Samson, and headed enthusiastically towards St Mary's.

'Here, take her,' said Mike, and Barry stepped up to the controls.

Over the stern I could still see Slim and Mark standing in the stationary *Whaler*, bobbing and swaying in the water-commotion we had left behind. Judging by the way they were waving their arms about, they were still arguing about that rum and shrub.

'What's it been like, then?' Mike emerged from the engine-room, looking entirely different in trousers and blue jersey with 'SEA-KING' inscribed across his chest. 'How were things topsides?'

'Fine, just fine! I've been telling Barry how useless it is to try and identify an underwater wreck by counting its guns. I've been boring him to death.'

'On the contrary,' intervened Barry, politely. 'It's been most interesting.'

'Well, I don't know if you knew,' said Mike, turning round to him, 'but when one of those old-time ships was at sea, in a fairly spanking breeze we'll say, and she was reaching before the wind, or otherwise straining herself unduly, the ship's carpenter went around with a bag of wedges. He'd artfully hammer in a wedge here and a wedge there, and generally tighten up the ship's hull. Later, when the strain was over, he'd go round and take them out again.'

'Well, I never knew that,' said Barry, 'but what's that got to do with guns?'

'If you'll only contain yourself a while,' said Mike, taking a bent cheroot from his hip pocket and eyeing it suspiciously, 'I'll inform you.'

'Thanks,' said Barry.

'It was also the ship's carpenter, Lord bless his soul,' Mike went on, 'who tended the ship's ballast-trim, and don't tell me that you don't know what that is!'

'Ballast-trim?' Barry was up to this one. 'Well, it's putting ballast, moveable ballast that is, where the ship most needs it, according to the conditions prevailing at the time.'

Rather taken aback, Mike drew a hand raspingly down over his beard, and threw the suspect cheroot overboard. 'Well, you know how easily the old-time gunners were able to place a gun anywhere they wanted in a ship. With ring bolts just about every-where, lifting and moving cannon was nothing to them. So, some carpenters might use iron ballast blocks for their ballast-trim, but, mostly, their favourite method was to use old clapped-out cannon barrels as moveable ballast in rough weather.'

Obviously Barry didn't see where the line of the argument was going, and would have broken in.

'No, no, hang on,' said Mike. 'If an underwater wreck had ten ballast-trim cannon on the site, it would rather put these gun-counting people's calculations up the spout, wouldn't it?'

The point was taken, but our attention was now diverted by the *Whaler* which was overtaking on the port side. Slim was driving, and still talking so earnestly to Mark that we got not a wave nor any other sign of acknowledgment from him or Mark, who was talking equally earnestly back. With bow bobbing in the air, and streaks of white and blue water flashing from that minimal area of her bottom which scorched over the sea's surface, the *Boston Whaler* had come and gone, leaving us in a giant furrowed wake, bucketing and wallowing.

Mike struggled with his wheel. 'Not a blind bit of notice of us, and I'll bet they'll still be arguing about that rum and shrub when we get back to port. Isn't it *marvellous*!'

10
The Satyr Face in the Sand

It could so easily have happened on a dull, rainy day. But, no. It was a day 'blessed' – and that is an appropriate day for finding sunken treasure.

May had gone, taking with it the strong east winds. The wind was now out of the west, soft and mild – a zephyr which gently stroked the face of the blue sea. What clouds there were floated high in the sky. It was June in Scilly, and, that morning, there was expectancy in the air. Not today was there the slightly jaded feeling that came with logging all the hundreds of nautifacts which made up the grave of the gigantic ship: all sorts and sizes of bronze and copper nails and spikes; a variety of lead and copper sheathing; glass, pewter, lead-shot, round-shot, iron-ballast blocks, pulley wheels and timber – not to mention the all-important guns.

When the divers poked their heads above water, at the end of the first dive of that beautiful day, they were some way from the boats. At that distance they resembled grey seals, and swam leisurely, their fins moving in slow, undulating variance. On reaching the boats, they pushed back their face-masks, and I could sense their excitement.

'What!' I said. 'No stern-board with *Colossus* carved on it in foot-high letters?'

'We've found something almost as good!' spluttered Mark, taking out his mouth-piece. 'We've found the rudder-pintles!' These were the short, chunky bronze bars forming the pivots on which the rudder turned, and a significant find.

'Welcome aboard!' I said, as they slip-slopped over *Sea King*'s gunnel and spread themselves around in the sunlight. 'Tell us, where?'

'To the extreme west of the West Side.' Mark pointed over the launch's bow to stress how far away they were, and took out his waterproof pad. 'Now, let's get this right. The last cannon we found were more or less in a triangle, they're quite badly corroded, by the way. They're lying on a ridge on top of the reef in shallow water – far shallower than any we've been in on the East Side. Well, this morning we continued on past the cannon, making our way due west through very dense weed. After about thirty metres of this we came to an even shallower ridge, and against the southern wall of this – in between the many boulders there – we found a mass of nautifacts. Then, another fifty metres further west still – just beyond the end of the ridge – lay the four pintles.'

I had spread our preliminary chart of the site across the roof of the engine compartment, which the sun had made too hot for us to lean on with our bare arms and chests.

'Hold hard,' I said, scrutinizing the drawing. 'That makes the pintles' – I marked off the details with a scale rule – 'that makes them 190 metres west of the carronades. Good law! Our site is getting larger every day!'

Mark nodded. It was no news to him.

I consulted my metric table. 'Why, 190 metres is round about 630 feet, or three and a half times the length of the Big C!' My surprise arose from the fact that, the carronades being taken as indicating the bow position of the wreck, it was reasonable to assume that the pintles did the same for the stern.

'Were the rudder-pintles originally made-fast the rudder or made-fast the ship?' asked Slim.

'A very good point indeed,' said I. 'If they were fast the rudder, which they certainly would have been originally, then the rudder – which we know was broken off – may have been washed over to the west'ard, carrying the pintles with it. Is that what you're thinking?'

Slim nodded and hunched his shoulders dejectedly.

'So, all we've found is the location where the rudder ended up!' Mark was equally disappointed.

'No, I don't think that at all,' Laughingly, I tapped my fore-head. 'This is where experience comes in.' I coughed modestly. 'When *Anson* went ashore her rudder was beaten off by the sea, and with her we found the braces, the pintles and the gudgeons – all the rudder hangings – fast the sternpost. So, let's assume the same thing happened here.'

Mark heaved a sigh of relief. 'So you think we've found the stern location of the Big C after all?'

'I'd say it was eighty to twenty in our favour,' I said. 'The Big C was cranky, as we well know, and I bet her rudder-timbers were as cranky as the rest of her. Probably fell to bits when she struck, leaving the bronze fittings behind.'

'But why *should* the pintles be so far to the west?'

'If we take it that the pintles do indicate the final lie of the stern,' I said, 'then there could be a number of reasons to account for the gap between that and the likely position we've established for the bow. As I was telling you the other day these old-time ships often broke into two, or even three, parts which went their separate ways. In the case of *Colossus* the bow, with its rounded shape to the sea, wouldn't be driven so far, but the stern – with its holds open to the waves – would catch their full force and go further to the nor'west, towards the reef. Of course, from our point of view, the precise position she was in when she broke is pretty important.'

'How's that?' said Barry.

'Well, so long as the ship herself was intact, the pottery might be in smithereens, but would all be likely to stay in the hold, even if *Colossus* was over on her side. Once she broke up, though, it would all come tumbling out.'

'At least we know that would have to have happened somewhere along a line between the carronades and the pintles,' said Mark.

'True.' I ran my finger down it on the chart. 'What we have to do now is survey the sea-bed there. Congratulations, boys! We've got ourselves a provisional *location*. If the material isn't somewhere in that area, then it's going to take a lot of finding.'

I slipped the elastic band from the rolled draught-sheer plan – a sectional drawing – of *Colossus*, and spread it over the site chart, holding the corners down with four copper spikes from her own great timbers.

With the sun's brilliant light reflecting back into our faces, we pored over the drawing with half-closed, protesting eyes. Except for the cries of the birds away over on Samson, and the chink of compressed-air bottles nodding together on the floor of the launch, the world was silent. We spoke in consciously subdued tones.

Mark crooked his little finger over the drawing to point to the after-hold. 'We know the Hamilton crates were probably here. . . .'

'And re-checking the measurement from the sternpost to the centre of the hold,' I applied my brass rule, hot from lying in the sun, 'gives us a distance overall of fifty-five feet.'

'And from the after-hold to the galley,' said Slim, 'can we just re-check that?'

'Ah, let's see,' I said. ''Ell, mm . . . that's all of eighty feet, measuring along the keel. Got that?'

'Right.' Slim was ready to go. 'We concentrate on the area fifty-five feet sou'east of the pintles – in way of our imaginary line pintles-to-carronades – and also have a look-see at the area eighty feet nor'west of those marble galley-slabs.'

Their preparatory routine gone through, the divers sat poised on the starboard gunnel, with the green of Samson behind them, and a fresh gleam of hope dancing through the visors of their face-masks. At a given signal, they departed simultaneously in a great commotion of disturbed water.

It was past low water, and the tide was 'making'. I could see its flow from east to west, marked by floating feathers and small wisps of weed below the surface. The launch, undecided whether to head into the gentle wind still, or to face about into the tide, took up a half-way position facing north towards Samson.

'There's more to this salvage lark than meets the eye,' said Barry, reflecting on our discussion now that we were alone again. 'Have you been in it most of your life?'

'Pretty well. And I've always gone back to it, even when other things intervened.'

'Such as?'

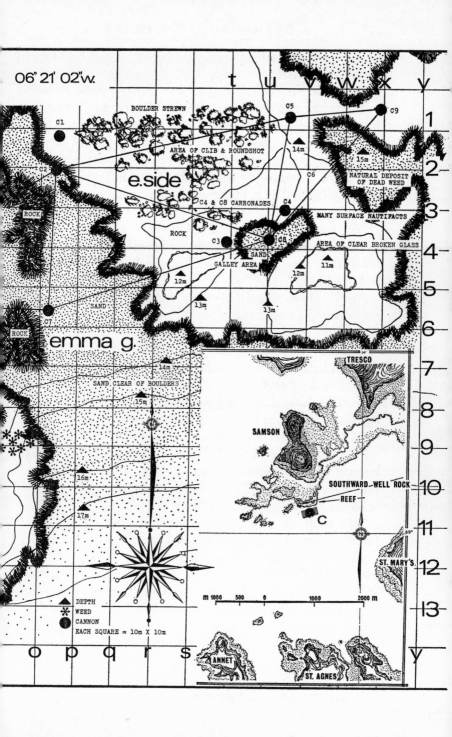

06° 21' 02"w.

t u v w x y

BOULDER STREWN

C1

C5

C9

1

AREA OF CLIB & ROUNDSHOT

14m

15m

C2

e.side

C6

2

NATURAL DEPOSIT
OF DEAD WEED

ROCK

C4 & C8 CARRONADES

C4

3

MANY SURFACE NAUTIFACTS

ROCK

C3

C8

SAND

AREA OF CLEAR BROKEN GLASS

4

GALLEY AREA

12m

11m

12m

5

13m

C7

SAND

13m

ROCK

emma g.

6

14m

SAND, CLEAR OF BOULDERS

7

TRESCO

15m

8

SAMSON

9

16m

SOUTHWARD–WELL ROCK

10

REEF

17m

C

11

ST. MARY'S.

12

▲ DEPTH
✳ WEED
● CANNON
EACH SQUARE = 10m X 10m

m 1000   500   0   1000   2000 m

13

o   p   q   r   s   y

ANNET

ST. AGNES.

'Bees,' I said, laughing at his dawning surprise. 'I kept bees for quite a few years.'

'Bees! They're the last thing I'd have thought you'd go in for!'

'It was just after the Second World War. I'd been doing more than enough diving, and when I went to my doctor for a routine check-up, he said I ought to get away from it for a while. Take up something completely different, just to take my mind off it. A hobby . . . and he just happened to mention bees. Not that he really thought I'd do it, I believe, but it just seemed to him to have the right sort of restful sound about it.'

'You knew something about it, I suppose. . . .'

'Not a bit. I bought a book which advised beginning with three hives at the most. In four years I had one thousand four hundred and fifty hives!'

Barry's sun-browned face was a study in incredulity – as I'd rather hoped it would be.

'Fourteen hundred and fifty! Not full of bees?'

'Rather,' I said. 'They were devils and nearly killed us in the summer, but they brought in the honey, all right. It's a marvellous way of making money. For a time we were the largest honey-farmers in the country, and were selling our honey in five-ton lots to the big dairies. Beeswax, too, by the ton.'

'Wax by the ton!' Barry was flummoxed.

'It was a wonderful life. We – my eldest son and I – ran the business with six or seven helpers, and we had apiaries from Land's End, right up through Cornwall, as far as Truro.'

'Where'd you get that many hives?'

'We made them. I set up a woodworking factory on the Penzance waterfront. Inland I built an enclosed apiary, where I could breed a hundred colonies of bees at one time – and all under cover. To begin with I bought my queens from Italy, five hundred at a time, but after a year I bred my own. Can you imagine me artificially inseminating queen bees at midnight?'

'I'm speechless! I really am.'

'At the time my indoor apiary was the largest in Europe, and all the best-known bee-keepers of the Continent used to come and see it. It was great.'

'There must have been some snags.'

'Oh, quite a few. For one thing, the work was terribly hard, and the hours were long – from sunrise to sunset in the summer months. Another worry was the way they bred so quickly. It was like one of those sci-fi horror stories – frightening at times – and you'd get the feeling the whole world could be taken over by bees.'

'What happened? Why did you give it up?'

'I had twin boys about seven years old at the time,' I said. 'It wasn't that they were frightened, for they used to play with the bees quite happily, believe it or not! They were stung now and again, of course, but without any ill effect. Then, they gradually became allergic, and a while later dangerously allergic, to being stung. I might call for them at school, and maybe there'd be a half-dead bee in the car somewhere, which one of the boys would put his hand on. I'd have to rush him to hospital at once. A doctor finally told me, give up your bees or lose your boys.'

'So?'

'We went to a Horticultural Show in London and had a gigantic sale, and sold everything off.'

'And you went back to salvage?'

'I'd never parted with my equipment,' I said, 'and I hadn't sold my honey-extracting works.'

'Your honey-extracting works? Surely that wasn't much good for salvage operations?'

'It was on the Penzance quayside, and good for more than honey. It was rather funny, really, for it was just then that a big seven-thousand-ton Liberian tramp steamer, the *Liberty*, was wrecked on the Cornish coast just to the north of us. The people I'd worked with during the war, the British Iron and Steel Corporation, rang me from London to ask if I'd cut her up for them and I agreed. The awkward part was that the salvage officers said they would see me in my office at eight the next morning. They were coming down on the night train.'

'Well, what was wrong with that?'

'Nothing, except that my magnificent office overlooking Penzance harbour was designed to put buyers in a good mood to sign up honey contracts – clinically clean, and all sweetness and light. Ever see a working salvage depot that looked like that? They'd think I didn't know what I was talking about.'

'What did you do?'

'Worked a transformation scene, that's what. We had one night to do it, and by eight o'clock that next day, you wouldn't have known the place. It was a busy salvage depot to the life, besmeared and soiled and with all the gear of the trade lying about haphazard. To get rid of the sweet smell of honey, I splashed some oil about to give the place the tang of diesel fuel. I looked as if I'd got a dozen contracts under my belt, instead of just the one I was hoping to get signed.'

'And you got it?'

'I did.'

'And that was the end of your honey-farming?'

'Yes. But if ever I'm born again that's what I'll go in for. I've always said I'll try anything twice. It's far harder work than salvage, though that's saying something! That doctor didn't have the right idea!'

We heard a shout and Barry checked his watch. 'They've only been down for forty minutes,' he said. 'If that's them it's either something wrong, or it's good news.'

By the sound of it, the news was good. Hurrying to the gunnel and looking overside, we saw the three heads – Slim, right up near us; Mark a bit further off, doing all the shouting; and quite a way behind him, Mike stolidly plodding towards us. Mark was upright in the water, waving his arms like a footballer who has just scored a goal.

'Yippee!' he cried. 'Yippee, we've found it!'

Slim paddled to the side of the boat. 'We've got it, and there's no mistaking it,' He calmly handed me a brown, shiny concave object. 'For land's sake don't drop it!'

An oval piece of pottery, a little less than the size of my hand, was placed in my outstretched fingers. Slim gave it to me with the ridged, reverse side uppermost. I turned it over and smoothed away the drops of water with my thumb: 'It's the face of a satyr!'

'What about my bloody bottles?' Slim's voice came indignantly from overside, where Barry had for once left him neglected in the general excitement.

We hauled him aboard, and he sat down beside me, breathing heavily still. 'Our first sherd,' he said.

It was brown, and striped with a darker tone, its broken edges sharply square, and the pottery having a very hard dense feel to it. The face was beautifully drawn. I felt the same wonder that Sir William had once known. He had never tired of remarking on the skill which enabled the old Greek artists to work with such freedom and mastery in a medium of such difficulty, though even he probably did not fully realize that the artists would have found it so hard to distinguish between background and figures as they worked, the overall red colour confusing the two to all except the expert eye.

'It's marvellous . . . stupendous.' For once, those well-used words meant what they said. 'This is really something worth all the work and the waiting.'

Mark and Mike had joined us now. Mark had already seen the find, and passed it to his team-mate: 'Here, Mike, have a look at this! Our first sherd. All of two thousand years old! Isn't that fab!'

'I'll say it is!' Mike looked at it eagerly. 'That's what you might call worth while! It really is!'

'I was swimming with my mask just about four inches above the sea-bed when I suddenly saw this face,' said Slim. 'It was just lying there in the sand on its own. I've searched the area round about, and so has Mark, but that's all there is.'

'Was it in the area sou'east of the pintles?' I asked.

'Yes,' said Mark, 'and that's the spot to start excavation, just as soon as the licence comes through.'

'What exactly are satyrs?' said Barry, looking over our shoulders.

'They were the sexy, bully boys of Greek mythology,' explained Mark.

'With horse's tails and ears, and pugilistic noses, and wild hair,' I added. 'They spent their time making music, dancing and chasing any maenads that were about.'

The finding of this figured sherd at this time was a heaven-sent piece of luck, for I was just completing my report on our pre-disturbance survey. The pieces of the ship's gear that we had recovered were convincing enough to us that this was the site of *Colossus*, but making a report which would convince members of the Runciman Committee, many of whom would have no direct experience of salvage, was another matter. The satyr's face was positive proof of the cargo the ship had had aboard, and no other wreck could have had anything like this in her hold.

Right from the inception of the project the British Museum had been interested in our work, and I – through me, the team – had rightly been subjected to a severe appraisal of our fitness to engage in it. Invited to the Museum to meet representatives of the trustees and other officials, I found the proceedings entirely friendly, but all the same I couldn't help feeling a bit like the little boy in silk breeches, standing on his mother's footstool and being asked: 'When did you last see your father?' Owing to the death of my father, I had left school at an age when all these people who were interviewing me had just started their serious education. I couldn't blame them if they felt that I was unlikely to reach the standard of knowledge that they were bound to ensure – for the sake of the vases and their value to research – that the person involved in the project should possess. Somehow I had to convince them that I had continued my own self-education to an extent that would enable me to cope. No one who has not been in that situation can appreciate quite how much at a disadvantage I felt.

The large, dim, high-ceilinged room, with its large polished desk and its heavy straight-backed chairs was intimidating, and my spirits sank to about zero among so many strange faces until I recognized Mrs Pam Vincent of the Marine Division of the Department of Trade, who was also secretary of the Committee, and Mr Brian Cook, then Assistant Keeper in the Department of Greek and Roman Antiquities, and soon to be promoted to the post of Keeper. Brian Cook had been among the first to be interested in our project, and I had met him when he was on holiday with his attractive wife in Penzance. It had been splendid to talk to someone with ample knowledge of precisely what we were looking for, and so willing to share it. He had even been so kind as to bring me a sherd from his own personal collection, which – in its scrupulous cleaning and the tiny provenance marked in the broken edge – was a lesson for us to follow in any future conservation. At the time it was like being presented with a fragment of the moon's crust, so rare a material was it, and it was also invaluable to be able to handle it and acquire familiarity with a sample of exactly what we were hoping to find, for no amount of gazing through the glass of a museum case gives quite the same sense of reality. We became friends in no time.

A little reassured by the presence of these two friendly souls, I managed to present a good case for myself before the august assembly in that handsome room, which included not only the then Keeper of the Department of Greek and Roman Antiquities, but the Director of the British Museum, also just about to retire, so that I was to meet neither of them again. Someone else who was present, and to whom I was introduced, was Dr Ann Birchall, another Assistant Keeper in the Department of Greek and Roman Antiquities, and though neither of us then knew it, we were to meet many times in the future.

It was impressed on me at the initial interview that, if the Big C were designated as an historic wreck, it would be for her cargo, not the vessel itself – the pottery was the thing. I could not have agreed more, for with my knowledge of the stout efforts of the *Fearless* official salvage crew, backed up by the work of the Scillonian wreckers, I could not imagine that there would be anything worth recovering of the actual structure of *Colossus*. Nor were any plans made to search for nautifacts until the excavation of the sherds was completed. However, we were to run into trouble in a way I had never expected when working in areas where nautifacts were mixed up with pot-sherds. It took no longer to put both in the collecting boxes, and bring them up together, than it would to bring up the pot-sherds alone: in actual fact, sorting them out would quite often have taken rather longer. We adopted the former method as a matter of course, but when the authorities realized that this was being done, we were told in no uncertain terms that the practice must cease. Pottery only must be brought up, the ship's nautifacts must be left on the sea-bed. Indeed, it was suggested that those nautifacts which had already been recovered should be returned whence they came!

It was cannon fins and scupper-pipes all over again, simply a lack of appreciation by people used to working on land of what really happens at sea. For a short period we reached an absolute impasse, for the divers had been trained over the years to recover everything they came across – or risk losing it for ever. It was the essential code of Atlantic diving, and there was no way in which that code might be changed. Those who contemplated instructing us to 'put it all back' did not even realize that their commands would be impossible to carry out: the place in which each item had been found no longer existed, the sea-bottom is an ever-changing place anywhere in the world, and nowhere more so than at the Scillies.

No doubt there was also a feeling among those intent on the recovery of the vases – and not unnaturally – that gathering copper tacks and domestic pins, clay-pipe fragments and buttons, buckles and lice-combs, spirit taps and pieces of wineglasses and the like, was a waste of time in a project so important as ours. I suspect indeed, for many of them, it seemed a waste of time to take account of such things in any circumstances: the vases were priceless and belonged to glamorous antiquity, but these homely articles seemed valueless, the personal possessions or working tools of people who were insignificant, and who (by comparison with the original owners of the vases) lived in an uninteresting 'yesterday'.

For me, and those working with me, they represent something quite different. They are part and parcel of the way Nelson's sailors lived and worked, and interest us enormously. A rather special example which particularly intrigues me is a wooden musket-ball pouch from *Colossus*. Previously, lead-shot had been carried in soft leather pouches with a cord draw-pull closure, but this new find was formed from a solid timber block $8\frac{1}{2}'' \times 4'' \times 2\frac{1}{2}''$, curved to fit the waist-belt. Eighteen holes, each $3\frac{1}{2}''$ deep and $0.58''$ in diameter, had been drilled in its upper side to take the shot, and the block was covered in fine leather with a G(3)R cipher in gilt, denoting George III, embossed on the front. I had never seen anything like it, and I am still trying to work out – from a jigsaw of many small brass fittings found with it – how the lead balls were retained in place.

Items that have a curiously personal appeal, too, are the remains of the shoes we found on both *Colossus* and the 1707 wreck sites. No boots were found of either period, but the shoes exhibit interesting differences. Those from the early wrecks are made from laminated layers of leather secured together by hand-stitching and also by oak sprigs, with a substantial oak 'nail' through the centre of the heel, and had a pronounced pointed toe. By the time of the foundering of *Colossus* fashion had changed, and the soft-leather shoes are more rounded in shape and completely hand-sewn throughout. To conserve the shoes, I first rid the leather of its salt-water contamination and then soak it under pressure in finely emulsified sunflower-seed oil, or olive oil.

Also found at the Big C site was a splendid little hand-carved model of a ship's boat. Well made, in spite of its crudeness, it has a little block of lead inserted in its keel to give it balance. Shaped by some sailor father for his little son, perhaps, the gift was never to reach the boy, but at least the man himself got home safely. The reverse is probably true in the case of a similar but sad discovery made on the *Association* site. In this instance, a little model boat was found on the sea-bed firmly adhering to a cluster of human bones, and nearby was a splintered leg-bone with the incongruous adjunct of a golden sovereign trapped in its fracture.

All the few hundred small articles relating to *Colossus* and the domestic life aboard her bristle with questions, or answers to questions that give insight into naval life in Nelson's day. One can sort them with quite a degree of certainty, in the case of personal belongings, into those of officers and men, the upper and the lower deck. Here an elegant silver spoon, and there one of common, battered brass; a gold-chain opera-cloak fastener found alongside a blackened clay-pipe crammed with partly burnt tobacco; the cut-glass base of a beautiful wine goblet set against the broken bottom of a homely, thick pottery mug; and – a far cry from that touching little present of a boat – a small, graceful swivelling castor, which once formed part of something perhaps intended as a present, too. Made of bronze, it bears traces of ormolu, or applied gold, beloved of eighteenth-century French furniture-makers. This, along with several small ornate drawer-pulls, are the only clues relating to the French furniture we know to have been taken from the prize ships after the Battle of the Nile. It is hardly likely that such a delicate piece of furniture, requiring gilded castors, would have had a permanent place on board *Colossus*. And this lone find, which ended on the sea-bed instead of in the drawing-room of some officer's wife, suggests that the rest of the furniture, broken as it obviously must have been, was successfully salved. I wonder how many pieces of it survive in the islands today?

Such items as these fascinate the visitors to my own nautical museum, and they will linger over them in a fashion that they tend not to do with some of the more technically 'valuable' saleroom items. They have a vital place in nautical museums everywhere, and I hope one day to produce an illustrated book, listing and describing every article we have recovered from old-time sunken men-o'-war. At least it would help to put an end to the kind of ridiculous speculation to which many marine archaeologists lend their names in cataloguing nautical gear they know nothing about!

However, such temporary disagreements as I have referred to – and, fortunately, they were only temporary – were in the future. Now, my great concern was the precious satyr sherd be taken to the Museum without further loss of time, for we were now in mid-season. If anything substantial was to be accomplished this year, there was a great deal of work to be done, and very little time in which to do it. Accordingly, it was agreed that Slim and I should meet at the Museum in two days' time: he was to travel by car, as he had equipment to collect, and I would take the overnight sleeper.

News of our project was now breaking in the national press, and the BBC was interested in making a television film. Among ourselves we debated the wisdom of allowing this to be done, for the return in cash would be negligible, the publicity double-edged, and the danger of the disruption of our work considerable – this last fear was irritatingly justified on several occasions. However, we signed, and the producer – the enthusiastic and meticulous Tony Salmon – did his first shooting for the film 'Colossus, the Ship that Lost a Fortune' to cover our Museum visit.

I'm always fascinated by the techniques of any profession, and television was no exception. The idea was that Slim and I should be shown arriving at the great wrought-iron gates, carrying a small leather case. Our taxi driver delivered us with aplomb, but the camera naturally hadn't caught us, and to his great astonishment the driver found himself and his taxi completely taken over. He was instructed to circle the Museum block and 'arrive' once again. Luckily, the weather was fine and sunny, but bad traffic conditions meant that it wasn't till the fourth 'arrival' and the fourth payment of his fare that the dramatic event was safely on film.

We were now able to advance across the forecourt with our little leather case in which, cradled in a container of water, our satyr was lying. In the foyer Dr Ann Birchall met us and took us up the great stairway that leads to the Department of Greek and Roman Antiquities – and never did such a treasure-house have such a sober name!

Anxious as Dr Birchall was to see the sherd, it took almost as many rehearsals as our arrival in the taxi before she had it at last between her hands. Her office was quite small, and the camera and its crew had to be fitted in between the filing cabinets. The script went like this:

Roland Morris, with leather case in right hand, knocks door of Dr Birchall's office with left hand.
Dr Birchall: 'Yes, come in!'
Roland Morris opens door and enters closely followed by *Slim Macdonnell*.
Roland Morris turns to his right and faces *Dr Birchall* who is seated behind desk. He says: 'Good morning? How are you?'
Dr Birchall: 'Oh, I'm fine! I hear you've been doing exciting things down in the Scillies.'
Roland Morris: 'Dr Ann Birchall, please meet *Slim Macdonnell*, our team's underwater cameraman.'
Slim Macdonnell: 'How are you!'
Roland Morris: 'Yes, we've got something here which we would like you to identify, if you'll be so kind.'
Dr Birchall: 'Sounds intriguing, what is it may I ask?'
Slim Macdonnell: 'It's a sherd which I found on the sea-bed –'
Dr Birchall: 'I trust there's been no excavating!'

Roland Morris: 'No, no; it was a surface sherd and the only one in the area.'

At a sign from the producer Roland Morris lifts with his right hand the small leather case, and deposits it on Dr Birchall's desk. He opens it with his left hand and allows the cover to fall back thus revealing the contents, which are one plastic 'snappy' bag half-filled with water. In the water may be seen the glimpse of a pottery sherd.

We were there! But, no. Both Dr Birchall and I reached for the bag at one and the same time.

'Cut!' rapped the producer. 'Pity! We should have rehearsed that. No, you, Roland, you take up the bag in your right hand and pass it to Dr Birchall, but slowly, mind, the camera will be following your hand in close-up. Dr Birchall, you take the bag from Roland and *slowly* take off its elastic band, slowly take out the sherd and lay it on your blotting-pad; right?'

With finger on lips the producer thought for a moment: 'Oh, and Roland, as Dr Birchall takes the bag from you, you with your *left* hand quietly remove the case from the desk.'

'What do I do with the water in the bag?' said Dr Birchall practically.

'Ah! Yes! That's a point, there's no ashtray is there? Well, just slide your *right* hand, with the bag, along your desk to the right, and when it's out of camera-shot I'll take it from you.'

'If that's so,' said Dr Birchall, 'I shall have to take the sherd from the bag with my *left* hand.'

And that is how the satyr sherd, painted some four to two hundred years before the birth of Christ, and which had lain in the murk of the sea-bed for nearly another two hundred, came to be deposited on the blotting pad of Dr Ann Birchall's office desk in the British Museum.

With the red indicator light of the camera blipping at a constant interval to remind us that its eye was on us, Dr Birchall explained how the sherd was undoubtedly ancient and a very good pointer to our being on the trail of the Hamilton pottery.

It was at this meeting, too, that we were told that Dr Birchall had been appointed archaeological adviser to the *Colossus* Underwater Excavation by the Runciman Committee. It was obvious that an expert in Greek archaeology should be charged to oversee this aspect of the work, but I was surprised that a non-diver had been appointed to what was, by force of circumstance, more of a salvage operation than an archaeological dig. It was, after all, 'salvage clues' which had made the location of *Colossus* possible, for to the land archaeologist the carronades, the galley tiles, and the rudder-pintles – let alone the significance of their location in relation to one another – would have had no meaning. Without that sort of insight the *Colossus* site would still be an undisturbed expanse of weed and rock, the haunt of conger eels!

Yet, in talking to land experts, I have again and again been struck by their total indifference to such things, even as vital clues to wreck locations. Their range of interest is incredibly concen-

A giant stem of oar-weed, the blotches of sea-mats on its blades, and the figure of a diver drawn on the same scale.

trated, confined to a particular period and – for preference – a completely remote one. Only within the last very few years, for example, has the value of medieval excavation as conveying information that no documents could provide, or the splendour of nineteenth-century industrial archaeology, been recognized, after the long efforts of the original devoted few. Undersea it is the same story. The nautifacts which meant so much to me, not merely as clues, but as relics of a past way of living and of the skills of shipwright and carver, smith and instrument-maker, left Dr Birchall quite unmoved. I could never persuade her to share my enthusiasm for this side of our work on *Colossus*, or do more than glance at these relics of life under sail, whereas my own curiosity and interest in her specialized field of Greek pottery was eager. It was a bone of contention between us that was also a source of amusement.

I've mentioned my surprise at Dr Birchall's appointment, but I'll admit to a certain relief as well. The sea-bed off the Scillies was regarded by the boys as their own particular stomping ground and a diver archaeologist who might have attempted to tell them how to set about work which they had so often done before, could well have had a walk-out – or, rather, a 'dive-out' – on his hands. Not that divers are interested in any trade union with a membership of more than one! Independence, risk-taking, and a hands-off-me approach to any attempt at organization are the hallmarks of a diver, and even the Inland Revenue has had to come round to that idea when trying to squeeze them into the regulation mould of taxation procedure. Even had she been a diver, however, Dr Birchall would have had some difficulty in supervising the underwater work at Scilly, since she was continuing with her normal full-time duties at the British Museum. This meant she was only able to visit us and the Big C site at very infrequent intervals during the excavation.

From the divers' reports it was clear that the satyr sherd had been found in the sand of what was at first thought to be one of several adjoining gullies, a gully which appeared to run east–west, and which was strewn with rocks and boulders ranging in size from 10 cm to 1·5 metres. On the strength of the pintles clue, and of the sherd having been found nearby, we mapped out our first excavation area. The hazard here was the very large weed – one species with round-section, knobbly stalks and the other with flat, oval stems – which had to be cut one at a time with a sharp knife. In fact, it was so tough that the only effective way of dealing with it was to bend each stem over into an acute straining curve, as close to the rock on which it grew as possible, and then hack the rubbery, tensioned strands one by one. By harvesting as close to the sea-bed as we could, we prevented it getting caught up in the protruding stalks, and the flow of the tide could carry it clear.

On our return to Scilly we began by clearing about half an acre of this weed, and arduous work the divers found it. They also found that their efforts were robbing the sea-bed of protection, the removal of the weed 'shelter-belt' allowing the sea-bed to be churned up even during the mildest ground sea. Consequently, it was decided to restrict the clearance to the area we might reasonably expect to be able to excavate during the remainder of the summer.

Initially we had taken the West Side site to have been made up of several gullies; it wasn't until the weed had been cleared that we realized that these were actually all part of one large feature, a gully running nor'west by sou'east and all of a hundred metres west of Emma Gully. The hard slog of the weed-clearing was enlivened by the discovery of several surface sherds of red-figure pottery, but it was among the stones and boulders, lying in the granite silt of the floor of the gully, that we found large numbers.

An exploratory trench excavated across the gully proved that, for every sherd on the surface, there would be dozens buried in the silt and rubble of the gully floor. The trouble was that, once disturbed, there was an ever-present danger of the whole location being scoured by ground-seas and tidal action, for the silt lay on comparatively smooth bedrock and could be swept away.

As a preliminary to excavation work in the gully, the team laid a 10-metre by 10-metre grid made of non-floating, non-stretching, fluorescent orange line. We chose an area where there had been numerous surface finds – all these having been duly marked with miniature, numbered, concrete blocks. The grid – known as grid A – was formed of a hundred squares, each a single square metre in area, so that the precise location of any find could be logged on a permanent record the moment it was discovered.

Our first square metre – A1 – proved immediately prolific in sherds, more than a dozen being found in the surface level. As the area was mostly granite, sand or silt, the divers worked as far apart from each other as the grid would allow, in order to avoid disturbing the visibility of the rest of the team by the milky opaqueness of the fog of tiny particles they dispersed into the surrounding water as they worked.

Water and air jets were at hand if the divers wanted them, but they found the most effective method of excavation to be fanning the silt layer with their bare hands. Many of the sherds might be very small, but they were nevertheless very important, and even an over-zealous fanning could drive them out of sight. It was a wearing method for the hands, because there were so many pieces of broken glass as well as sea-urchin spines among the silt. Gloves couldn't be worn as protection against cuts because tiny sherds could not then be felt.

We were fortunate in finding a depression nearby with a floor of bedrock which we could use as a 'spoil' area, and scores of tons of rock and silt were transported there by the indefatigable team, and safely retained away from the site. The sherds themselves were collected in rigid polythene containers, which were sent to the surface with waterproof tags indicating where they had been found, and once aboard the boat they were permanently marked with the appropriate grid number.

We made the most of our opportunities in that glorious summer, and in the comparatively short time between receiving the licence to excavate and the close of the 1975 season, when storms and gales drove us from the site, we amassed a total of eight thousand sherds. The quantity rather took the British Museum aback, and after conserving the first few hundred, the department there found they were too busy to continue doing so, and the task devolved on me. My feelings were somewhat mixed, for it was very time-consuming and I, too, had a pretty full schedule. But the fascination of restoring these precious fragments of the past to as near pristine condition as possible kept me for increasingly long hours hard at work. The decision was also to the benefit of the sherds, for with so many calls on its funds the Museum could not have provided the specially equipped laboratory I set up at the Benbow.

So, we left Scilly with our hopes high for the 1976 season, and on one of our last evenings on the islands we had a mild celebration in one of the crowded bars of Hugh Town. Slim is an inveterate leg-puller, and he enlisted the help of a friendly potter to make a 'red-figure pot' for the occasion. It certainly looked authentic, and in case anyone should have any doubts, he made sure that everyone heard his loud 'asides', entreating us to be most careful with it, as we each drank in turn.

'Emma could very well have set her own rosy lips to that,' he would say, or 'Tastes a bit salty, but what can you expect after a century and a half on the sea-bed,' and so on.

The next morning I received an urgent telephone call from the Department of Trade. Was it true that the team had been drinking out of one of Sir William Hamilton's priceless vases last night? And that the fragile antique had been passing carelessly from hand to hand in a public bar?

Luckily, the expensive call was the Department's for it took me some considerable time to explain the incident away. When I took the matter up with Slim, he smiled his Mona Lisa special, hunched his shoulders and threw out his hands:

'Can I help it if people get the wrong impression?'

I I
The Smith-God's Return

Marine salvage depends, more than any other kind of work, on fine weather. We'd had a good summer in 1975, and, though we looked forward to the season of 1976, we could hardly hope for such luck again. Instead, the weather was better than ever.

Day after day the sun rose into a clear blue sky, and day after day it beat down on the sub-tropical islands with a tropical intensity. Night after night the stars made their glittering appearance on the soft, deep-purple of space, there to show off their mystic, gyratory rites.

The sea responded magnificently, remaining calm and unruffled for most of the summer. True, the plankton hordes, enticed by the sun-drenched water, gathered in impenetrable clouds during the early days of the season, but even these soon dispersed to leave the sea as clear as anyone could ever hope to see it.

My role was now a more active one, since I was not only keeping an eye and the lens of my camera on the salvage side, but had taken over the conservation of the priceless sherds the divers were raising in thousands. I spent the splendid days shuttling between the Big C site in Scilly and my laboratory in Penzance, my work in one as exciting and intriguing as in the other.

Of all my experiences on the Big C site, however, one stands out in the eye of memory over all the others, simply because of the depth – or, rather, the lack of it – of the water at the time. It was the time of the August spring-tides, when the sea rises exceptionally high and then falls correspondingly low. This meant that when the tide was right out, there were only two fathoms of water – a mere twelve feet – over the site.

The sea was as clear as champagne, not a speck of plankton marring the limpidity of the shallows, and the *Whaler* and the *Sea King* seemed to float in air. To me, used as I had been in my diving days to poor visibility, it was an exhilarating experience. I was alone in *Sea King*, with Mark, Slim and Mike down below me on the sea-bed, but I could watch them as easily as if I were leaning over a wall on land. There they were, just below the keel of the launch, spread-eagled on their stomachs with their arms stretched out before them.

I could see them fanning the silt with their hands, plucking the colourful sherds from the 'smoking' sea-floor, and placing them in an open-topped container. Even the silt fug cleared as soon as it was raised by the ground-tide running that day. And I could also see another phenomenon, caused by the steady tidal flow of water, which most people don't know anything about – the mystery of the 'mobile rocks'. In spring a baby seaweed plant will attach itself to a rock, and will then sprout ahead at such a rate that by midsummer it will have outgrown the retaining weight of its host anchorage, so that in a tide-way the rock will no longer be capable of holding it down. The result is that rocks – varying in size from pebbles to rugger balls – get towed along by their large heads of weed. Dragged willy-nilly across the soft sea-bed, they leave deep furrows in the sand behind them. Many holidaymakers, looking down through the clear shallow water and noticing these long straight lines, rather like a miniature railway junction, are sorely perplexed.

Turning back to watch the divers, and their patient, repetitive movements, I saw a red-suited one roll over on his back. Looking up at me, he raised his arms in quick movements, like a conductor urging his orchestra to greater efforts – it was Slim giving me the go-ahead to haul up.

There is a kind of serene magic in recovering beautiful things from the sea's underwater world, more especially so on a fine, sunny day. I shall never forget hauling that bucketful of priceless Grecian pot-sherds – my first – to the surface. Usually the divers bring up their own finds.

As the green plastic container neared the surface the brilliant sunlight spilled into its interior. Holding the line in a tight grip, I let it rest just below the surface for a full five minutes – just for the thrill of it. They were minutes to relish, for that pottery had been buried under the sea and silt for one hundred and seventy-seven years. The last sunlight that had fallen on it had come from an Italian sky as Sir William, and maybe Emma as well, stood by to watch it packed. And before that, it had been in darkness again for more than a millennium, maybe buried in a grave to which it had been consigned to accompany the beloved dead to another world. Cherished possessions, used two thousand years ago in festivities such as those painted in the bright colours that looked up at me now, had lain beneath the soil awaiting the plundering hands of the peasants who sold them to Sir William.

The launch gently dipped and rolled, contentedly scratching her back on the surface of the sea. The water chuckled under her counter, and the pottery, in its sparkling wetness, glowed in the brilliant light like a casket of gems.

Treasure! And, moored as we were on the northern boundary of St Mary's Pool in the centre of the Islands of Scilly, what better surroundings could there be in which to find it? The isles, islets and rocks formed a two-mile circle round me, lying mist-blue and shimmering away in the sun-tinged haze. There was not a breath of wind to riffle the sea's surface, yet high overhead in the cloudless sky the gulls hovered with stationary wings, on thermals of which they alone were aware.

The sea barely moved, its colour the blue-green of deep ice. Far to the west, menacing and sombre, stood the serried ranks of the Western Rocks. I raised my head to the north and looked across the blue water to the island of Samson, the sun hot on my bare back and shoulders, and saw – away beyond the sand-flats, left drying by the ebb-tide – the pale silver beaches of Tresco. To my left, and quite near, reared the weed-festooned head of Southward Well, the rock which pinpoints the last resting-place of the old man-o'-war – *Colossus*.

With the exception of the distorting shapes of the divers down below, there was not a soul in sight. I seemed completely alone in a brilliantly colourful world. Except for the soothing slap of water on the hull, and the tropical-sounding, far-away cries of seabirds, there was no sound. The scent on the air was of hot seaweed, the warm unmistakeable tang of hot, sunburnt weed which is unaccustomed to any lengthy exposure above water. It invariably brings back to me memories of the war years when we cut up into very small pieces half-submerged iron ships.

With a heave I brought the container of sherds inboard, chill water slopping and splashing over me as I did so. After stowing it carefully on the hot, slatted seat, I took out a glistening, black, spherical pot. It was quite small, about the size of a golf ball, and its miniature spout was chipped. On its side was a figure, looking to my inexperienced eye rather like a mandarin in a loose-fitting robe, and outlined in black by the sure hand of a craftsman on the enriched colour of the base clay. I found it beautiful, exquisite. Later Dr Birchall was to tell me that it was a Grecian perfume jar.

As I replaced the pot in the water – to avoid damaging it by too rapid a transition to life in the air again – and watched the air bubbles fussing out of its small neck, I wondered who the original owner had been. Its history ranged over two thousand three hundred years, and the marvel to me, which I found a little difficult to get used to, was that we – Mark Horobin, Slim Macdonnell, Mike Hicks and I – were actively involved in that history.

Leaning back in the launch, with my cap tilted over my eyes, I looked at the little perfume jar and the fragments of red-figure ware, and understood very well how the decorated vases from the potters' quarter of Athens had come to dominate the export trade of their day. A few potters and artists from Athens settled in southern Italy from the middle of the fifth century BC, and produced work to rival the home workshops, but most of the items in the Hamilton collection would have originated in that single city-state which gave the world so much in every field of art and intellect – Athens.

Greek merchants bringing black-figured and red-figured pottery to Italy found two main classes of customers: Greek colonists and native Italians. The natives included the Etruscans, whose influence extended as far south as Capua. Sir William Hamilton was fortunate in the location of his diplomatic post in that Naples was a Greek city originally – Nea-polis = New-city –

and there were other Greek settlements in the area, but some of his collection, especially the Apulian vases, must have come from farther afield. Most of his collection would have been specimens which had gone with their owners to their graves. Hidden over the centuries, they were from time to time accidentally discovered by peasants, but it was not until the eighteenth century that a craze for antique relics began on a grand scale. Like that sixteenth-century connoisseur, Benvenuto Cellini, Sir William developed his own contacts with the peasantry who were now finding a welcome source of income in a more systematic raiding of ancient graves and disposing of their contents to connoisseurs who asked no questions. In the process they destroyed much invaluable archaeological evidence.

However, granted that the 'treasure-hunt' could not be prevented, Sir William – as Envoy Extraordinary to the Kingdom of the Two Sicilies – was from his own point of view the right man in the right place at the right time. From the point of view of the authorities of the Naples Museum he most certainly was not, for many of the treasures which should have found their way into the museum display cases were undoubtedly sidetracked into the cellars of the Palazzo Sessa.

The painter Philip Hackert was a close friend of Sir William, and through his intervention, Goethe was allowed to visit the ambassador's 'secret lumber-vault'. 'Everything was in a state of terrible confusion', the poet later wrote.

Products of every epoch were thrown together at random: busts, torsos, vases, bronzes, paintings, and chance bargains of every sort: even a small chapel. Out of curiosity I pushed aside the lid of a long case on the floor; in it were two magnificent bronze candelabra. I caught Hackert's eye and asked him in a whisper if these were not very much like those in the museum at Portici. He silenced me with a look; no doubt they had strayed here from the cellars of Pompeii by a sideward path. Doubtless these and other lucky acquisitions are the reason why Sir William shows his hidden treasures only to his most intimate friends.

At least, however, Sir William appreciated what he bought from more than the financial point of view. Museums elsewhere in the world had eventually benefited, and little though he could ever have thought of that, he had given us one of the greatest adventures of our lives.

I was now jerked back to the present by the surfacing of the divers, all complaining bitterly of the cold.

'You're lucky,' I said. 'You ought to have been up here, it's been sweltering!'

They all gave me an 'old-fashioned' look, so I piped down and changed the subject.

'We'll cut the diving today to three hours,' said Mark.

'Suits me!' Mike, ready to go back to work again after these few words, leant over the side a moment. 'Look at it. Clear as gin. The clearer it is, the colder it is, that's the trouble!'

Slim nonchalantly shrugged his shoulders, raising his hands palms uppermost. 'It can't always be perfect!'

With a rattle of air bottles they were gone again, and I amused myself by seeing how many rock outcrops were in my view. Clear-cut and unmistakeable on the convexed line of the horizon, though it was all and more of five sea miles away, was the Bishop Light. To the left, from where I sat, but only half the distance away, were the Haycocks, their appearance living up to their name. Then I looked for Rosevean, but decided it must be out of sight behind the island of Annet.

The thought of Rosevean always brings back a memory that makes me smile. I've never told the story before, but I find it as intriguing as it is amusing. Rosevean is a small, low-lying islet, less than two sea miles from the Bishop Light and less than a thousand metres from the Gilstone Ledges where we worked on the site of the wreck of *Association*. I'd never believed what the old-time records told me, that Admiral Sir Cloudesley Shovell took his entire fortune to sea with him. However, when pieces of eight, louis d'or, Portuguese gold reis and English sovereigns began to turn up, it seemed they were right after all. Whatever could possess a man to do such a thing? The banks of those days might not be all that reliable, but a ship . . .

Not that we found anything like a fortune. What we found – and others after us – was a mere drop in the bucket, taking into account the enormous mass of gold and silver reckoned to have been aboard. In addition to ten chests said to have held specie to the value of over three million pounds sterling, the admiral is said never to have sailed without two sets of gold and silver plate – an official one carried for the liberal entertaining he did in his capacity as roving ambassador, and his own personal one.

What we found was almost less interesting than where. The prime reason for our *Association* project had been the raising of three fine bronze cannon from the darkness of the Gilstone depths. One of them lay with its entire 9-foot length prone on the sea-bed, and when we lifted it, pressed into the silt beneath was a ribbon of coins – about 4 inches wide and with the coins lying three to four deep – over three hundred coins in all.

None of the others seemed unduly surprised, but I found it odd, very odd. Up till then in this series of dives the coins we had found had had to be searched for, and, except for a cache found in a small grotto in the rocks which had been very difficult of access, they had been picked up in ones and twos. When Mark had found the admiral's silver plate – which must have been one of a large set – it was hidden from sight between a gun and a rock.

When we lifted a second cannon – an iron one this time, with a topside weight of 3 tons – there again, lying in a long line and impressed into the silt – were over 300 coins. Then I remembered that, earlier in the project, one of the divers had reported how he had found two hundred and sixty pieces of eight.

'Stuck to the sea-bed in a straight line, they were,' he said. 'Just as if someone had deliberately laid them in a row.'

I had asked him then: 'Was there a cannon nearby?'

'The nearest was about three metres away,' he had said.

'Now I was certain what had happened. As *Association* broke apart and the admiral's treasure chests burst open, the hundreds of thousands of coins had scattered like leaves in an autumnal forest. The sea-bed would have been carpeted with them three to four deep, just as we had found them under the guns, and once upon a time they would have lain in the silt at the rate of three hundred to every 9 feet by 4 inches of sea-bed.

The very fact, as I have explained elsewhere in the book, that guns of three tons and more in weight can be taken up by the sea, as if they were mere timber logs, and put down somewhere else – in this case on a bed of treasure – provided the vital clue.

Without it, the final links in the story of Sir Cloudesley's treasure would never have been complete.

The next link of the chain was Rosevean, which is not only a mere gun-shot distance from Gilstone Rock, or *Shovell* Rock, as it was long known in tribute to the admiral's demise, but less than two miles east of the Bishop Light. In 1851, being so close and handy, it was used to accommodate the men who built the first stone lighthouse there to the design of the great engineer Sir James Douglass. The ruins of the little houses built for them can still be seen today.

The first contingent to arrive were naturally the helmeted divers and their attendants who were to carry out the prodigious task of levelling the rock, and bolting together and cementing into place the enormous ring of interlocking granite blocks which formed the foundation. It was a task that took them a full year, and no wonder, for there's many a day when, though diving would be possible elsewhere, the sea would 'have too much of a run' to work at the Bishop.

The key word here, of course, is *elsewhere*. Sitting round the fire at night, quaffing their beer and sucking their clay-pipes, these large barrel-chested men would have settled down to talk. And what would their talk have run to? Precious little else but women and wreck, I'll be bound. They were not exactly surrounded by females, the nearest being miles away and only to be met with on Saturday nights, but shipwreck was all about them. And with the name Shovell Rock to prompt their memories, and the famous tale of the wreck of the *Eagle, Romney* and *Association* fresher in local minds than now, I'll bet my bottom piece of eight, they found good use for their spare time. They had the best of boats, gear and equipment for their official job, and once they found the site would have only had to drop over the side to pick up gold and silver by the handful, for the depth was a mere 100 feet – 30 metres.

I would sooner they had left it for me to find, but I don't grudge them their good fortune: they had a hard and hazardous life, those early divers and – as diving casualty figures show – it hasn't changed much today.

During that splendid summer of 1976 we had many visitors

on the *Colossus* site. The Duke of Gloucester was one of the
Trustees of the British Museum, and he and the Duchess, with
the little Earl of Ulster – just coming up to his second birthday –
came along to see us at work. Another Trustee who paid us a
visit was Lord Fletcher, himself a lawyer and former chairman
of the Management Committee of the Institute of Archaeology,
and so well able to understand the twin aspects of our problems.
He came with his wife and Dr Ann Birchall, and then took us
for a return visit to his own field of land archaeology. Using
Sea King we went to see the ruins of St Ilid hermitage on the isle
of St Helen's.

We also had a visit from Lord Runciman, the chairman of the
Advisory Committee on Historic Wreck Sites, who anchored
his superb motor yacht *Bondicar* in the channel between Tresco
and Bryher, and invited us aboard. She had the largest pitchpine
mast I've seen in a long while, and her engine room was a sight
worth looking at, too. Having Lord Runciman behind us to deal
with cowboy 'wreck-rustlers', we could congratulate ourselves
on a 'sheriff' well able to use the law in the worthy task of
protecting the remains of historic ships.

Protection was also needed once the 'remains' were recovered,
for Dr Ann Birchall had impressed on me, when it was agreed
that I should take over the task of conservation of the sherds, that
the material was almost priceless. My usual conservation laboratory was inadequate, especially in view of the publicity now
attending our project. I needed somewhere larger and less vul-
nerable to intending burglars.

During the winter months I had been building a new bar-
lounge at the Admiral Benbow. It was to be something special,
with large blown-up photographs of wrecked ships by my friend
Frank Gibson of Scilly, and a window commanding a spectacular
view of the harbour and the anchorage beyond. The latter
feature was essential to the well-being of my many French,
German and Spanish yachting customers, for it would enable them
to keep one eye on their moored craft and the other on their
drink.

I was very proud of the new addition, and anxious to open it,
for little remained to be done to make it all ship-shape and Bristol

fashion, bar a few additions to the nautical décor. However, I could see that the room would make the most beautiful and secure laboratory, so I delayed the opening for eighteen months. I use the word 'laboratory' advisedly, for the conservation of nautifacts is a subject to which I have devoted a great deal of study and practical experiment over many years, and on which I read a good proportion of the many articles and books published.

Faced with an accumulation of sherds, and the prospect of a constant incoming flow, I had to establish at the outset the right method of not merely cleaning the surface, but removing the salt which would have permeated the entire body of the pottery. Hamilton had been right enough when he had said that 'salt water will not damage the pottery' when he was hopeful of salvage in the period immediately after the wreck. Even in the long term, it would do no damage so long as the pots remained submerged, but if the sherds were to be brought back into the atmosphere without the salt being removed they would be like the salty-plaster walls of old Cornish cottages – always 'damp' and with the salt eventually appearing in the form of a grey discoloration.

One of my worries was whether ordinary sluicing with fresh water would be enough to rid the sherds of the chlorides which had been forced into them over nearly two hundred years. I am always surprised that little, if any, mention is made in the literature on conservation of the question of pressure. The sherds, for example, had not been lying in the equivalent of a bucket of sea-water all that time. At the depth they were found, they would have been under a sustained pressure of about 7 kg (15 lb) a square inch, and I wondered whether, like some of the timber nautifacts I had treated, they would have to be washed under the same pressure which they had endured while submerged.

In the event, tests showed that sluicing was effective, which simplified the installation of my desalination tanks. These were tables one metre by two, made of bonded marine 8-ply, glued and brass-screwed together, and with the shallow – six centimetre deep – trays forming their tops waterproofed with seven coats of varnish sealer. They were arranged so that water would flow across them at a rate of roughly five gallons an hour, and the sherds were to stay in them for a minimum of a hundred hours.

This 'magic' figure was not arrived at by guesswork, of course, and I took test after test during the washing of the final total of 35,000 sherds to determine whether they were certainly 'salt-free'. To the layman it would seem an impossible task, for one has to test the water content of the sherd for salt, and the only obvious way is to get the water out of a sherd is to dry it, which just as obviously means good-bye to your water sample. Fortunately, there are other ways.

First, I would select a sherd with a good thick section, such as a rim or base fragment, for test purposes, for if a piece of this thickness had been rendered salt-free, then it was certain that the thinner pieces would have been made safe as well. Then, having transferred it from the water-table to a small pressure container filled with distilled water, I was ready for action. The container was made of heavy-duty perspex 4-inch diameter tube, so that I could now, with the aid of a foot-pump, subject the soaking sherd to an absolute pressure of about 10 kg (20 lb) per square inch. This pressure was maintained for ten days before the sherd was removed from the distilled water, and placed in a tightly sealed ordinary plastic bag.

Then came the extraction of the sherd's water-content. Condensation was one of the two methods I used. The water-soaked sherd, still inside its plastic bag, was placed on a laboratory 'drying tray', which in this instance was rather more than the words conveyed. For drying the sherds I had decided to use 'dimple' panel heaters, which are designed for use upright, but which were shaped in just the right way when adjusted to an almost horizontal position to take a sherd in each dimple. In the case of the test sherds, still in their plastic containers, the heat conveniently condensed the liquid on to the inner surface of the container, from which it could be drained off into a test-tube. The large amount of liquid obtained, in comparison with the size of the sherd, never ceased to surprise me.

The second, and most satisfactory, method I used to obtain the water content of the sherds, along with any contamination it had in solution, was by centrifugal force. The Department of Trade once invited Mike Hicks and myself to a meeting of the Runciman

Committee in the lecture hall of the National Maritime Museum, where the many divers engaged in work on protected wreck sites had the opportunity of talking about their conservation methods. My contribution was advocacy of the merits of 'spin-drying' when dealing with materials brought up from the sea-bed. The word prompted an absolute shout of laughter, with its association of wives and girl-friends washing out their smalls and drying them in those screaming machines which inhabit the corner of the kitchen, but although 'centrifugal' sounds more grandly scientific, spin-drying is still exactly what it means. The difference between the machine in the kitchen and the one in the conservationists' laboratory is chiefly that of size – the marine archaeologist may be drying something that is no larger than the space taken up by a bikini brief, or he may be coping with giant ship's timbers – and speed. Household machines are commonly high-speed, but centrifugal force may be exerted to draw water from any soaked article at quite low speeds. When extracting the water-content of a sherd, I revolve it at 500 revolutions per minute in a perspex container attached to the face-plate of a lathe. It is a matter of fine judgment to place the container at precisely the right distance from the centre, adjust the speed of the revolutions and give the process exactly the right time to be completed satisfactorily.

The water content having been obtained by either method, the next step was to test in the usual way for the presence of chlorides. A drop or two of nitric acid first ensures that the water is freed of carbonates, and then a small amount of silver nitrate in solution is added. If chlorides are present a precipitate of silver choride will cloud the liquid – proof that the process of desalination is not yet complete, and back went the sherd with its companions in the water tables for a further period. It was interesting that my experiments showed that sherds could be desalinated more quickly by washing them under the same pressure they had known on the sea bottom, rather than by sluicing at atmospheric pressure, but the latter is equally effective though taking longer, and is happily also more economic.

Before their immersion in the water tables for desalination, however, the sherds had first to be washed clean by hand. 'By hand' meant just that – rubbing them individually between finger and thumb to remove the slime accumulated during a couple of centuries in the sea. Warm water only – no soap or detergents – was used, and a sherd was only clear of slime when it could be felt to be so. It was then ready for its next stage.

The advantage of the large, shallow open tanks was that every piece being treated could be seen all the time, and could even be photographed under water, so that I could feel completely in control throughout. The 35,000 pot-sherds we eventually recovered each passed thrice through my hands – once for the initial cleaning, again when they went into the desalination tanks, and yet again when they were taken out for careful drying. It was no wonder, therefore, that they began to fall into a kind of pattern in my mind, and in particular I became aware of what I called 'special fragments'. Many others came very close to being as hard, as dense, as lustrous, and as shiny-black – but not quite. These were 'special'. Early in the excavation they were nearly all plain black, but even then, among many hundreds of plain black fragments, they stood out. As the project progressed, however, figured fragments with the same characteristics began to appear. Their curvature indicated that they came from a large pot, and in texture they had the feel of plate-glass, polished on both sides. Even though the inside bore the potter's 'wheel-marks' it still shone brilliantly when held at an angle to the light. I grouped them together, and even began to make 'joins' of matching pieces, so that the nucleus of a painted scene began to emerge, and to help in the reconstruction I fashioned a curved sheet of lead approximating to a vase shape, so that I could place the pieces more accurately.

'Wheel-marks' can be invaluable in this process. They are the grooves and ridges – rather like the enlargement of grooves on a gramophone record – which are produced by the wet fingers of the potter, as he 'throws' the pot on the revolving wheel. Even when a pot is finished off inside, while still on the wheel, with a pad of wet leather (to get a more level surface) wheel-marks are still formed. They vary with the pressure and movement of a potter's hands, so that even a plain, undecorated pot may be reassembled from its fragments by picking up the clues of the wheel-marks on the inner surface. As they can be no other than horizontal, you have only to bring them level to know that you have the pot sherd in a vertical position – though whether it is right-way up or wrong-way up will remain to be discovered. The next thing is to get the marks to align themselves on adjoining pieces – when they do, you know you've got a match, even though the straight edges of the piece might give you very little help if you were looking at them from the 'right' side.

There are also a number of other useful clues. The outstanding quality of the fragments I have just mentioned is an extreme example, but the fact that the pots were all individually created means that there are subtle differences in the texture of the clay from which they were made – notably between that of mainland Greece and southern Italy – and a degree of sorting is possible on the basis of this, the absence or presence of 'glazing' and so on, to decide which pot an undecorated fragment may belong to. Once the fragments of a particular pot are collected the varying thickness and curvature of them enables them to be subdivided, not only according to whether they come from the rim or foot, but from the top, middle or bottom section of the body of the pot. A degree of 'hand mass-production' was involved, and the master artist responsible for the principal design on the side intended for display would often hand the pot to his assistants for the completion of the remainder of the decoration, so that less perfect work can usually be ascribed to the 'back' of the pot.

By the early summer of 1976 the laboratory contained many thousands of sherds. Hundreds upon hundreds were in the desalination tanks, with water flowing slowly over them. Hundreds were on the drying grids, with their true colours coming back to them as they became free of their water content. And thousands on the sorting tables. They were of all shapes and colours. Some were fragments of vase bodies, others obviously formed parts of rims, bases or handles. But besides vases, we clearly had pieces of many other types of pottery – parts of the neck of a slender flask; portions of jars, pitchers and wine jugs; and small delicate handles from cups or perfume bottles.

Then there were the figured pieces. We had a multitude of irregular fragments portraying male and female heads, faces, eyes, noses, arms, legs, hands, feet, thighs, torsos, breasts, and what we called 'unmentionables'. Then there were the 'dress' fragments, with their tantalizing glimpses of elegant falls of drapery, or scraps of body-armour, shields or helmets. And also the decorative motifs, rhythmic designs of palmettos and lotus – the latter symbolic of luxurious dreaminess and distaste for the active life – or bands of geometric invention.

The whole presented a loose mosaic of colour, not one puzzle but a perplexing jumble of enigmas for the British Museum experts to solve when they came to piece the fragments together. Meanwhile, it was impossible to have so many sherds passing through my hands without saying, every now and then, 'Hang on, there's another piece about somewhere like that one.' A search would reveal the piece one had in mind, and if the two joined, that was a marvellous moment.

The only people allowed in the laboratory – apart, of course, from the team – were three people very close to me: Elisabeth, Denise and Ian, my younger son. All four of us would often be engrossed to the small hours in this giant and intriguing puzzle.

By the time Dr Ann Birchall made her first visit to the laboratory, I had many hundreds of fragments conserved and ready for her to see. Best of all, I had my assembled 'specials' which we at the Benbow had managed to join together to make sections of what was obviously a continuous picture – the bare chest of a man with his arms raised, a right shoulder, a male left thigh, and so on. I hoped, of course, that this would prove to be one of the designs in the Tischbein volumes. These books are now collectors' items beyond the range of my library, nor had I been able to spare the time in the midst of my work on the sherds to consult them elsewhere, but at the British Museum they would be among the reference tools of Dr Birchall, and I was hopeful that she would recognize my partly assembled picture.

Her usually serious face was alight with intense anticipation as she walked towards the laden tables, where the sherds were laid out like some glorious antique patchwork quilt. She spent a whole day examining the fragments, holding them up before her one at a time in deep thought, and giving extra attention to my 'specials'.

'I'm not at all sure,' she said, at last, thoughtfully, 'but I may be able to identify this. I shan't know until I get back to the Museum.' Like me, she suspected that the intriguing combination of 'specials' came from one of the vases portrayed by Tischbein, but archaeologists never commit themselves until they are dead certain. It was to be some days before I heard that the picture we had begun to piece together matched with the central details of a Tischbein drawing of the 'Return of Hephaistos' – the Greek god of fire and metals. This put us into a state of gleeful excitement, for it showed that we had recovered part of one of Hamilton's finest vases, for only the cream were selected for the artist to record. It was the high point of the project so far.

As I have mentioned earlier, we had recovered a substantial number of fragments in our first season in 1975 – 8186 to be precise. But this was nothing to what we had by the summer of the following year when the sherds were virtually pouring into the laboratory. The small scattering of 'specials' from the Tischbein pot gradually rose to over thirty pieces, which I carefully set aside for delivery to Dr Birchall at the Museum, excitedly matching them up to the copy of the Tischbein drawing (see endpaper drawing) which I now had before I handed them over, and noting with delight how greatly artistic skill and creative zest of the original Greek artists excelled the rather flat copy drawings made by Tischbein and his students.

We had promised to keep Tony Salmon, our film producer at the BBC, in touch with progress and, on hearing this news, he decided to use it to provide a spectacular ending to his film, and brought his team post-haste to the laboratory at the Admiral Benbow.

The divers came over from Scilly, and were glad of a few days away from grubbing about on the sea-bed.

'I don't pick the sea-urchin spines out of my fingers any more,' said Slim. 'To save time, I just shave them off.'

'You're lucky to have any fingers left,' retorted Mike. 'I think I'll take a week off to let mine have a chance to grow back to normal.'

So, we had a convivial filming re-capping get-together, which put everyone in a good mood. The filming could be a mite

39 cm

With the discovery of the rim-sherd which completed the thyrsus in the main design, and the legs of the satyr and mule, which linked with decorative band on the inward curving lower part, it was possible to start calculating the size of the bell-krater.

The Tischbein drawing of the design on the Colossus Vase, and (below) the design with the completed parts blacked out, which I used to aid me in the search for the still missing pieces.

tedious, but at the Benbow it was only a matter of calling Ida, or Jackie, or Doris, or Christine, or Dot, or Jean, or Silvia, or Marlene, or Barbara, to bring some refreshment, and any one of them would come a-running, bless her!

As the prime stars of the show, the sherds were filmed under water in the tanks, out on the drying racks, during the sorting process, and being packed ready to be taken to Barclays Bank in Penzance before their final transport to the British Museum itself.

When it came to the divers' turn, they were asked their reactions to the project, and said how honoured they were to be associated with it, and how they had never dreamt that salvaging pottery would come to seem more of a historically exciting event than recovering pieces of eight. At the end of his interview, Slim slapped his ample chest with outspread fingers and declared: 'If I'm to become a millionaire, I'd just as well do it this way as not.'

Dr Birchall had chosen some of the choicest fragments for display before the cameras, and after speaking of the importance of the team's work in rediscovering the Hamilton collection, she went on to speak in detail about the selected pieces:

'For example, here we have one of the earliest pieces – early Attic black figure – which means that it was made in Athens in the sixth century before the birth of Christ, and this [holding up another piece] is from a certain kind of storage jar which was made in about the fifth century B C.

'We are talking about pottery that is over two and a half thousand years old. It really is incredible. Here is the top of a jar, the neck rising up there and underneath are bands of decoration. This is a lovely little piece. See this little dancing reveller, and underneath there would have been bands of animals, which we have here. Those are the earliest, now we have the southern Italian which is much later. But we are still talking in terms of two and a half thousand years ago. Here we have one of the regional styles of pottery; the Paestan style, and I think I can say who painted it. He was Python, one of the two great vase painters of that regional style. This is the banquet scene, a drinking scene, there are three pieces here. We have not yet got them complete, but we have a figure reclining on a couch, and they're all drinking and enjoying themselves. And underneath is this little old satyr poking his head up from under the couch.'

All that was done in a fairly simple take, but the final camera-take set a poser for both the producer and his cameraman, Peter Watson-Wood, whom I had known for many years. The plan was that a copy of Tischbein's drawing of Hephaistos's return from Olympus should be spread on the table, and Dr Birchall would then place the pottery sherds on the related section of the drawing, commenting at the same time on what she was doing. The idea sounded simple enough, but to get the eye of the cameraman and that of his complex, sophisticated and heavy camera united in the essential position to let the viewers follow this manoeuvre was not so easy.

After several rehearsed attempts, it was finally arranged that Dr Birchall should be seated directly beneath the camera, which had to be lowered bodily over her where she sat, so that she was pinned beneath the centre of the camera tripod, with her body and left arm immobilized, and only able to move her right arm a few centimetres.

'Quiet everyone!'

The clapper board snapped down in front of her face, the take-number was called, and Tony gave the command: 'Action!' The camera's telltale light blipped like a sparkling red jewel, and the tape-recorder slung over my shoulder took in every sound. Peter, the cameraman, interrupted with a sign. 'Cut!' said Tony. 'What went wrong?'

'It would be better if Dr Birchall kept her wrist parallel with the drawing,' explained Peter. 'By raising her wrist from the table we lose sight of the fragment at the crucial moment.'

'Can you do that?' Tony asked. Dr Birchall, under the hot glare of the lights, agreed, and after the ironing out of another snag connected with shadows in the wrong place, we were away.

'Over here,' Dr Birchall began, 'we have the most interesting and exciting finds of the whole season.' She indicated the drawing and the small pile of sherds. 'I've brought with me a copy of the drawing by Tischbein, because when I was here a few weeks ago I picked out some sherds which I recognized as coming from a vase as illustrated by him. And, rather like a jigsaw puzzle, what I'm going to try to do now is to fit some of these pieces to the drawing.'

I should mention that the background story of the picture Dr Birchall had in front of her was that of Hephaistos having been thrown out of heaven by the goddess Hera, who disowned him as her son because of his lameness. In revenge he sent her a beautiful throne which magically held her fast the moment she sat down, and refused to return to heaven to release her until Dionysos – the god of wine – broke down his resistance by making him drunk and brought him back in triumph.

'Here I'm putting in the elbows of the figure riding on a mule,' continued Dr Birchall. 'It is in fact Hephaistos the smith-god. He is being brought back to Olympus in an advanced state of intoxication by Dionysos and satyrs. I put in this bit of drapery there . . . bits of the mule there . . . with his knee . . . and here . . . beautifully conserved, his head . . . and shoulders . . . that fits just there.

'What is he carrying over his shoulder? . . . a thyrsus . . . we have two tiny fragments which fit together to complete that.

'Behind him one of the satyrs . . . these two sherds give us most of his head . . . the satyr is playing the double pipes . . . another indication of the good time they've been having drinking. A little bit of his leg there . . . behind the satyr comes Dionysos . . . and there's his head . . . a lovely head, this, a beautiful drawing . . . we have his eye . . . and his hair . . . in fact, he has a very modern hair style . . . these pieces fit here . . . and show us his beard . . . long ringlets . . . another piece with his shoulder . . . and some of his drapery.

'Behind him again one of the maenads . . . the attendants of Dionysos . . . a little bit of her drapery there . . . and then, only just last week, the very last piece of the season's recoveries, and terribly exciting . . . it's discoloured because it is still damp, in fact . . . the lower part of the maenad . . . carrying her wine jug . . . with the tail and leg of the satyr . . . then this little piece that just fits in. . . .

'This vase, which of course we never expected ever to see again, the Tischbein which we had thought to have gone for ever with *Colossus*, this vase is a very fine vase. It was painted in Athens in about 440 BC. In fact, at the time that Pericles was building the Parthenon – fine period, fine style. These fragments are in a lovely state of conservation and I think we here have the finest illustration of the justification, if there need be any, for the whole season's work on the sea-bed.'

That splendid performance by Dr Ann Birchall brought Tony Salmon's film to a dramatic conclusion. The smith-god had appeared at just the right moment, and it seemed appropriate that in my schooldays he had been my favourite character in the complex and wondrous world of Greek mythology. What I liked was his magical practical jokes, and the way he could make things with his hands – something which I early discovered that I could do, too.

It was a tremendous help to us, of course, that the drawings executed by Tischbein and his students – he became director of the Neapolitan Academy of Painting – were full-size and probably taken directly from the vases by an initial tracing. However, the vases being in the round and the drawings of necessity flat, no exact copy was possible. The drawings, too, are in outline only, ignoring the contrast between the dark and light areas of the paintings.

The one which incorporates the smith-god's return to Olympus was included in the third of the four volumes of Hamilton's *Collection of Engravings from Ancient Vases mostly of Pure Greek Workmanship discovered in Sepulchres in the Kingdom of the Two Sicilies*, published in Naples between 1791 and 1795. The mention of 'sepulchres', of course, is no certain guide to the source of all the vases illustrated, since Hamilton could hardly attribute them to sites which were the subject of 'official' digs.

The Hephaistos drawing was taken from a 'bell-krater', rather than what we nowadays think of as a 'vase'. This was a vessel used as a wine-mixing bowl, for the Greeks and Italians were as fond of adding water to their wine then as they are now. The Tischbein rendering was beautiful, but I did rather regret the absence of any indication of gaiety on what had obviously been a very jolly occasion, and so I redrew the scene for the team's

The smith-god's return, as I redrew it for the team's Christmas card, to the scandal of the academic recipients.

Christmas card. Unfortunately, it met with a very cold reception from some of my academic friends to whom it was sent.

Before the fragments of the precious vase were finally taken off to the British Museum, I took the precaution of drawing each of them on card life-size. I then cut out the shapes, placed them on my own copy of the Tischbein drawing, and so was able to monitor the progress of the reconstitution of our 'bell-krater', as I must learn to call it. I could also work out the areas of it which were still to be filled in. It was tremendously exciting to watch the pieces gradually falling into place. Some versions of the Hephaistos legend have it that, when he was thrown from heaven, he fell for the length of a day, and was only rescued by sea nymphs in the nick of time. From his second descent to the sea, in the hold of *Colossus*, it was taking us many and many a day to retrieve him, and I often chuckle at the idea of Mike, Slim, Mark – and myself – in the role of latter-day sea nymphs!

12
A Phoenix from the Sea

With the season of 1977 drawing to an end, and the flow of sherds reducing to a trickle as the project was coming to its close, Dr Birchall found it ever more frustrating during her brief visits to us that her role was limited to peering over the gunnel, waiting for the divers to return. As a land archaeologist she had been used to stepping down into the trenches the moment a discovery seemed imminent, and to handling material the moment it was found, and it was naturally irksome to have to leave the whole of the marine excavation to be organized by the divers themselves. Obviously, they followed her directions as to recording the position of finds in relation to a plastic tape grid layout, but it was actually only the comparatively sheltered nature of the site and the excellence of the weather we had which enabled this to be kept in position. I often thought with a quiet smile of the other sites, and very different sea conditions, in which my previous salvage operations had been carried out, and how that tape would have been tangled into the next-best thing to a piece of knitting.

Dr Birchall longed to be down with the divers to see for herself just how it was all done, and decided in the September of 1977 to make at least one personal visit to the sea bottom before our work was completed. It was a courageous decision, especially for someone who had never swum the length of a swimming bath and who had always kept within her depth, and the venture would lend a touch of drama to the second *Colossus* film being undertaken by Tony Salmon, which in other respects was more academic than the first. The divers and I were entirely sympathetic to both their wishes, but on practical grounds our enthusiasm was bound to be a trifle muted, for an effective diving schedule and filming are two things which we knew from experience don't mix.

With my knowledge of the Scillies, I was always conscious that any sherds we missed in the disturbed area during these precious closing days of the season were likely to be lost for ever in the winter storms ahead, and from the point of being cost-effective, outlay on a day's diving needed to be offset by a constant inflow of sherds. At the end of the day, when I read the divers' reports, my eyes would first of all scan the recovery column and I would judge the success or otherwise of the day's work by the number of sherds brought up. During filming the reports would state laconically, 'Performing for the BBC. Sherd recoveries – nil.'

For her training, Dr Birchall went to the Fort Bovisand Diving School at Plymouth, and, Slim having filmed her beginner's underwater exercises there for the BBC documentary, she was ready for her great adventure. Mike and Mark were to dive down ahead of her, while Slim waited underwater with his camera at the ready, and they carefully explained to her before they submerged that they would be waiting for her at the bottom of the mooring line. Back in the boat, her instructor, whom she had brought with her from Plymouth, would put her down at the surface (buoy) end of the line, so that she had only to follow the line down to be safely guided to the nervously waiting Mike and Mark. They were more greatly concerned about her than she knew. Used as they were to the chill of the depths, they did not forget the effect of it on someone encountering it for the first time, and the twenty minutes that she spent on the bottom obviously seemed longer than it was – and not only to her but to them.

In spite of the brief time she spent on the site, Dr Birchall surfaced so incapacitated by cramp that the divers had difficulty in bringing her back on board, since she had been rendered incapable of helping herself over the ample freeboard of the launch. They only breathed normally themselves when they had her recovered, getting on for half an hour and a hot cup of tea later. When she was, once again, able to face the cameras and the microphone, she told Mike: 'It was fantastic! I felt quite euphoric! It wasn't quite really what I'd imagined.'

'It never is!' said Mike, helpfully.

'I had that incredible feeling of being suspended in space!' went on Dr Birchall. 'A sort of euphoric feeling – then suddenly there was a sort of reality of it all, you know when the proverbial dying man sees everything flashing in front of his eyes. I thought of the ship, the wreck and the boats and Hamilton and the pottery, it all came back in such a tangible moment! It was *so real* it was fantastic, you couldn't possibly describe how I felt!'

Dr Birchall was never to dive on the *Colossus* site again, but she had achieved what she had set out to do and discovered that the sea-bed at the Big C site was 'rougher and tougher' than she'd expected, even on a day when – for a professional diver – conditions were idyllic.

My chief regret of the 1977 season was that Slim had not been able to be with us, except on these special photographic sessions. He had already sacrificed many other filming ventures to work on *Colossus*, and had now to catch up on some pressing commitments on the other side of the world. In his place we had taken on another Mark as relief diver – Mark Groves – a master of his craft and another Scillonian.

At the British Museum, the experts continued the work I had begun of piecing together the fragments of the bell-krater decorated with the painting of the 'Return of Hephaistos'. I was able to speed and simplify the work for them by sorting out the 'special' sherds from the others, just as I had originally done, and, of course, continued to monitor progress by making cardboard copies of each piece to fit over my own copy of the Tischbein drawing of the vase before despatching them in their separate container. By constant handling of the pieces I developed an instinct for them, and felt quite put out when one piece was rejected by the Museum as 'not belonging', but not for long – further examination proved me right after all. A small triumph enough, perhaps, but in the hard slog of hour after hour in my laboratory, such things gave a lift to the day.

The completeness of the reconstruction we were beginning

jointly to achieve was in itself a tribute to the thoroughness of
the work of the divers, for the fragments had not been found in
one location, but scattered far and wide throughout the site. It is
interesting to note that this variation in location can be traced
in the variation in condition and colour of the adjoining pieces.

And now, at last, the stage had been reached at which the vase
could be re-created more permanently in the round than I had
naturally been able to do by using my vase-shaped lead sheet,
and, for good measure, two other vases of a different type were
to be reconstructed as well – a jug and a mug.

The first step in the restoration of the major vase – the Colossus
Vase, as I like to think of it – was the making of a friable-clay
core on the potter's wheel, corresponding as nearly as possible
to the estimated inner shape of the original. This was done by
taking an approximate 'profile' at a point where the pieces made
a nearly complete outline from rim to base. This drawing was
then transferred to a metal template which, when rotated, cut
away the superfluous plaster from the roughly moulded shape
built up (for the sake of lightness) on a plastic bucket 'core'.
When this had dried, the sherds were placed in position on it,
the surface being scraped away or added to in order to accommodate them comfortably, and any spaces being filled in with plaster,
ready for a discreet top coating of shellac and ground pigments
to give a tint toning in with the rest of the pot and a texture closely
resembling the original fired clay. Any missing decoration was
faintly and unobtrusively sketched in on the plaster, not to
conceal the incompleteness, but to indicate just that, while at the
same time giving an idea of how the pot once looked. Completion of this work rather outran events, for yet further sherds of
the Colossus Vase came to light early in the 1978 season, 'Too
late!' And I had visions of someone eventually having to get to
work with a dentist's drill to fit in my unseasonable finds in the
appropriate places.

While this work went on at the British Museum – a delicate
and time-consuming process – I had a final chore to tackle, too.
It was time-consuming all right, and though superficially like
old-time hard labour in the Dartmoor stone quarries, it called for
delicacy of touch as well, in its own peculiar way. As the sherds

had grown satisfyingly fewer at the end of the diving season, I had asked the divers to send over to Penzance some samples of clib from the Scillies site. As I have mentioned earlier, every wreck, whether ancient or modern, has its clib plateaux. Those at the site of the Big C were less extensive than many we had seen because the wrought-iron fittings, responsible for most clib-growth where wrecks lie, had been salvaged in the early days after she first sank. Nevertheless, we estimated that there were at the least ten to twelve tons of the gritty, granite-like material adhering to the sea floor.

Removing it involved careful leverage with wrecking bars to break it up into handy-sized pieces, and the first samples arrived at my lab in chunks of half a hundredweight. I knew, of course, that I was faced by a 'lucky dip'. Maybe there would be something of value inside, and maybe not. There was only one way to find out. It had to be squeezed apart in a hydraulic press, using a 5-ton lifting jack, and I held my breath as I awaited the result, only too conscious of the extraordinary nature of my task. It isn't often that one looks for something without being sure whether one hopes to find it or not! Did I want to find sherds embedded in it? If I did find any there would be nothing for it but to raise the rest of the twelve tons of clib glued to the sea-bed at Southward Well. Months of work! Yes, even if just one sherd turned up, the lot would have to be broken up with every golf-ball-sized piece reduced to dust, just in case.

The first chunk crumbled in the press – silt, pebbles, small shells and rust dust lay before me, and over me such a deluge of gritty dirt that I felt like cheating and putting the lot back where it came from, on the model of marine archaeological rules! Not a single sherd. But, on I went, through the rest of that first half-ton. The odds on finding a sherd were fifty-fifty either way, and it was 'no' at the end of the first few days of black, grimy crunching. Then, as I pressed apart my umpteenth clib nugget in the midst of my sample delivery – and did so with the same care as I had done my first – there came a particularly teasing 'crunch' from the press and out fell a glistening painted pot-sherd. Part of a male torso! The edges were as sharply squared as when it had first broken nearly two hundred years ago. The clib had done its stuff and protected that sherd to perfection, and would have done so for ever.

My discovery was immediately reported to the authorities, and at a meeting at the Department of Trade, attended also by all the people at the British Museum who were interested in the project and myself, the vital decision was taken to continue the work of diving through the winter and raise the remaining tons of clib. It is usually quite uneconomical to carry on after the end of the diving season, but the urgent importance of the work, and the fact that raising the lumps of clib wasn't the sort of delicate salvage we had been doing in the summer, bringing up individual fragments of pottery, made it worth while. So, our plans were made.

Nature, having pampered us in our summer labours, decided otherwise. The winter of 1977–8 was one of the worst I remember. There was gale after gale. Ship after ship was wrecked, the last and most famous being the oil tanker *Amoco Cadiz*: 190,000 tons of pollution menace as she struck the rocks on the other side of the Channel, less than a hundred miles from my Penzance home. The weather was so appalling that the divers never once managed to get even as far as putting on their suits. The ground-seas did their damndest at Southward Well, and a harvest of giant kelp lay, piled high, along the rocky southern shore of Samson.

In spite of our intensive search, there may still have been a few pot sherds for the seas to force loose from the grip of the weed holdfasts, but I rejoiced in the thought of the 35,000 saved from what would have been their inevitable fate had they remained where they were all through that worst of winters, with the sea whipped to maximum force by the unending gales.

Nor did spring bring much improvement. Conditions were to be bad throughout the 1978 season. Fortunately, I was confident that little still lay down below to be recovered, and was not all that anxious to make an early start, but Dr Birchall was understandably impatient. The weather topside looked reasonable enough, and on a site nearby, where the East Indiaman *Hollandia* had come to grief, visibility was perfect because the area was swept free by currents. But, on the more sheltered *Colossus* site, plankton reduced the visibility to about four feet, and groping about down there was the equivalent of working in an old London pea-soup fog. In the end we started work before it was really suitable because we were afraid that we might lose our licence to some other team if we didn't go ahead.

Meantime, during that winter it was brought home to me exactly how the raging seas would have served the sherds, as I worked on the rest of that first consignment of clib. I was to find many beautiful sherds intact, but I was also to discover how untold numbers had been destroyed – ground back to the clay from which they had started their existence, as if the ocean were a gigantic pug-mill, which indeed it is. In my time I have come across tons of clib of every kind – silt-clib, sand-clib, gravel clib, and (on one occasion) copper-tack-clib, but to be confronted by Hamilton-vase-clib was pretty near heart-breaking. Several blocks of the clib from one area of the site were particularly heavy and dense, defeating even my press. They were composed of solid pottery, clay and silt, set to an incredible hardness by the rust fixative, and I had to cut them open with a diamond saw.

This vase-clib was, of course, predominantly clay-red, but there were also thin strata of the various colours used by the original artists – the black, grey and blue of pigments ground so many centuries ago. As every one of the thousands of pot sherds we had recovered passed through my hands, I had found, as had been expected, that many had been abrased by the action of the sea, as they washed about in the sand at sea-bed level. They had been left glazeless, unrecognizable, round-edged, and unusable for reconstruction purposes. It was to be expected, too, that some should have been milled down even further, but the granite hardness of this creation of the sea – the vase-clib – was something of a surprise even to me.

We shall never know, of course, how many of the Hamilton vases were entirely lost in this way, and only partial reconstruction can be expected for many, but knowing the site as I do, it sometimes seems like a miracle that we should have been able to recover from such a place the host of beautiful sherds that we have. There is a strange fascination, too, about these incomplete vases. They are rather like the Parthenon, more beautiful and stimulating to the imagination in ruin than when it was first built. The Greeks themselves were familiar with this idea, as with most others, and even there left certain features unfinished, never wishing to usurp the place of the gods and create the perfect.

There was a chance of further stray sherds coming to light at the site, even after the completion of our work in the 1978 season, when the rest of the clib, as well as the cannon and the surviving timbers, were raised. So, to enable us to make reconnaissance dives to round these up, the protection order was to remain in force for three further years.

On the October day when we lifted the guns the sea and the sky were interfused into one by low-lying 'misk', as the old-time fishermen used to call the 'fine weather' haze that rises from the sea. The sun was hidden from view, but its brilliant, diffused white light penetrated everywhere. After a whole summer of continual harassment by clouds of plankton in the water, we were able to look down through a calm sea and pick out every detail of the rugged bottom. We used the *Swordfish*, a sturdy Kelvin-engined boat owned by Mike's father, Mr G. Hicks, which 'Gee' has used hundreds of times in the 'relief' of the Bishop Light. It has a capstan set in its forepeak, and so is a splendid work-boat.

The carronades, festooned with hand-sized weed holdfasts, broke the surface, one after another, like two short, fat, powerful killer whales. Clearing them of their crud encasement, when I got them back to Penzance, was a great thrill. Their casting numbers and the place and year of their manufacture were laid bare in clear-cut detail on their undersides: CARRON – 1794, and they weighed fifteen hundredweight each. Both had a tampion in their muzzles, an oaken spile in their vents and an oiled round-shot in their barrels.

The project was now essentially at an end. On the twenty-seventh day of September 1978 I walked across the forecourt of the British Museum carrying with me the last one thousand and thirty-six sherds, plus the interesting addition of a little lion's head made of modern Wedgwood basalt pottery – our final offering from the Big C. Recently cleaned, the great façade, with its pediment of sculpture depicting the progress of civilization, glowed in the mid-morning sunlight. Yet, as I walked up the

twelve great grey steps to the main door, picking my way between the blue or pink jean-clad legs of the many students
lounging in the sun, I felt a pang of regret. Twenty-seven had
till now been a lucky number for me, but on this – probably the
last of my many visits to the Museum in connection with the loss
of old *Colossus* – I felt nothing but despondency.

The security guards had come to know me and my mystery
parcels over the years, and as I put my attaché case on the table
for the routine examination, they cracked the usual joke.

'Still having a smashing time? How much more is there?'

'This is it. This is the lot,' I answered, with a wry smile, and
went on into the great front hall. There, opposite the Museum
bookshop, in the far right-hand corner, was the showcase con-
taining the *Colossus* exhibit. And there, looking larger and heavier,
and somehow more magnificently monumental than I had imagined, was the great bell-krater – the Colossus Vase. I could
recognize the first sherds I had so painstakingly pieced together,
remember this piece of the base, or that fragment of the rim, as
I had picked them out, and biggest delight of all, the moments
when I came across another element in the jigsaw of its main
design. Yet, somehow, the impact of the reconstructed object
was curiously different, and much greater than my first sight of it
during the second of the BBC television films. I remembered,
even now with a shudder, how I had seen it being manoeuvred –
during the process of the attempted removal of the clay core
used in rebuilding it – into a position of no return, and how it
had crashed to the floor in almost as many fragments as there had
been originally. In my mental ear, the exclamation of the young
man superintending the reconstruction, short and sharp, like the
sound of a knife jabbed into a gale-strained spinnaker, still re-
echoed. 'Shit!' he had said – which was nothing to what I had
shouted at the screen at the same moment.

In my present mood of despondency I studied the great vase
in its clinical glass case, fully prepared to criticize, but instead I
admired. The reconstruction was splendid indeed, I could not
fault it. The artist who painted the design had been identified as
one of the chief members of the Polygnotos Group in Athens.
(This Polygnotos is not the celebrated wall-painter of the same

name, active in the earlier part of the fifth century BC, but a member of the next generation, possibly the son of a vase painter, named after the great artist.) The Colossus Vase was the work of the so-called 'Peleus Painter': Greek artists whose personal name is unknown are frequently denoted by the subject matter of their best-known work – Peleus was the mortal husband of the goddess Thetis, and father of Achilles. The Peleus Painter worked in Athens c. 440–430 BC, which meant that this vase, gathered piece by piece by the torn hands of our diving team from the rocky bottom of the Scillonian seas, had been created some two and a half millennia ago under the warm sun of the Mediterranean. As he paused in his work, the artist may have looked out towards a Parthenon still being built, and perhaps seen Pericles going up to check on its progress. The Colossus Vase is a relic of Athens at the height of her power, both politically and culturally, and the artist who worked on it is no stranger to the British Museum, for there is a neck amphora also painted by him in the 'Room of the Harpy Tomb'.

The Colossus Vase naturally held pride of place in the exhibit, but alongside it was a very clever partial reconstruction of a red-figure volute krater – one with high, curly handles. Two-thirds of the original had been painstakingly reconstructed from 175 sherds, and we had recovered a further large number of sherds, as yet not placed in position. The museum has a similar one from Sir William's First Collection, and like a little wine jug and mug also displayed in the central part of the case, this new krater is classed as Apulian, suggesting that they were collected by him from the 'heel' of Italy, or at least that his contacts spread down so far.

I was then pleased to greet as an old friend the little 'golf-ball' perfume jar – the painted figure now recognized as a woman running – which I had first held in my hand that perfect day in the Scillies when it first came to the surface, restored to light for the second time since the artist painted it c. 430 BC. And there, ranged at the foot of the case, were three of my little haunting faces – mascaroons, to give them their proper title.

Too big in design for its partially reconstructed sides and rim to be set in their natural position, a Paestan red-figure bell-krater was displayed in a side section. On one side there is a banquet scene, and on the reverse two draped women on either side of a nude youth, who have been identified as maenads with Dionysos. This piece – as was mentioned in the BBC film – has been recognized as the work of Python, one of the great early Paestan vase painters, active about 340 to 325 BC. The British Museum already possesses a bell-krater by him in the Payava Room, his workmanship being guaranteed by a signature. In yet another side section of the display were two Attic red-figure amphorae, also 'twins' of perfect specimens in the British Museum's existing collection.

It was good to see this handful of reconstructions, and yet they were a scant display when I compared them in my mind's eye with the treasure-hoard of sherds which had been spread out in my laboratory. Many will certainly never be part of a reconstructed vase, but undoubtedly the sea has in the case of many proved a greater preserver of the original colours of what it has shattered than the atmosphere on dry land has been for the tints of many Greek vases that have survived intact. I should have liked to see a larger show, and perhaps to have been allowed – with the rest of the team – to have some share in what show there was.

I felt as if the team and I had carried the burden of performing the first two long and difficult acts of a stage play, and had yet had no place in the line-up at the end of their brief third act. It had not occurred to me that there would be no joint celebration between Dr Birchall and the other members of the *Colossus* unit and the salvors when the great bell-krater was complete, nor that when I handed over my sherd consignments for it, that would be the last I would see of them. Neither I, nor any of the team, knew of the successful outcome of the work on the material we had provided until we were invited by the BBC to the preview of the second film the week before the television broadcast to the public, so that the camera team and the technicians with no special interest in the matter had been better informed than we, on whose toil over the years the whole exercise was based. Perhaps archaeologists and salvors will never see eye to eye but, when they do, perhaps we can look forward to 'salvage directors' in charge of underwater archaeological digs.

Small wonder then that my feelings were mixed on that day as I stood in front of the glass case among the many other members of the public, looking at the Colossus Vase for the first time, just as they did, months after completion of the work and separated from it by the glass barrier as firmly as if it had never been my hands which had washed and cleaned every last sherd. I would have needed to be more than human if I had not felt a touch of bitterness as I read the printed explanatory material on the sides of the exhibit prepared by the unit and saw that, although my name was included in the list of 'divers', no mention was made that it was I who had started the quest all those many years ago, and had carried it through against much discouragement and very long odds. No reference here to the underwater exploratory work of myself and the team which had ended in our location of the site, or of the endless hours of physical labour which I had devoted to the wearisome cleansing and other early stages of the conservation of those thousands upon thousands of sherds. No explanation that, but for all this, the display-case would have been empty, and the world's knowledge of Greek art that much poorer.

Small wonder, too, that the comments of the public round me, who could only draw for their knowledge of the project on the little exhibit, and on the BBC films, revealed all sorts of misconceptions as to the discovery of the wreck site, the way in which the sherds had been recovered, and much else besides. Something of my feelings may have shown upon my face, revealing my personal interest in the vases, for it was now that several people began to recognize me as having been a subsidiary character in the film drama, and I had to take refuge in retreat and a pair of disguising spectacles.

Yet, as I stepped aside, it was the interest which ordinary people were taking in the vases, even more than that shown by the members of the International Congress of Classical Archaeology held in London in 1978, which somehow revived my spirits. There was a mingling of accents from all parts of Britain, some from the Continent, and more than a sprinkling of American voices. One couple from the States had encountered the BBC films while at Southampton at the start of their tour, and had set out for the Scillies on the strength of them. These people were full of questions, too, which neither the films nor the exhibit answered. All the kinds of practical question that I have in my time asked, too, and which I hope this book will answer.

On one of them – the final fate of the vases and sherds – I am almost as much in the dark as they were. This will depend in part on the Department of Trade, and the British Museum, which made a loan towards recovery costs and provided a lot of staff time for sorting and the final stages of conservation, also has an interest in the matter. As to the value of the finds – the question everybody inevitably asks – the diving team and I had been too much absorbed in the fascination of the project to devote much time to calculations of the worth of what we had recovered. In our leisure moments, of course, we did leaf through the catalogues issued by the specialist dealers in such large cities as Geneva, London and Paris, which are centres of the international trade in sherds. The legal position varies in the many countries round the Mediterranean where antique Greek pottery remains are found. In some places sherds can be legally purchased in the country, though the police may step in to prevent their being openly exhibited for sale, and it isn't legal to take them out of the country without a permit. In Italy and the Greek mainland the export of pot sherds is simply illegal, no permits being issued for these or any other antique object. The only result of all this is a great deal of black market dealing which makes the prices even higher, and we found that plain, ordinary pottery sherds – that bore no comparison with what we had recovered – were listed at astronomic prices. In our case, too, the Museum's reconstruction of three vases, including the magnificent bell-krater, as well as the partial reconstruction of others, enhanced the value of our finds.

The only decisive answer to the question of value can be given in the auction room, and that is a solution I should myself welcome. Inquiries have already been made to me by a number of museums, and the British Museum is perhaps the only one in the world to which our finds could add comparatively little. Even Sir William, when his Second Collection was in its perfect state, did not offer it to them after having sold them his First Collection, since it would for the most part have been a matter of duplication.

In conclusion I can say only that *Colossus* is the fifth and last in the series of sunken men-o'-war – on each and every one I obtained permission to dive – of which I have salvaged the remains, and it is my last. I have realized my teenage dreams, accomplished what I set out to do, and in all this world there is nothing more satisfying than that. Adventure has followed adventure for me in the underwater world of the Scillies and south-west Cornwall, and as a Cornishman born and bred, I can think of no better place to follow and find one's heart's desire. And though *Colossus* is the last of my warship projects, a good salvor always has a shot or two by way of wreck ideas in his locker, and there's a chart right now on my study table . . . but that would be telling! One thing I can say: the first thing I did, when I got back from my trip to deliver those final sherds and take a look at the exhibit, was to arrange a champagne celebration party of our own for the divers and all those at the Benbow who had helped me, and we toasted *Colossus*, those who sailed in her, and her cargo, until the timbers of my old inn rang again.

Sources

80 Letter: Sir William Hamilton to Charles Greville, 25 January 1800

All from Alfred Morrison *Collection of Autograph Letters and Historical Documents: The Hamilton and Nelson Papers*, vol. 2, 1798–1815. Privately printed 1893–4

100 Wreck site of Frigate H M S *Anson* – further details of the salvage operations are contained in my earlier book *Island Treasure*, Hutchinson 1969

102 'Clib' and 'crud' – a more extended account of my research into the formation of these is to be found in my article 'The formation of marine organic and detrital concretion in Cornwall and the Scilly Isles', *International Journal of Nautical Archaeology and Underwater Exploration* (1976), 5.4: pp. 333–43

123 Letter: Sir William Hamilton to the Countess of Lichtenau, May 1796

E. Edwards *Lives of the Founders of the British Museum*, vol. 1, p. 357, 1870

128 Draught-sheer-plan of *Colossus*
Royal Maritime Museum, Greenwich

132 Pryse Lockhart Gordon *Personal Memoirs*, vol. 1, pp. 201–11, 1830

150 Extract from Parliamentary Debates (Hansard), Wednesday, 11 March 1970, pp. 1366–71

186 ff BBC film Colossus: *The Ship that Lost a Fortune*, Part I Expectation, Part II Realisation. Producer, Tony Salmon

Index